MW00686343

Cambridge English

Business
BENCHMARK

Upper Intermediate

BULATS

Student's Book

Guy Brook-Hart

2nd Edition

CAMBRIDGE
UNIVERSITY PRESS

University Printing House, Cambridge CB2 8BS, United Kingdom

Cambridge University Press is part of the University of Cambridge.

It furthers the University's mission by disseminating knowledge in the pursuit of education, learning and research at the highest international levels of excellence.

www.cambridge.org
Information on this title: www.cambridge.org/9781107639836

© Cambridge University Press 2013

First published 2006
Second edition published 2013
6th printing 2015

Printed in the United Kingdom by Latimer Trend

A catalogue record for this publication is available from the British Library

ISBN 978-1-107-63983-6 Upper Intermediate BULATS Student's Book
ISBN 978-1-107-68098-2 Upper Intermediate Business Vantage Student's Book
ISBN 978-1-107-63211-0 Upper Intermediate BULATS and Business Vantage Teacher's Resource Book
ISBN 978-1-107-68660-1 Upper Intermediate BULATS and Business Vantage Personal Study Book
ISBN 978-1-107-68003-6 Upper Intermediate BULATS Class Audio CDs (2)
ISBN 978-1-107-63315-5 Upper Intermediate Business Vantage Class Audio CDs (2)

Introduction

Business Benchmark Second edition Upper Intermediate, is a completely updated and revised course at CEFR B2 level, reflecting contemporary international business in a stimulating way both for people already working and for students who have not yet worked in business.

It teaches the reading, speaking, listening and writing skills needed in today's global workplaces, together with essential business vocabulary and grammar.

Business Benchmark Upper Intermediate is also the most complete preparation material available for Cambridge Business Language Testing Service (BULATS) and is officially approved as an exam preparation course by Cambridge ESOL.

The book contains:

- **24 units for classroom study** covering all four skills in a dynamic and integrated way, together with essential business vocabulary and grammar.
- Authentic listening and reading material, including interviews with real business people.
- Six **Grammar workshops** which explain and extend the grammar work covered in the units and which are informed by the Cambridge Learner Corpus (CLC) – see right.
- A nine-page **Writing reference** covering emails, memos, letters, reports and proposals, and a function bank.
- A fully referenced **Word list** with definitions, covering key vocabulary from the units and the transcripts.
- An **Exam skills and Exam practice** section, which gives students detailed guidance on how to approach each exam task, the skills required and what the exam task is testing, together with exercises to build up students' exam skills. The Exam practice pages contain **the parts of a past BULATS test relevant to B2-level students**, with answers.
- A **full answer key** for all the exercises in the Student's Book, including **sample answers** to all the writing tasks.
- Complete **recording transcripts**.

New features in the 2nd edition

- **Updated grammar and vocabulary** exercises based on correcting common grammar and vocabulary mistakes made by Business English students at this level, as shown by the CLC (see below). Exercises based on the CLC are indicated by this symbol: ⊙
- New **Writing reference** section with guidance for each type of writing task and sample answers.
- New topics, texts and recordings reflecting the realities of contemporary international business.
- **Complete revision of all exam-style tasks**, making them closer to real exam tasks.

The Cambridge Learner Corpus (CLC)

The Cambridge Learner Corpus (CLC) is a large collection of exam scripts written by candidates taken from Cambridge ESOL exams around the world. It currently contains over 220,000 scripts which translates to over 48 million words, scripts and is growing all the time. It forms part of the Cambridge International Corpus (CIC) and it has been built up by Cambridge University Press and Cambridge ESOL. The CLC currently contains scripts from over:

- 200,000 students
- 170 first languages
- 200 countries.

Find out more about the Cambridge Learner Corpus at www.cambridge.org/corpus.

Also available are:

- **two audio CDs**, which include authentic interviews with real business people.
- **Teacher's Resource Book**, which includes detailed lesson notes plus photocopiable activities and case studies.
- **Personal Study Book**, which includes activities and exercises, as well as a **self-study writing supplement**.

Map of the book

	Unit	Reading	Listening	Writing
Human resources	**1** Staff development and training 8–11	• Recruitment brochure • Training at Deloitte in China	• Training course: Skills Development College	
	2 Job descriptions and job satisfaction 12–15		• A human resources manager • What I like about my job	• Staff training report
	3 Getting the right job 16–19	• Job satisfaction at Sony Mobile Communications	• Advice on job applications • What is important when doing a job interview?	• A website entry • A short email and an email of a job application
	4 Making contact 20–23	• A telephone quiz • Phone-answering tips	• An occupational psychologist • A phone call to a hotel • Enquiring about a job	
Grammar workshop 1 (Units 1–4) 24–25 Countable and uncountable nouns; Past perfect and past simple; Talking about large and small				
Marketing	**5** Breaking into the market 26–29	• Promoting AXE • Going viral in India and China	• Supermarkets' own brands	
	6 Launching a product 30–33	• The Drink Me Chai success story	• Developing and launching Drink Me Chai • Launching and promoting a new product	• A marketing report
	7 A stand at a trade fair 34–37	• The London Contemporary Design Show • Preparing an exhibition stand • A reply to an email	• Phoning 100percentdesign	• An email giving information • An email making an enquiry • An email answering enquiries • A memo to staff
	8 Being persuasive 38–41	• The art of agreeing • An email summarising an agreement	• What makes people persuasive • People negotiating a sale at a trade fair	• An email correcting information • An email confirming terms
Grammar workshop 2 (Units 5–8) 42–43 Infinitives and verb + -ing; Prepositions in phrases describing trends; Formal requests; First and				
Entrepreneurship	**9** Starting a business 44–47	• An international franchise • A letter to a franchiser	• Why start your own business?	• A letter of enquiry
	10 Financing a start-up 48–51	• Raising finance	• Setting up a food consultancy • Carter Bearings	
	11 Expanding into Europe 52–55	• Heidelberg Technology Park vs. Biopôle, Lausanne • A proposal	• A new location in Europe	• A proposal
	12 Presenting your business idea 56–59	• Making the most of presentations	• Signalling the parts of a presentation	
Grammar workshop 3 (Units 9–12) 60–61 Prepositions in time clauses; Linking ideas; Can and could				

Speaking	Vocabulary	Language work
• Discussion: job benefits • Discussion: who should pay for training? • Role-play: planning a training course	• Recruitment brochure: *ability, certificate, course,* etc. • *work, job, training, training course*	• Countable and uncountable nouns
• Discussion: activities you would enjoy in a job • Discussion: first impressions and enthusiasm • Discussion: what I enjoy about my job/studies	• Job responsibilities • *staff, employee, member of staff*	• Asking questions • Expressing likes • Introducing reasons
• Discussion: things which make somewhere a great place to work • Dicussion: the format of letters and emails • Short talk: what is important when doing a job interview?	• Phrases expressing enthusiasm • Adjective forms	
• Discussion: first impressions • Role-play: phoning a hotel • Short talk: what is important when making a business telephone call? • Role-play: enquiring about a job • Discussion: deciding who should go on a course		• Talking about large and small differences

differences

Speaking	Vocabulary	Language work
• Discussion: advantages and disadvantages of different promotional methods • Role-play: launching a shampoo • Short talk: a clothing brand	• *launch, ploys,* etc.	• Infinitive or verb + *-ing*
• Discussion: new products • Role-play: an interior design company		• Prepositions in phrases describing trends
• Discussion: how companies can promote products at trade fairs • Discussion: choosing a design	• *find out, learn, know, teach*	• Formal requests
• Discussion: what makes people persuasive • Role-play: breaking the ice • Role-play: exchanging information about a product • Short talk: what is important when negotiating? • Role-play: negotiating a deal		• First and second conditionals

cond conditionals

Speaking	Vocabulary	Language work
• Role-play: buying into a franchise	• *concept, gross revenue,* etc. • Financial terms	• Prepositions in time phrases
• Role-play: advice about starting a business • Short talk: what is important when looking for finance?	• Raising finance • Noun phrases connected with starting companies • *assets, collateral,* etc.	
• Discussion: what factors are important when choosing a location? • Discussion: choosing the best location	• *place, space, room; opportunity, possibility, option*	• Making recommendations
• Discussion: which things are important when giving a presentation? • Structuring a presentation • Giving a short presentation • Role-play: presenting your business idea		• Phrases signalling parts of a presentation • *Can* and *could*

	Unit	Reading	Listening	Writing
Business abroad	**13 Arranging business travel** 62–65	• How business travel is changing	• A sales manager talking about business travel • Conference problems	• Arranging to travel: an email agreeing to a request and making suggestions • An email giving information and instructions
	14 Business conferences 66–69	• Making the most of business conferences	• Arranging conference facilities • Networking at a conference • A destination management company (DMC)	• An email giving instructions
	15 Business meetings 70–73	• A survey of meetings	• Talking about meetings • Looking for solutions	• An email about a business trip
	16 Spending the sales budget 74–77	• DF Software	• Spanish sales • A report on the use of private company jets	• A report on the use of private company jets
Grammar workshop 4 (Units 13–16) 78–79 Modal verbs: perfect forms; Referencing; Passives				
Change	**17 Social media and business** 80–83	• Some ways of using social media • An email introducing a company	• Social media and customers	• An email arranging a meeting • An email introducing a company and asking for information
	18 Business and the environment 84–87	• The green office	• An environmental consultant	• A memo asking for suggestions • An email giving suggestions
	19 A staff survey 88–91	• Reading a report	• Staff reactions • Calls to HR	• A survey report
	20 Offshoring and outsourcing 92–95	• When should we outsource?	• Outsourcing IT	• A proposal for outsourcing
Grammar workshop 5 (Units 17–20) 96–97 The definite article; Tense changes in reported speech; Third conditional				
Customer relations	**21 Customer satisfaction and loyalty** 98–101	• From satisfaction to loyalty • A memo	• Encouraging customer loyalty	• An email apologising and explaining why you'll be late
	22 Communication with customers 102–105	• Training in customer communication skills • Turning complaints to your advantage	• Customer communication at Not Just Food	
	23 Corresponding with customers 106–109	• A letter about a new service • An email from a dissatisfied customer	• Preparing a letter or email of complaint	• A letter informing about a new service • A letter of complaint
	24 Business across cultures 110–113	• Working in another culture • A job advertisement	• A short talk • Working in China and working in Europe	• An email announcing a job opportunity
Grammar workshop 6 (Units 21–24) 114–115 Relative clauses; Which pronoun: *it, this* or *that*?; Expressing results				

Speaking	Vocabulary	Language work
• Discussion: why business people need to travel • Short talks: what is important when deciding when to travel on business? • Discussion: social media • Discussion: planning a business trip	• *travel, journey, trip*	• Modal verbs: perfect forms
• Discussion: why business people go to conferences • Discussion: selecting staff to go to a conference • Role-play: networking at a conference • Discussion: organising a conference		
• Discussion: how meetings should be conducted • Summarising results of a survey • Role-play: a meeting at a medical equipment company	• Collocations describing reasons for meetings • Collocations with *meeting* • *crucial, priceless*, etc.	• Referencing
• Discussion: aspects of sales		• Making recommendations • Using the passive to express opinions and ideas
• Discussion: how social media can help people in their jobs • Discussion: how to use social media	• Verb–noun collocations	• When to use *the*
• Discussion: how to make offices more environmentally friendly • Short talk: what is important when making a workplace environmentally friendly? • Discussion: how work will change in the future	• *issues, impact*, etc. • *way* or *method*	• Expressing causes
• Discussion: the advantages and disadvantages to changes in working conditions • Discussion: improving working conditions	• Words and phrases expressing numbers	• Reporting verbs and reported speech
• Discussion: advantages and disadvantages of offshoring and outsourcing • Short talk: what is important when deciding what business activities to outsource? • Discussion: outsourcing and offshoring: the pros and cons		• Third conditional
• Discussion: dissatisfied customers • Discussion: relationships with customers • Short talk: a staff meeting	• *revenue, outcome*, etc.	• Relative clauses
• Discussion: the best method of communicating different things • Discussion: why companies lose customers • Discussion: complaining	• Adjective–noun collocations	
• Discussion: launching new services • Discussion: what you should put in a letter of complaint	• *last* and *latest*	• Expressing results
• Discussion: typical parts of business culture • Presentation: what is important when going to work in a foreign country? • Discussion: selecting staff to work abroad		• Phrases followed by a verb + *-ing*

Staff development and training

Getting started

Work in pairs. Which of these benefits of working for a company would you find most attractive? Why?

- a bonus scheme
- responsibility
- a high salary
- an in-house training scheme
- the opportunity to travel
- a permanent contract
- long holidays
- rapid promotion

> **Useful language**
> **Giving opinions – agreeing and disagreeing**
>
> I think .... would be the most attractive because ...
>
> I'm not sure about that. For me, ... would be more useful than .... because ...
>
> Perhaps you're right. And I don't think .... is as important as ...

Recruitment brochure

Reading

1 Work in pairs. You are going to read an extract from the recruitment page of a travel company's website. Before you read, discuss what training you think university graduates might need when they first join a company like this.

2 Read the text below quite quickly.

    1 What training does Flight Centre offer new staff?

    2 Why does Flight Centre think staff training is so important?

> **Flight Centre**
>
> This company has been offering advice and making travel arrangements for customers since it opened its first store in Australia in 1981. It is now one of the world's largest and most successful independent travel retailers, with 1,700 stores around the globe.

GO ANYWHERE
YOU WANT TO GO

At Flight Centre, we believe in giving you a lot of responsibility from day one, so one of our main priorities is to make sure you get the training and support you need to **1** .... the skills which will allow you to succeed.

Training starts as soon as you **2** .... – and it never stops. The initial programme is **3** .... partly at your office and partly in our dedicated Learning Centre. For the first 12 months, you'll have a regular programme of training, **4** .... topics as diverse as Advanced Sales, Goal Setting and Time Management.

After that, you can develop in any direction you choose by **5** .... a range of courses and events in key areas: Sales and Service, Products and Airfares, Systems, and Personal Development. All this is provided at no **6** .... to you. We have a consistent **7** .... of promoting from inside the company; currently about 90 per cent of our Team Leaders have come through the ranks, and we want to keep it that **8** ....

We're also keen to train the leaders of the future with our Leadership Development programme. It's an intensive training course **9** .... up by specialist project work. After all, becoming a high flier in any company shouldn't be about just waiting to shuffle up the ladder. Here, the best people develop as far as they like, as fast as they like. We hope you'll be one of them. And the success of our philosophy of cultivating personal and **10** .... development, as well as promoting from within, has earned us a Training and Development award for excellence, as voted by our employees.

adapted from www.therecruitmentcentre.com

3 Read the text again and choose the best option – A, B, C or D – for each gap.

1 A win	B gain	C earn	D collect
2 A join	B recruit	C contract	D employ
3 A situated	B located	C based	D fixed
4 A dealing	B covering	C learning	D working
5 A going	B assisting	C having	D attending
6 A money	B payment	C cost	D price
7 A record	B reputation	C activity	D standard
8 A type	B sort	C kind	D way
9 A set	B backed	C held	D kept
10 A career	B work	C life	D profession

Speaking

Work in small groups.

1 Would you like to work for a company like Flight Centre? Why? / Why not?

2 Which of these statements do you agree/disagree with? Why? / Why not?
- Companies should pay for training to do the job, but staff should pay for training which gives them qualifications.
- Training should be done in employees' free time.
- If a company trains you, you should agree to work for that company for a number of years afterwards.
- All staff need continuous training – not just new recruits.
- It doesn't matter what you study. The important thing is to get a good degree.

> **Useful language**
> **Saying how much you agree/disagree**
>
> I partly/completely/totally agree with .... because I think/feel that ...
> I completely/totally disagree with .... because ...

Vocabulary 1

Check the meanings of these words, then use them to complete the sentences below.

> certificate   course   degree   development
> experience   knowledge   qualifications   skills

1 Our training programme aims to teach you key _skills_ such as using spreadsheets.

2 Although he lacks any formal ...., such as a university degree, he's now one of our best managers.

3 The .... you study for at university is likely to decide the sort of job you do afterwards.

4 At the end of the four-week training ...., you will receive a .... You'll gain a thorough .... of the company's activities. However, there are a lot of things which you can only learn from the .... you'll get working here.

5 With our policy of professional ...., we expect him to soon become a manager.

Grammar workshop

Countable and uncountable nouns

- Countable nouns [C] often use a or an in the singular (a company, an office) and can be plural (companies, offices).
- Uncountable nouns [U] do not use a or an and are always singular (information, advice).

Find these words in the reading passage on page 8 and decide whether they are countable (C) or uncountable (U).

1 responsibility U   2 training   3 programme
4 training course   5 work   6 excellence

> **page 24** Countable and uncountable nouns

Vocabulary 2

Business students often confuse these words: *work* and *job*; *training* and *training course*. Look at these extracts from the *CALD*. Then choose the correct alternative in italics in the sentences below.

> **work** [U] – something you do to earn money: *He's looking for work.*
> **job** [C] – used to talk about a particular type of work activity which you do: *He's looking for a job in computer programming.*
> **training** [U] – the process of learning the skills you need to do a particular job or activity
> **training course** [C] – a set of classes or a plan of study on a particular subject

1 Due to your excellent *job / work*, you have increased productivity by 25%.

2 She has also done an excellent *job / work* with our staff, who are now working as a real team.

3 We haven't enough people to deal with this amount of *job / work*.

4 Wish me luck in my new *job / work*.

5 I have to go on a *training course / training* to learn about the new safety regulations.

6 We need to give health and safety *training course / training* to eight senior executives.

7 Is it possible to hold this *training course / training* with just six trainees?

Training course

Listening

1 Work in pairs. You are going to listen to a short conversation about a training course. Before you listen, read the notes below and decide what type of information you need in each gap.

> **Skills Development College**
>
> - Had an enquiry from **1** .... Company.
> - Want an advanced computer course for their **2** ....
> - Require a course lasting **3** ....
> - Director of Studies should:
>   - conduct needs analysis
>   - give a **4** ....

2 (1) 01 Listen and write one or two words or a number in the numbered gaps in the notes.

3 Match these phrases (1–6) with their definitions (a–f).

1 tailor-made   a practical, not theoretical, training
2 learning goals   b able to use a computer
3 training budget   c basic, essential skills
4 hands-on training   d money reserved for training staff
5 computer literate   e specially designed to meet your needs
6 core skills   f your objectives when doing the course

Training at Deloitte in China

Reading

> **Deloitte**
> A worldwide company offering management consultancy, auditing and financial advisory services

1 Work in pairs. Read the article in the next column, ignoring the gaps and the underlined words. What is the subject of each paragraph?

Encouraging employees

In each of the main offices in Shanghai, Beijing and Hong Kong, Deloitte China has dedicated facilities known as the Deloitte Institute training centres. Employees who develop their careers within Deloitte believe that the benefits are multiple. 'In Deloitte, some managers are only in their early thirties, and this encourages young people like me,' says Shawn Su from the Tax Department. 'I think Deloitte offers employees a clear upward path for development. **1** _G_ '

Charlotte Chen says, 'I knew Deloitte was different when I first came here for interview.' During the interview, Charlotte was impressed by the professionalism of the Deloitte interviewers. 'They didn't act in a superior manner; they were friendly and patient. **2** ....' When Charlotte was about to take her professional exams, her manager said, 'With the test coming in June, you should take some days off. You will have a better chance of passing if you have time to study.'

Attention from managers often works better than material incentives. Jessica Li from the Audit Department recalls, 'The third year with Deloitte was crucial, and passing my exams was essential for my career. **3** .... What touched me most was that they came to wish me good luck the day before I took my study leave. I was very emotional to see their concern.' **4** .... Jessica says, 'Deloitte cares about my personal development, and that suits me. Now, when I get calls from headhunters, I tell them, "I really like working here and can develop my career within Deloitte. I don't need to change environment."'

Attention and recognition by management are elements of Deloitte's corporate culture. Shawn Su, who is about to be promoted to manager, says he always gets an immediate reply from his supervisors, no matter how late. They always say, 'Thank you for working so late.' Shawn says, '**5** ....' Now a manager-to-be, Shawn says, 'I'll follow in the footsteps of my bosses, encouraging and paying attention to my staff.'

This is how Deloitte's corporate culture is passed down through the company. Every new recruit has a 'counsellor', who guides them, helps them at work and cares about them. **6** .... Counsellors are like Deloitte second bosses. Although they don't necessarily lead you directly when it comes to work, they guide every Deloitte employee with their own professional experience.

adapted from www.topemployers.com.cn

2 Work in pairs.

1 Look at the example given in gap 1. Why is sentence G below the correct option to fill the gap?

2 Choose the best sentence (A–G) to fill each of the gaps. Use the underlined words and phrases in the sentences and in the text to help you.

A <u>At the time</u>, my managers helped me apply for training courses, and they let me take time to attend training and to study.

B <u>Interest and commitment</u> from the management retains talent.

C I thought, if my bosses are <u>like these people</u>, I'll feel comfortable here.

D Jessica Li believes that it was <u>a recommendation from hers</u> that gave her the chance to work abroad.

E <u>This policy</u> has led to a great expansion in Deloitte's services.

F Young people <u>don't mind doing overtime</u>, but we tend to feel frustrated when what we've done is not recognised.

G This gives everyone the chance to ascend to the top, as long as they remain committed and perform well.

Task tip

- Consider the subject of each paragraph.
- Look at words in the sentences which refer to other things in the passage.

3 Discuss in small groups.

1 What positive aspects of working for Deloitte are mentioned in the text?

2 Which ones do you think are most attractive? Why?

Vocabulary

Match these words and phrases from the text (1–6) with their definitions (a–f).

1 dedicated facilities
2 material incentives
3 headhunters
4 corporate culture
5 commitment
6 overtime

a people who try to persuade someone to leave their job by offering them another job with more pay and a higher position

b buildings and equipment provided for a particular purpose

c something, especially money, which encourages a person to do something

d the beliefs and ideas that a company has and the way in which they affect how it does business and how its employees behave

e time spent working beyond the usual time needed or expected in a job

f when you are willing to give your time and energy to something that you believe in

Training scheme for new staff

Role-play

1 Before you do this task, work alone and prepare by making some brief notes about your ideas.

You work in the human resources department of a company. Your company has decided to provide a one-week training course for new employees. You have been asked to help prepare the programme. Discuss the situation with a partner and decide:

a what things the course should include;

b whether the course should be given by people inside the company or by an outside organisation;

c whether the course should happen during work time or free time.

2 (1) 02 Two business students discussed the task in Exercise 1. Match these sentences (1–6) from their discussion with points in the task (a–c). Then listen to check your answers.

1 <u>How about</u> getting them to spend two days learning how our computer systems work?

2 <u>Why don't we</u> ask an external organisation?

3 <u>I think another useful thing is to</u> explain what to do when they have a problem.

4 <u>We could</u> also spend some time introducing people in the company.

5 <u>What about</u> holding the course for two hours every day, from nine to 11 in the morning?

6 <u>I suggest that</u> on the first day, <u>we should</u> explain what the company does.

3 Study the underlined phrases in Exercise 2 and think how you could use them when you discuss the situation.

4 Work in pairs or small groups. Discuss the situation using your own ideas and some of the language from Exercise 2.

UNIT 2

Job descriptions and job satisfaction

Getting started

1 Work in pairs. Which of these activities would you enjoy in a job, and which would you dislike? Why?

1 working with figures
2 dealing with customers
3 supervising staff
4 taking important decisions
5 writing reports
6 working with new technologies

2 Which of the activities in Exercise 1 (1–6) are part of these jobs?

a receptionist
b marketing assistant
c accountant
d human resources administrator
e logistics controller

Job responsibilities

Vocabulary

1 Underline phrases in these statements which are useful for talking about jobs.

1
<u>My main responsibilities are</u> to keep financial records, make sure the company pays its taxes by the deadlines and supervise how funds are used. I deal with financial paperwork, and look after budgeting and planning any future investment.

2
I help to recruit new employees, keep staff records and reports, help to plan staff training, and organise team-building activities. I also participate in evaluating the performance of junior members of staff.

3
I work as part of a team promoting the company's products. We have a budget for advertising and promotion and we work with outside agencies to design effective promotional campaigns.

4
I'm really the first person visitors see when they walk in through the door, so I have to look good, be polite and efficient, and pass them on to the right person. I answer the phone, issue visitors' passes, organise meeting rooms and make sure that mail and other messages are distributed correctly.

5
My job involves ensuring that goods are transported to and from our factories and warehouses in an efficient and co-ordinated way. In other words, I'm responsible for goods arriving at their destination on time and in good condition.

2 Match the statements above (1–5) with the jobs (a–e) in Getting started Exercise 2.

3 Find words in Exercise 1 to match these definitions from the *CALD*.

1 to plan how much money you will spend on something budgeting

2 to persuade someone to work for a company or become a new member of an organisation

3 judging or calculating the quality, importance, amount or value of something

4 encouraging the popularity or sale of something

5 the act of putting money into something to make a profit

6 money needed or available to spend on something

7 how well a person, machine, etc. does a piece of work or an activity

8 times or days by which something must be done

4 Check how the phrases in the Useful language box are used in Exercise 1. Then work alone and think of a job (not the job you do now). Write a short paragraph like the ones in Exercise 1 to describe the job, but without mentioning the job title.

> **Useful language**
> **Talking about jobs**
>
> | | |
> |---|---|
> | My main responsibilities are to … | My job involves … (+ verb + -*ing*) |
> | I help to … | I'm responsible for … |
> | I participate in … | I deal with … |
> | I have to … | I look after … |

5 Work in small groups. Take turns to read your paragraphs. The others in your group should guess what job you are talking about.

6 Complete these questions by writing one word in each gap.

1 What _does_ your job consist _____ ? / What _____ you studying?

2 How long _____ you _____ in your present job? / How long _____ you _____ studying?

3 When _____ you first become interested in your present job/studies?

4 What _____ your goals and ambitions _____ the future?

7 Work in pairs. Take turns to ask and answer the questions.

A human resources manager

Listening

1 You are going to hear Christina Bunt, a human resources manager for Tesco, talking about her job. Before you listen, underline the key idea in each of these questions.

1 What part of her job does Christina <u>enjoy most</u>?
   (A) teaching job skills
   B challenging tasks
   C maintaining discipline

2 What, according to Christina, <u>makes managing people easy</u>?
   A strong discipline
   (B) recruiting the right staff
   C having friendly staff

3 How did Christina become a personnel manager?
   A Tesco recruited her as a personnel manager.
   B She trained in another company as a personnel manager.
   (C) She started at the bottom and came up through the ranks.

4 What would she like to be doing in ten years' time?
   A opening new stores
   B working as a store manager
   (C) continuing her present job

5 What advice does Christina give for job candidates?
   A Dress very smartly.
   (B) Try to look relaxed.
   C Behave in a friendly, casual way.

6 How does she know when a candidate will be good at the job?
   A They are ambitious about their career.
   B They express interest in their other activities.
   C They are good at the other things they do.

2 (1)03 Now listen and choose the best answer – A, B or C – for each question.

> ### Task tip
> Before you listen, underline the key idea in the question, but not in each option. This will help you to focus when you listen.

Human resources

Speaking

Work in small groups.

1 Do you agree with these opinions?
- First impressions are really important. Be totally natural and don't try to put yourself forward as something you're not.
- I'll always know that I'm talking to somebody that's going to be enthusiastic, because they're enthusiastic about the things they like in their normal life.

2 Do you think enthusiastic people are more successful? Why? / Why not?

3 What other interview advice would you give?

Tesco
Britain's largest chain of supermarkets and the biggest food retailer in the UK

Vocabulary

1 Business students often confuse these words and phrases: *staff*, *employee* and *member of staff*. Read Speaker 2 on page 12 again, then match these words (1–3) with their definitions from the *CALD* (a–c).

1	staff	a	one person who works for a shop, company, etc.
2	employee	b	someone who is paid to work for someone else
3	member of staff	c	the group of people who work for an organisation

2 ⊘ **Correct these mistakes made by students in Cambridge business exams. More than one answer may be possible.**

1 I'm pleased to announce that every ~~staff~~ will be given a bonus.
member of staff / employee

2 Around 70% of customers felt that the staffs were generally unfriendly.

3 She's a very hard-working staff.

4 In fact, we need 35 new staffs.

What I like about my job

Listening

1 **Work in pairs. Look at these reasons why people might like their jobs. Which, for you, are more important, and which are less important?**

a balancing working life with family life
b being my own boss
c building customer relationships
d finding solutions for customers
e improving my staff's performance
f observing trainees' progress
g seeing the success of my company
h having a variety of tasks

Useful language
Talking about yourself

I (would) find .... very interesting/enjoyable because …

For me, ... is very important because …

I wouldn't be / I'm not so interested in .... because …

.... is something I'd really enjoy / find challenging / find exciting because …

---

2 ①04 **Listen to five people talking about why they like their jobs. What reason does each person give? Choose from the reasons (a–h) in Exercise 1.**

1 Jane Milton ....
2 Amanda Hamilton ....
3 Rob Liu ....
4 Adam Evans ....
5 Harriet Barber ....

Task tip

When you listen, you won't hear exactly the same words as in Exercise 1 – you have to listen for the same idea to be expressed.

3 ①04 **Complete these sentences by writing one word in each gap. Then listen again to check your answers.**

1 I love being able to .... out what a .... needs and … and do it.

2 I absolutely thrive on the .... , just being able to make, you know, my own ....

3 You sort of somehow don't mind those longer hours because it's ....

4 You see people, sort of, improve, really, within a short, quite a short time sometimes. That's very, um, ... , I think.

5 I'm getting their future ready, so when they arrive, there's a job there for them, and that's .... I enjoy – that's .... of the main things.

6 It's .... to see, like, how these projects are progressing,

---

Speaking

1 Work alone. Imagine you are going to an interview for a job. Look at these questions and think how you might answer them, using words and phrases you have studied in this unit where possible.

- What do you most enjoy about your job/studies?
- Is there anything you dislike?
- What do you regard as your most valuable job skills?
- What other job skills would you like to acquire? Why?
- What sort of job would suit you best? Why?

2 Now work in pairs. Take turns to ask and answer the questions.

Staff training report

Writing

1 Read this extract from a report and put the verbs in brackets into the correct tense.

Two years ago, PDQ **1** ..spent.. (*spend*) 200,000 CHF on staff training. The main reason for spending so much money was that the company **2** .... (*take*) on 40 new employees who **3** .... (*need*) training. However, last year, the training budget **4** .... (*fall*) to just 80,000 CHF because the company only **5** .... (*recruit*) seven new members of staff. Recently, PDQ **6** .... (*sign*) an agreement to work on a major project with an Indian company, and because of this, staff now have to learn new working methods. For that reason, the company **7** .... (*set*) its training budget for this year at 300,000 CHF.

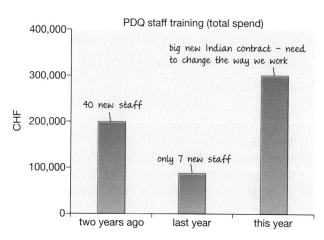

PDQ staff training (total spend)

big new Indian contract – need to change the way we work

40 new staff

only 7 new staff

CHF

❯ page 24 Present perfect and past simple

2 Find words or phrases on the chart above which mean the same as the highlighted words and phrases in the report.

3 Underline four words or phrases in the report which introduce reasons.

4 Work in pairs. You work for the Bank of Veronezh. Your line manager has asked you to write a short report on in-house training.

- Study the chart opposite and the handwritten notes.
- Discuss what the chart shows and what you can say in your report.

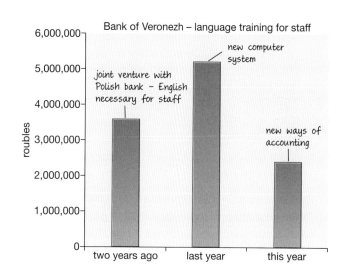

Bank of Veronezh – language training for staff

new computer system

joint venture with Polish bank – English necessary for staff

new ways of accounting

roubles

5 Work alone. Write a paragraph for the report, including all the handwritten notes on the chart.

 page 120 Writing reference

Getting the right job

Getting started

Work in small groups and discuss this question.

What, for you, would make a company or organisation a great place to work?

Here are some ideas to help you:

- opportunities for promotion
- a good salary
- opportunities to travel
- working in teams
- challenging work
- friendly colleagues
- developing new ideas
- taking responsibility

Job satisfaction at Sony Mobile Communications

Reading

1. **Work in pairs. You are going to read what four employees say about their jobs at Sony Mobile Communications. Before you read, discuss the advantages of working for a multinational company.**

2. **Work in pairs. Underline the key idea in each of these statements, then express the key idea using your own words.**

   1. I like to see how <u>the people I work with evolve</u>.
      my colleagues develop
   2. I like producing things which people will enjoy.
   3. It's important to continually improve our ways of working.
   4. My team's work affects the whole company.
   5. Recent recruits are encouraged to contribute ideas.
   6. The company wants its employees to have a variety of attitudes and opinions.
   7. To survive in this industry, you continually have to be producing new products.
   8. We need to be aware of our customers' different ways of thinking.

3. **Read these opinions expressed by Sony Mobile Communications employees. Which person does each statement from Exercise 2 refer to?**

> **Useful language**
> **Talking about importance**
>
> I really like …
> For me, ……… is very important because …
> One of the things I think is essential is ……… because …
> I don't think ……… is so important because …
> For me, ……… would be / is a priority because …

Task tip

Make sure you are familiar with the questions before you read. That way, you will only need to read the paragraphs once.

A Gurshan Kaal, Senior Manager Android Software, United States

The employees here are from very diverse cultural backgrounds. It all makes for a really open workplace where different views and mindsets are accepted and encouraged. Mobile technology has been evolving fast. As soon as you've mastered a technology, a new one crops up. There's also fierce competition that's always changing, forcing us to stay on our toes and innovate. Ever-changing technologies and new ideas keep my job intellectually stimulating and really satisfying. I've always been interested in mobile technologies. Sony Mobile Communications attracted me because it's a leader in communication technologies. The people here are passionate, fun-loving, hard-working and looking to make a difference. They're not intimidated by change, but they do understand the importance of being able to adapt.

B Katie Wu, Head of Engineering and Material Management, Beijing

I never feel work is just about eight hours a day. Everyone here's so passionate, positive and full of energy. We love our work and we also have a lot of fun together. I think what I contribute most to Sony Mobile Communications is bringing an analytical mindset to my team. We work hard, but also we want to do it more intelligently, more efficiently and effectively. We like to challenge the status quo. I have a real passion about people. Developing my team and seeing them grow is what makes me happy – seeing them change over time.

Vocabulary

Find words or phrases in the first two sections of the text which mean:

1 learned how to do something well (A)
2 appears unexpectedly (A)
3 to continue directing all our attention and energy to what we are doing (A)
4 having a way of thinking which examines facts and information in a very careful way (B)
5 to question the present situation (B)

Speaking

Work in small groups.

1 What impression do you get of Sony Mobile Communications?
2 Which of the jobs mentioned sounds most interesting to you?
3 On their website, Sony Mobile Communications say, 'Sony Mobile Communications is a global company and our corporate language is English.' What are the advantages and disadvantages of working in English?

C Hikaru Kimura, Software Developer, Japan

There's a great culture here where you can really discuss things with all your colleagues, even if you're a newcomer. It's a very open atmosphere. For the last four years, I've been working in software development. I take real pride in creating applications that are fun and satisfying for our customers to use. It's great working for such a diverse company where you can learn a lot and get inspired by sharing ideas with other cultures and mindsets. I also value having the chance to suggest new ideas and speak out freely.

D Sarah Hewitt, Senior Global Brand Manager, London

The strength of our brand is hugely important. It isn't just a logo or an advertising campaign: it's who we are and what we do. I'm lucky to have a role that touches every part of the organisation. It's <u>rewarding</u> to see our team's thinking and plans <u>shaping</u> and changing all parts of the company from internal culture through to packaging, product design and advertising. I love working in Global, as we get to interact with people from all over the world: it's about understanding the cultural sensitivities of different markets.

Sony Mobile Communications
A leader in communication technologies

SONY

A website entry

Writing

1 Find these phrases in the texts on Sony Mobile Communications and note how they are used.

I've always been interested in …
I think what I contribute most to … is …
I have a real passion about …
… is what makes me happy.
I take real pride in …
It's great …
I also value …
I'm lucky …
It's rewarding …

2 Imagine you have been asked to write a paragraph about yourself for your organisation's website (your college or your company). Write the paragraph using four or five of the phrases in Exercise 1.

3 Work in small groups and compare your paragraphs.

Advice on job applications

Listening

1 Underline the key ideas in these pieces of advice.

a Include a photograph with your application.
b Send your application by email.
c Make sure your application is not longer than one page.
d Mention your interests outside work.
e Ask someone else to check your application before sending it.
f Phone your prospective employer.
g Tell the truth about yourself in your application.
h Include names, addresses and telephone numbers of referees.

2 ①05 Now listen to the five speakers. For each one, decide what advice from Exercise 1 is being given.

1 Jürgen   2 Marta   3 Alex   4 Luli   5 Ivan

3 Which of the pieces of advice from Exercise 1 would you give someone applying for a job in your country? Why? / Why not?

A short email and an email of a job application

Writing 1

1   Work in small groups. Read the job advertisement below from Sony Mobile Communication's website and discuss what sort of person this job would suit. Think about:

- age • studies/qualifications
- previous work experience
- personality

Team Assistant

(Job ref.: 23998G)

JOB DESCRIPTION

- Handle phone calls and visitors, compile documents for approval, organise and co-ordinate Team Leader's daily routine/ biz working schedule and travel arrangements.
- Initiate and organise internal and external meetings, write follow-up reports etc., act as department facilitator to co-ordinate within team and with other departments when needed.
- Plan, organise and improve administrative services and implement company policies.
- Carry out tasks assigned by Team Leader according to business needs.

2   Mia Zhang saw the job advertised and thought it would suit a student doing an internship in her department. Complete the email she wrote by writing one word in each gap.

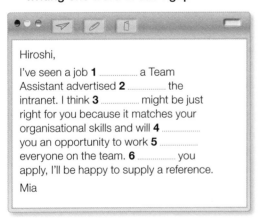

Hiroshi,

I've seen a job **1** .... a Team Assistant advertised **2** .... the intranet. I think **3** .... might be just right for you because it matches your organisational skills and will **4** .... you an opportunity to work **5** .... everyone on the team. **6** .... you apply, I'll be happy to supply a reference.

Mia

3   You have seen a job advertisement on your company intranet. Write an email to a colleague (40–50 words).

- Explain where you saw the advertisement.
- Say why it suits them.
- Offer to help them with their application.

4   Work in pairs. Imagine you have seen the job of Team Assistant advertised on the company's website and are thinking of applying. Choose which of these things you should mention in an email of application.

1 a summary of relevant work experience
2 how you heard about the job
3 references from your employers
4 the other jobs you're applying for
5 the reason for writing the email
6 what you studied
7 why you're applying
8 when you are ready to be interviewed
9 your CV
10 your free-time interests

5   Write a plan for your email, deciding in which paragraph you will put each of the things you chose in Exercise 4.

6   Read this email, ignoring any mistakes you see in the English. Was Christa Schmidt's plan the same as yours? In what ways was it different?

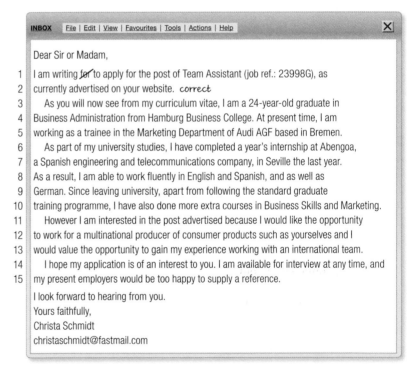

INBOX   File | Edit | View | Favourites | Tools | Actions | Help   ✕

Dear Sir or Madam,

1   I am writing ~~for~~ to apply for the post of Team Assistant (job ref.: 23998G), as
2   currently advertised on your website. *correct*
3   As you will now see from my curriculum vitae, I am a 24-year-old graduate in
4   Business Administration from Hamburg Business College. At present time, I am
5   working as a trainee in the Marketing Department of Audi AGF based in Bremen.
6   As part of my university studies, I have completed a year's internship at Abengoa,
7   a Spanish engineering and telecommunications company, in Seville the last year.
8   As a result, I am able to work fluently in English and Spanish, and as well as
9   German. Since leaving university, apart from following the standard graduate
10 training programme, I have also done more extra courses in Business Skills and Marketing.
11   However I am interested in the post advertised because I would like the opportunity
12 to work for a multinational producer of consumer products such as yourselves and I
13 would value the opportunity to gain my experience working with an international team.
14   I hope my application is of an interest to you. I am available for interview at any time, and
15 my present employers would be too happy to supply a reference.

I look forward to hearing from you.
Yours faithfully,
Christa Schmidt
christaschmidt@fastmail.com

7   In most of the numbered lines in the email above there is one extra word. It is either grammatically incorrect or does not fit in with the meaning of the text. Some lines, however, are correct. Find and delete the extra words.

▶ page 118 Writing reference

Speaking

Work in pairs. Look at the two emails in this unit.

- In what ways are the beginnings and endings different? Why?
- What other ways are there of beginning and ending business letters and emails?
- Underline words and phrases in the emails which you think would be useful when applying for a job.
- How are emails applying for jobs different in your country?

Vocabulary

⊘ **Business English students often form adjectives incorrectly. Correct each of these sentences.**

1 Could you also give me more ~~detail~~ information about working conditions? *detailed*
2 I have selected two recruitment agencies which seem interested possibilities.
3 If you are interest in working for us, you should send us your CV with a photo.
4 Our offices are opened each day from 08:00 till 20:00.
5 Please let us know if next week is not convenience for an interview.
6 She never has been absence from her work for more than a few days

Writing 2

Write an email applying for a job you would like to do. Use the email on page 18 as a model.

Doing interviews

Speaking

1 **Work in pairs. Imagine you are human resources officers and you are going to give a short talk to university students entitled 'What is important when doing a job interview?'. Decide and make notes on:**

- two or three points you want to make
- reasons for each point you make
- examples to support your ideas.

2 (1)06 **Listen to Adam Evans, a promotions manager, and Harriet Barber, an environmental consultant, answering the same question.**

1 Do Adam, Harriet or both Adam and Harriet express each of the ideas below?
2 They support some of their ideas with reasons. What reasons do they give?

		Adam	Harriet	reasons
1	Be confident of your value to the organisation.	✓		
2	Behave in a friendly way.			
3	Don't pretend to be someone you aren't.			
4	Find out about the organisation in advance.			
5	Get to know people in the organisation.			
6	Work with the company in advance.			

3 **Add any ideas you want to the notes you made in Exercise 1. Then change partners and take turns to give your talks.**

Making contact

Getting started

1 **Work in small groups. Look at the options in italics in each of these sentences and discuss which one you think is true.**

In a business situation:

1 when you meet someone face to face for the first time, your body language and appearance is *much more important than* / *not nearly as important as* your choice of words.

2 making a good first impression for most people takes *a little more* / *a lot less* than five minutes.

3 it's far *easier* / *harder* to make a good first impression than to change a bad one.

4 when you go to a first meeting, you should dress *a little more* / *slightly less* formally than usual.

5 when your first 'meeting' is on the phone, your choice of words is *considerably more important than* / *not quite as important as* how your voice sounds.

2 **①07 Listen to Chandra, an occupational psychologist, talking about first impressions in business and see if she shares your opinions.**

3 **Discuss these questions.**

1 What is good body language for a first business meeting in your culture? Think about how you stand, the expression on your face, where you look, your handshake, etc.

2 How can you make a good impression:
   • on the phone?
   • using Skype or video-conferencing?
   • by email?

3 In general, why is talking on the phone more difficult than talking face to face?

Grammar workshop

Talking about large and small differences

Look at these phrases from Getting started Exercise 1. Which phrases express a large difference (L), and which express a small difference (S)?

1 much more important than L
2 not nearly as important as L
3 a little more formally than S
4 slightly less formally than S
5 a lot less L
6 far easier L
7 considerably more important than L
8 not quite as important as S

❯ page 25 Talking about large and small differences

A phone call to a hotel

Listening

1 **Work in pairs. You are going to hear a telephone conversation between a customer and a hotel receptionist. Before you listen, look at this form and decide what type of information you need to fill the gaps.**

PRINCES HOTEL

RESERVATION FORM

RESERVATION MADE BY:	Alexei **1** kutsov
COMPANY:	**2** Bentfly International top flight
TYPE OF ROOM:	a small **3** meeting room
PURPOSE:	**4** Job interviews
DATE:	**5** May 13 from 9 a.m. to 8 p.m.
OTHER REQUIREMENTS:	**6** Cofee and tee

Task tip

Before you listen, think what information you need to fill each gap.

2 **①08 Listen and complete the form in Exercise 1. For each gap, write one or two words or a number and a word.**

Role-play

Work in pairs. Each take one of the roles and prepare some of the language you want to use before you speak. You can do this by looking at the transcript for Track 8.

Student A: See below.   Student B: See page 22.

Student A

You work as PA to the Human Resources Manager. Read this email which she has sent you, plan what you are going to say and make the phone call.

I want to hold interviews for the post of Production Controller (Gdansk, Poland) on Friday 14 June in the morning. As you know, there are three candidates. Can you ring the Ritz Hotel in Gdansk, please, and book two rooms for the night of 13 June and one meeting room for the morning of 14 June? The Production Manager (Poland) will be accompanying me, and we will be interviewing together.

We want to start at 9.30 and finish at 1.00 with a half-hour coffee break at 11.00.

Also, can you find out the prices and let me know?

Thanks

A telephone quiz

Reading

Work in pairs. Answer these questions about how you should speak on the phone in English. In some cases, more than one answer is possible.

1 Which do you think is the best way to answer the phone at work?
   A by saying *Hello!*
   B by saying your name
   C by saying your name and the name of your department or company
   D by saying the name of your company

2 Which of these do you think would be the best way to reply when someone on the phone says *Can I speak to (your name)?*
   A *That's me!*
   B *Speaking.*
   C *Yes, I am.*

3 How should Alberto Costa introduce himself for the first time on the phone?
   A *It's Alberto Costa.*
   B *I'm Alberto Costa.*
   C *My name's Alberto Costa.*

4 How should Lucia Falcone introduce herself on the phone to someone who already knows her?
   A *This is Lucia Falcone.*
   B *I'm Lucia Falcone.*
   C *It's Lucia Falcone here.*

5 When you ask someone to wait on the phone, which of these is quite formal, which is informal, and which would you probably never say?
   A *Could you hold on a minute, please?*
   B *Hang on!*
   C *Wait, please.*

6 When you want to know who is calling you, which of these is formal, which is informal, and which sounds rude?
   A *Who's that?*
   B *Who are you?*
   C *Who's calling, please?*

7 Which of these is the most formal way to introduce the subject of your phone call?
   A *I want to talk about the sales conference in March.*
   B *I'm calling in connection with the sales conference in March.*
   C *Let's talk about the sales conference in March.*

8 Which of these would you say when you want to find some information on your computer while you're on the phone?
   A *Wait while I get it on my computer, please.*
   B *Just a moment while I get it up on the screen.*
   C *I'm just bringing up your details now.*

9 What should you say when you don't understand something?
   A *What?*
   B *Could you repeat that, please?*
   C *I'm sorry, but I don't know.*

Student B

(page 21 Role-play)

You are a receptionist at the Ritz Hotel in Gdansk, Poland. Study this information and prepare to take a phone reservation.

Ritz Hotel ROOM PRICES

Double room:	500 Polish zlotys per night
Single room:	380 Polish zlotys per night
Conference room:	210 Polish zlotys per hour
Large meeting room (max. 25 people):	125 Polish zlotys per hour
Small meeting room (max. 10 people):	100 Polish zlotys per hour

Speaking

1 Work in pairs and discuss this question.

What's important when making a business phone call in English?

Use these ideas to help you if you like.

- preparation
- speaking clearly
- checking understanding

2 Change partners. Imagine you are giving a brief talk at a business meeting. Take it in turns to explain what you think is important when making a business phone call in English. Try to talk for a minute. As in a business meeting, your partner should listen and not comment until you have finished.

> **Useful language**
> **Listing and giving examples**
>
> I think there are three important things to remember when making a business call in English: …
> The most important thing is ……… because …
> For example, …
> Another thing which is important is …
> For instance, …
> Finally, you should …

Enquiring about a job

Listening

1 ①⁰⁹ You are going to hear a man phoning a company to enquire about a job. Listen and tick (✓) the phrases the speakers use from the quiz on page 21.

2 ①⁰⁹ Listen again and complete the man's notes below with one or two words in each gap.

> **Amposta Metals, S.A.**
> Post: **1** ……………
> Working hours: **2** ……………
> Duties: office admin, typing and **3** ……………
> Starting date: **4** …………… of September
> How to apply: **5** ……………

> **Role-play**
>
> 1 Work in pairs. Juanita is also recruiting for the job of Marketing Assistant at Amposta Metals. Read your role card below.
>
> **Student A**
>
> You are Juanita. Invent details of the post. Answer the phone and give information about the job. Use the conversation you have just listened to as a model.
>
> **Student B**
>
> You are interested in the job at Amposta Metals. Prepare some questions and phone to find out details of the job. Use the conversation you have just listened to as a model.

2 Juanita also needs an accountant. Change roles and find out / give details about the post.

Phone-answering tips

Reading

1 Work in small groups. You are going to read some advice about how to use the telephone to improve your business.

   1 What things annoy you when you phone companies or other organisations?
   2 What problems have you had when phoning companies, either in English or in your own language?

2 Read the article below without paying attention to the gaps. While you read, note down the main idea of each paragraph.

   Example: 1 *The importance of first impressions*

PHONE-ANSWERING TIPS TO WIN BUSINESS

Phone-answering skills are critical for businesses. The telephone is still many businesses' first point of contact with customers, so the way you answer your company's phone will form your customers' first impression of your business. These phone-answering tips will ensure that callers know they're dealing with a winning business.

Answer all incoming phone calls before the third ring and when you answer the phone, be warm and enthusiastic. Your voice at the end of the telephone line is sometimes the only impression of your company a caller will get. Welcome callers politely and identify your organisation and yourself. Say, for instance, *Good morning. Cypress Technologies. Susan speaking. How can I help you?* No one should ever have to ask if they've reached such-and-such a business. Keep your voice volume moderate and speak slowly and clearly. 1 .... Train your voice and vocabulary to be positive, even on a 'down' day.
2 ....

Always ask the caller if it's all right to put him or her on hold and don't leave people on hold for longer than is necessary. 3 .... Offer them choices such as, *The line is still busy. Will you continue to hold, or shall I ask Mrs Lee to call you back?*

Take telephone messages completely and accurately. If there's something you don't understand or can't spell, such as a person's surname, ask the caller to repeat it or spell it for you. 4 ....

Respond to all your calls within one business day. 5 .... The early caller can get the contract, the sale, the problem solved and reinforce the favourable impression of your business that you want to circulate.

Train everyone else who answers the phone to answer the same way. 6 .... If they don't pass the test, go over these telephone-answering tips with them.

adapted from *Your Guide to Small Business: Canada*

3 Read these missing sentences and underline a word or phrase in each one which might refer to something in the article.

   A Call in to check and see if <u>this</u> is being done in a professional manner.
   B For example, rather than saying *I don't know*, say *Let me find out about that for you.*
   C You really should not leave it any longer.
   D If possible, provide these callers with progress reports every 30 to 45 seconds.
   E However, research carried out in Hong Kong and Singapore has shown this is not usually true.
   F Then make sure it gets to the intended recipient.
   G This will help your caller to understand you easily.

4 Now choose the best sentence from Exercise 3 (A–G) to fill each of the gaps in the article.

   Task tip

   When you have finished, quickly read the text again with your answers to make sure it makes sense.

5 Work in pairs or small groups. Discuss which advice is very useful, and which is not so useful.

Speaking

Work in pairs or groups of three. Your company has decided to run a one-day course on effective telephone skills at work. You have been asked to prepare the course. Discuss the situation together, and decide:

- which staff in a company would most benefit from this type of course
- what advice and training should be given during the course.

   Task tip

   Before you speak, think of different possibilities to discuss for the two parts of the task.

Grammar workshop 1

Units 1–4

Countable and uncountable nouns

Nouns are either countable [C], e.g. *a job, two jobs*, or uncountable [U], e.g. *work*.
The grammar for countable nouns is different from the grammar for uncountable nouns.

Countable nouns
- use *a* or *an* in the singular: *a job, an employee*
- can be made plural: *jobs, employees*
- use *some* and *any* in the plural: *some customers, any emails*
- use *few* and *many* in the plural: *few clients, many complaints*
- use *a lot of* + plural noun:
  Manfred did a lot of jobs while he was at university.
- use *a number of*:
  We've had a number of complaints.

Uncountable nouns
- do not use *a* or *an*
- cannot be made plural: *work, furniture*
- use verbs in the singular: *The money is in the bank.*
- use *some* and *any* in the singular: *some information, any money*
- use *little* and *much*: *little information, much work*
- use other words to refer to a quantity:
  a piece of advice, an amount of money
- use *a lot of* + singular noun: *I've got a lot of work on at the moment.*
- use *an amount of*: *It's difficult to deal with such a large amount of information.*

1 ⊙ **Business English students are often not sure if these nouns are countable or uncountable. Write C (countable) or U (uncountable) for each one.**

advice *U*　budget *C*　car　computer　equipment
feedback　freight　information　knowledge　parking
programme　recruitment　report　research
software　spending　team　teamwork　training
training course　transport　travel

2 **Choose the correct option in italics in each of these sentences.**

1　He put *advertisement / an advertisement* for a sales director in the paper.
2　During the training course, you'll learn how to use some new *equipment / equipments*.
3　Our *research / researches* show that 90% of our students find *work / a work* within six months.
4　You'll find a large *amount of information / number of informations* on their website.
5　We can give you some *advice / advices* on how to apply.
6　During the first year, the job will involve *little travel / few travels* but *much training courses / many training courses*.

Present perfect and past simple

- We use the **past simple** for things which started and finished in the past:
  *Two years ago, PDQ **spent** 200,000 CHF on staff training.*
- We often use the past simple with time adverbs which indicate past time, e.g. *ago, last week/year, in the past, in 2005/January.*
- We use the **present perfect**:
  - for things which started in the past and are still happening now:
    *In the past three months, I've **been given** a lot more responsibility (which I still have).*
    *I **have had** this job since I left university.*
  - for things in the past where the exact time is not clear:
    *The company's training budget for this year **has been set** at 300,000 euros.*
  - for things which happened in the past but which have a present result:
    *PDQ **has** recently **signed** an agreement ... and because of this, staff now have to learn new working methods.*
- We often use the present perfect with time adverbs which indicate something started in the past and is still continuing, e.g. *since, in the last year / three weeks, this morning/year.*

1 Put the verbs in brackets in to the correct tense (present perfect or past simple).

1 I .... (work) for the company for only three years, but I'm already a senior manager.
2 I .... (go) on a training course during my first month at work, but I .... (not go) on one since then.
3 My first boss .... (be) very friendly, but she .... (leave) the company last year and I .... (not see) her since she .... (go).
4 They .... (change) the way we work completely in the last six months. Now we have flexible working, whereas before we .... (start) at nine and .... (finish) at five.
5 In 2004, they .... (post) him to Japan. He .... (be) there ever since, and during that time, he .... (get) married and .... (start) a family.
6 I .... (write) an email applying for the job several days ago, but I .... (not receive) a reply yet.
7 The company .... (grow) because we .... (take on) new staff every year since we .... (open) in 2005.

2 ◉ Business English students often make mistakes with the present perfect and the past simple. Choose the correct option in italics in each of these sentences.

1 The profits are higher than we *have expected / expected*.
2 We can advertise in daily newspapers, as we *have done / did* on many previous occasions.
3 I am writing to inform you that the board of directors *has decided / decided* to introduce identity cards in our department.
4 I want to tell you that I *have arranged / arranged* a meeting with the senior staff. It will take place on Thursday at 11 a.m.
5 I'm very glad to tell you that last month's profits *have increased / increased* by ten per cent.
6 It *has become / became* clear in the last few days that we need the new staff as soon as possible.
7 Last week, we *have decided / decided* that the company will need new premises if it is going to expand.
8 Last year, we *have made / made* a profit of eight million euros.

Talking about large and small differences

Here are some ways of expressing:
■ **large differences:**
  • *much / far / a lot / considerably larger than*:
    Our workforce is **far larger than** it was five years ago.
  • *not nearly as large as*:
    Five years ago, our workforce was **not nearly as large as** it is now.
■ **small differences**
  • *a little / slightly / somewhat more efficient than*:
    This year, our factory is **slightly more efficient than** last year.
  • *not quite as efficient as*:
    Our factory was **not quite as efficient** last year **as** this year.
We can express the difference more exactly using:
■ *twice, two-and-a-half times, three times as* + adjective/adverb + *as*:
  This machine produces **twice as many** components **as** the machine we had before.
  The lorry can carry **three times as much as** the van.
  (Remember: *many* is used with countable nouns and *much* with uncountables.)
■ *two-and-a-half times, three times more than* (but not *twice more than*):
  The lorry can carry **three times more than** the van.

1 This table shows average statistics for communications from a Spanish engineering company per week. Study the table and complete the sentences below.

	ten years ago	this year
emails	2,000	12,000
letters	850	230
meetings	70	75
phone calls	6,800	3,400
text messages	500	520

1 Staff write ~~far more~~ .... emails than ten years ago.
2 They don't write ~~nearly as many~~ .... letters ~~as 10 years ago~~ ....
3 Ten years ago, they didn't hold .... meetings ~~quite as many~~ ....
4 Ten years ago, they made ~~many more~~ .... phone calls ~~than this year~~ ....
5 They send .... text messages now .... ~~slightly more than 10 years ago~~.

2 Use language describing large and small differences to write four or five sentences describing how:

1 working/student life has changed in your country
2 the town or city where you live has changed.

Breaking into the market

Getting started

1 Work in pairs. Match the promotional activities (1–7) with the photos (a–g).

1 direct mail
2 free samples or gifts
3 leaflets and brochures
4 point-of-sale display
5 sponsorship
6 television and radio advertising
7 website

2 What are the advantages and disadvantages of each method of promotion?

Example 1: Direct mail is expensive, but you can target individual customers.

> **Useful language**
> **Discussing advantages and disadvantages**
>
> One advantage of (direct mail) is that …
> Another good thing about it is that …
> The main disadvantage of (sponsorship) is that …
> They also have the drawback that …

a

b

c

d

e

f

g

Promoting AXE

Reading

1 Work in pairs. You are going to read an article about Unilever's promotion of their AXE deodorant spray in the USA. Before you read, discuss these questions.

1 How are deodorants and toiletries promoted in your country?
2 Which promotional activities do you think would be suitable for promoting a deodorant spray? Why?

> **Unilever**
> A large multinational company based in Britain and Holland which produces foods, cleaning products and toiletries
>
> Unilever

2 Read the article on page 27 quickly to find out which promotional activities were used.

THE AXE EFFECT

When Unilever wanted to launch its AXE deodorant spray for men in the United States, it combined young men's natural interest in pretty girls with the attraction of a great house party. The idea was simple: boy buys AXE, boy
5 meets girl, boy smells nice, girl likes boy.

The product, which was already popular in other parts of the world, was launched in the United States with a powerful promotional plan to make it appeal to American male youth culture. Using the slogan 'the AXE effect', the company
10 used a number of marketing ploys to bring the product to the attention of the public. These included playing an online game, free samples of the deodorant handed out by attractive female models in retail stores, point-of-sale displays, media advertising and public relations (PR), all of
15 which hyped the centrepiece of the promotion: a once-in-a-lifetime party at a Florida mansion.

Unilever began by direct-mailing millions of college students and young males aged between 11 and 24. They received free samples and information about the event,
20 which was advertised as the AXE House Party: crowds of attractive people, rock stars and a beach house. A radio advertising campaign and online publicity called for young men to log on to the Internet to play a video game on the AXE website. Participants had to apply their dating skills to
25 score points. If the player reached a certain level, he entered a lottery to win a trip to the party.

AXE focused on the intrigue and discovery of the party. Leaflets similar to ones made for a party by a group of college students were posted in relevant locations such
30 as men's toilets at nightclubs. There were also print ads in *Rolling Stone* and *Spin* magazines.

'It was all about getting into the mind of the 20-something guy,' says Mary Drapp, Manager of Strategic Alliances and Sponsorships for Unilever. And they succeeded in doing
35 that. Their website received more than 943,000 hits, or 20% more than the goal. Some 100 lucky young men were flown in to attend the party, held near Miami. Hundreds of young people were invited to dance and enjoy musical acts by well-known rock bands. Guests could use the pool, go to a game
40 room or play air hockey, cards or billiards.

The party was filmed and made into an hour-long show broadcast on TNN. 'To our knowledge, nobody has ever taken a consumer promotion and turned it into a television show,' says Steve Jarvis, the marketing consultant for AXE.
45 'That was something completely original.' After the party, AXE continued to capitalise on the event. Some 500,000 special packs went on sale in retail stores, offering two cans of the deodorant spray with a free AXE house-party CD that featured songs from the artists who had appeared at the
50 party.

Following the promotion, results included a 22% increase in general brand awareness among males aged 11 to 24 and a 3.0% to 3.7% increase in antiperspirant and deodorant market share.

adapted from Promo

UNIT 5

Task tip

Read the question, then find the answer in the text. After that, read the options A–D and choose the one which matches what you read.

3 **Now choose the best answer – A, B, C or D – for each of these questions.**

1 Who were the target audience in Unilever's promotional campaign?
   A young women
   B young men
   C men of all ages
   D men and women

2 How did people get an invitation to the house party?
   A by receiving direct mail
   B by answering an advertisement
   C by applying through an internet site
   D by participating in a game

3 What was the aim of the publicity for the party?
   A to show an exotic location
   B to improve men's dating skills
   C to excite people's curiosity
   D to show people they needed AXE

4 According to Mary Drapp, what was the aim of the promotional campaign?
   A to increase brand awareness
   B to encourage people to visit the website
   C to change the target customers
   D to show the effectiveness of the product

5 What was unique about the promotion of AXE?
   A the house party
   B the television programme
   C the free CD
   D the use of the Internet

6 What was the effect of the marketing campaign?
   A Twenty-two per cent more people knew about AXE.
   B Sales of AXE increased by 22%.
   C There was an increase in the percentage of young men who knew about AXE.
   D Brand awareness rose to 3.7%.

Vocabulary

Match these words and phrases from the text (1–6) with their definitions (a–f).

1 launch (line 1)
2 ploys (line 10)
3 hyped (line 15)
4 hits (line 35)
5 brand awareness (line 52)
6 market share (line 54)

a how much of the market is taken by a particular product
b knowledge that a certain brand exists
c publicised strongly
d tactics/tricks
e visits (to a website)
f start selling for the first time

Grammar workshop

Infinitive or verb + -ing

Choose the correct option in italics in these sentences. (Sentences 1–5 are from the article you have just read.)

1 The product was launched with a powerful promotional plan *to make / making* it appeal to youth culture.
2 The company used a number of marketing ploys *to bring / bringing* the product to the attention of the public.
3 These included *to play / playing* an online game.
4 They succeeded in *to do / doing* that.
5 Hundreds of young people were invited *to dance / dancing*.
6 We are considering *to use / using* television advertising to promote the product.
7 It's important *not to let / not letting* advertising costs get out of control.
8 *To build / Building* a brand takes time and imagination.
9 We decided *to launch / launching* the new product during the summer.

❯ **page 42** Infinitives and verb + -*ing*

Role-play

Work in groups of about four. You work on the creative team in the marketing department of a large multinational company. The company has decided that it is time to launch in your country a shampoo which has been very successful in the United States and Canada. The target customers for this shampoo, called *Imagination* in the US and Canada, are young women aged 12–25. Your job is to prepare a promotional campaign for the launch.

You should:

- brainstorm ideas for possible promotional activities
- evaluate the ideas and decide which ones you want to use
- produce a plan of action
- compare your plans with other creative teams.

Supermarkets' own brands

Listening

1 Work in pairs. You are going to hear Christina Bunt talking about Tesco's own brands. An 'own brand' is a product which a supermarket sells with its own name on it, e.g. Tesco washing powder or Tesco coffee. Before you listen, discuss why supermarkets have own brands.

2 ①10 Listen and choose the best answer – A, B or C – for each question.

1 Why did Tesco originally introduce its own brand?
   A to increase sales
   B to reduce reliance on suppliers
   C to reduce costs
2 What is the main reason for supermarkets having own brands nowadays?
   A They bring customers back to their shops.
   B They have a higher profit margin.
   C They don't depend on outside suppliers.
3 Tesco can sell its value brands more cheaply than other brands because …
   A it pays suppliers less.
   B they sell in large quantities.
   C they don't need advertising.

Going viral in India and China

Reading

1 Work in small groups. You are going to read extracts from an article about Levi's marketing strategy in India and China. Before you read, look at the company background box and discuss this question.

How do you think the Indian and Chinese markets are different from Levi's traditional markets?

> **Levi's**
>
> Levi Strauss (Levi's) is a clothing manufacturer established in 1873 and based in San Francisco, California. Known particularly for their denim jeans, their traditional markets have been North America and Europe.

2 Look at these descriptions (1–8) and the paragraphs (A–D) in the article. Which paragraph does each description refer to?

1 a market which can't be ignored D
2 a marketing strategy which attracted negative comments
3 a new location for bringing a new product to market
4 a product which can now be worn in the office
5 a strategy to keep customers loyal
6 advertising that suggested that people should change their behaviour
7 employing people to express their emotions about the product
8 following their competitors' example

Speaking

Work in pairs. Prepare a short talk about a clothing brand you are both familiar with. Take notes while you discuss these questions. When you are ready, change partners and take turns to give your talks.

- What image does it have?
- How do you feel about the brand?
- How is it marketed?

A When Diesel launched its 'Be Stupid' campaign to encourage consumers to take risks and move beyond the smart and sensible life, the viral video got everyone's attention. Word got around, and the video stacked up to 700,000 views on YouTube, even though it was criticised widely in the media. 'Going viral' is the new watchword for clothing brands. Most, if not all, have gone digital, and Levi's now seems to be doing the same.

B At the launch of Denizen, its low-cost brand, in India, Levi's has brought in what they call the 'Denizen 8', a team consisting of a software developer, a media planner, a property consultant, an app developer, a writer and a student, all aged between 18 and 28. 'We're getting eight denim lovers from all over the country to become our brand ambassadors,' says Sanjay Purohit, MD, Levi Strauss India. Eight might not seem to be a very large number in a country of millions, but this team aren't just ordinary brand ambassadors. The brand has them activated on the social media space. They blog about the brand and how the brand makes them feel.

C The launch of Denizen in China last month was the first time that Levi's has moved outside the United States for the global launch of a brand. Levi's has been known for its strength in the premium and super-premium denim price segments and is now keen on expanding the price ladder lower to prevent consumers from crossing over to competitors. Through Denizen, the company seeks to attract the 18–28 age group with affordable pricing. 'We are targeting consumers who are just out of college or have taken on their first jobs and want a brand that could fit into their lifestyle and budget needs. It made more sense to launch Denizen in emerging markets, particularly in Asia first,' said Tod Gimbel.

D Denizen is the first clothing brand to have been built for the digital medium, as most of its target group uses social media, Internet and mobile. India, being among the three largest markets for Levi's in Asia, is also a market where denim is the fastest-growing clothing category, producing 35 to 40 million pairs a year. With work environments becoming more casual, for the younger generation, denim is the clothing of choice. These consumers are typically young, middle-class, probably the first generation to be university educated and the first to work in a foreign multinational.

adapted from *The Economic Times*

Launching a product

Getting started

Work in pairs. Talk about two or three new products that have appeared on the market in the last ten years. Discuss:

- how you first heard about them
- if you think they are useful or desirable (if you would like to have them)
- where you can buy them
- how they are marketed
- how they are packaged.

Developing and launching Drink Me Chai

Listening

1 Work in small groups. You are going to hear Amanda Hamilton, Managing Director of Drink Me Chai, talking about how she developed a new tea product. Before you listen, make a list of the steps you would take before launching a new drink on the market.

2 ①11 Listen and choose the best answer – A, B or C – for each question.

1 What was *chai* originally?
  A an Indian drink
  B an American drink
  C a drink Amanda invented

2 Why did she start importing *chai*?
  A for selling to people travelling to work
  B for herself
  C for selling in shops

3 Why did she decide to develop her own *chai*?
  A She couldn't afford to import it.
  B She couldn't depend on her suppliers.
  C She enjoyed experimenting with different flavours.

4 How did she test her product?
  A by using a market-research company
  B by giving it to her own customers
  C by trying it in the USA

5 What was the supermarket buyer's reaction to her product?
  A He fixed another meeting for six weeks later.
  B He agreed to try selling it in a few stores.
  C He agreed to sell it in a large number of stores all over the country.

3 Work in small groups. Were any of the steps Amanda took the same as your list from Exercise 1?

> **Useful language**
> **Saying what you would do**
>
> The first thing we could do is …
> After that / Next, we could …
> We could also … / Another thing we could do is …
> I think we should also …

> **Drink Me Chai**
> An award-winning UK-based company that produces a range of authentic Indian *chai* in an instant form

Reading

1 Read the article on the right about Amanda Hamilton quite quickly and answer these questions.

1 When did she realise there was a larger market for her product?
2 In what way(s) was her deal with Tesco remarkable?

2 Work in pairs. Six sentences have been removed from the article.

1 Underline words or phrases in the sentences (A–G) which refer to something in the article.
2 Discuss what the words/phrases might refer to.

A He liked it and came back, saying Tesco wanted to put it into 230 of its UK stores.
'He' is someone mentioned in the text and 'it' may be chai.

B However, getting a good cup of tea for the journey was a real struggle.

C I started importing it, but it cost me an absolute fortune, so I worked on a range of different recipes for my own *chai* and did some testing.

D But the major problem was raising finance and setting up a production facility.

E It really transformed the business.

F Since then, Drink Me Chai has been taken up by Waitrose, another supermarket chain.

G As a result, her *chai* latte product, and her company Drink Me Chai, had instant access to retail customers across the UK.

3 Choose the best sentence (A–G) to fill each gap. There is one sentence that you will not need.

The **Drink Me Chai** success story

For businesses that are starting out, it can take years to achieve a national distribution deal, and many never do. Amanda Hamilton, however, managed to get her ready-to-drink tea into 230 Tesco stores before she had even settled on branding and packaging for the product. **1** ___G___

Like many business ideas, Hamilton's came out of a personal need. She started by working firstly in advertising and then for the BBC, commuting by train into London. **2** _____ Eventually, with the help of the Prince's Youth Business Trust and a Business 2000 loan, she raised funds to open tea bars at railway stations offering a range of gourmet teas to travellers. Tea was regarded as downmarket, but the tea bars were really trendy mobile bars, offering lots of tastes and flavours.

It was on a visit to the US that Hamilton discovered that *chai* latte, a tea made from a powdered mix of tea and spices, milk and sugar, was the fastest-growing drink in the US. '**3** _____ Customers kept saying they preferred my version, so I stopped importing US *chai* and sold my *chai* through the tea bars.'

Hamilton's customers also started to say that they would like to drink the product at home, which gave her the idea of sending a sample to a Tesco buyer. 'I had no branding and no packaging, but I managed to get through and spoke to the buyer,' she says. '**4** _____ It was a massive deal for me, but at that stage I could not afford my own factory, so I had to source a co-packing facility to mix it and pack it for me.'

The drink was launched by a new company under the same name and produced in spiced *chai* and vanilla *chai* flavours. **5** _____ Tesco has recently launched Spiced Chai Light, which comes in individually wrapped 20g sachets, and Drink Me Chai is also on sale in Caffè Nero coffee bars, taking the brand into the catering market and bringing Hamilton's success story full circle.

Hamilton's aim is for Drink Me Chai to be the number-one instant *chai* latte brand in the UK and Europe in both the catering and retail markets. She still regards the Tesco deal as the one that started everything, however. '**6** _____ It's highly unusual for a national supermarket chain to take a product without any packaging or branding,' she says. 'The taste was so good that we managed to get a deal without those things.'

adapted from the Daily Telegraph

Launching and promoting a new product

Listening

1 Work in small groups. Discuss and take notes on this question.

What is important when launching a new product?

2 ①12 Listen to Amanda Hamilton talking about the same topic. Does she mention anything which did not arise in your discussion?

3 Now work with a partner from another group and take turns to talk for a minute about what is important when launching a new product.

4 Work in small groups. Look at these promotional methods.

internet advertising	viral marketing
word of mouth	point-of-sale displays
stand at food fair	social media

Can you add other promotional methods to the list? How could they be used to promote *chai*?

5 ①13 Listen to Amanda Hamilton talking about how she has marketed *chai*. Make brief notes on the following:

1 the promotional methods she has used
2 the reasons she uses each promotional method

A marketing report

Writing

1 **Work in pairs. You work in the marketing department of Turbodrinks, a company which produces sports drinks.**

1 Look at the charts on the right for Turbofizz, one of the company's sports drinks (but not the handwritten notes).
2 Study sentence 1 below.
3 Complete sentence 2 by writing prepositions in the gaps.
4 Complete sentences 3 and 4 with your own words.

> 1 Spending on advertising in sports magazines has risen by 150,000 Australian dollars from 300,000 to 450,000 Australian dollars.
> 2 We have raised spending on free samples at sports events .... 150,000 Australian dollars .... 50,000 .... 200,000 Australian dollars.
> 3 We have reduced ....
> 4 Our total promotional budget this year ....

 page 42 Prepositions in phrases describing trends

2 **Work in pairs. The Marketing Manager has asked you to write a report on the promotional budget. Discuss what you can say to deal with each of the handwritten notes and note down your ideas.**

3 **Read the report below. Which ideas were the same as yours, and which were different?**

4 **Read the report again. In most of the lines, there is one extra word. It is either grammatically incorrect or does not fit in with the meaning of the text. Some lines, however, are correct. Find and delete the extra words.**

Task tips

Read the whole text first so you know what it's about. Then read it sentence by sentence to recognise the extra words.

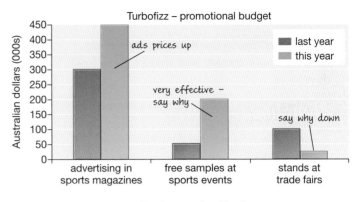

Turbofizz – promotional budget

ads prices up
very effective – say why
say why down

advertising in sports magazines · free samples at sports events · stands at trade fairs

last year / this year

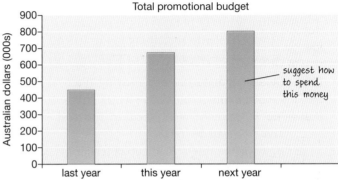

Total promotional budget

suggest how to spend this money

last year · this year · next year

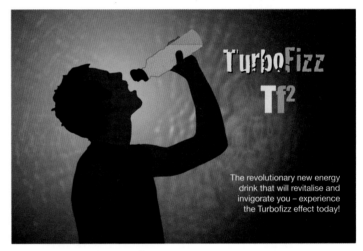

TurboFizz Tf²

The revolutionary new energy drink that will revitalise and invigorate you – experience the Turbofizz effect today!

INTRODUCTION

1 The aim of this report is for to summarise our spending on Turbofizz in the last two
2 years and to make recommendations for the future budget allocations.

PROMOTIONAL ACTIVITIES

3 Spending on sports magazine advertisements has risen by 150,000 Australian dollars
4 to 450,000 Australian dollars this year due as a result of an increase in advertising rates.
5 Over the same period only, we have raised spending on free samples at sports events by
6 150,000 Australian dollars to 200,000 Australian dollars because we have attracted too
7 many new customers as a result.
8 We have reduced down our spending on stands at trade fairs from 100,000
9 Australian dollars to 25,000 Australian dollars because trade customers are already being
10 very familiar with the product.

RECOMMENDATIONS

11 Our budget will rise up to 800,000 Australian dollars next year. I recommend
12 cutting the amount we spend on free samples and starting off advertising on television
13 in order to reach a wider public.

5 Work in pairs. You work in the marketing department of Slimchocs, a company which makes low-calorie sweets. Your line manager has asked you to write a report on the promotional budget. Look at the information below, on which you have already made some handwritten notes, and answer these questions.

1 How has spending on different types of promotion changed between last year and this year?
2 What can you say to complete the comments on the first chart (you will have to invent ideas)?
3 How has the total budget changed, and how will it change next year?
4 What recommendations can you make for spending next year?

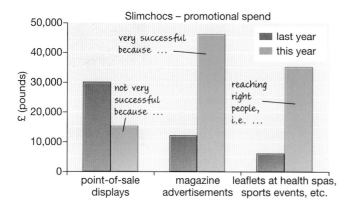

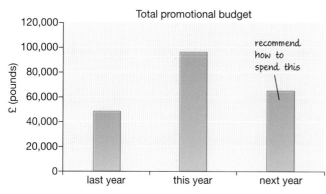

6 Work alone. Using all your handwritten notes, write your report.

An interior design company

UNIT 6

Role-play

1 Work in groups of four. Read this situation.

You work for an interior design company in your city (you decorate and furnish the inside of houses and offices) and until now, you have only worked with architects and builders. Now you would like to sell your services directly to the general public as well, and you are having a meeting to decide how to promote yourselves.

2 Each of you should take one of these roles and prepare what you are going to say.

Managing Director

You know you can find good staff and you are confident that there is a large market for your services, so you want to expand the business quickly. You would like to use some form of advertising and also direct mail. You are ready to invest heavily in promotion.

Finance Director

You are cautious about expanding the business too fast, having a marketing budget which is too large, taking on too many new employees and having cashflow problems. You would like to distribute leaflets around shops and offices and also have some advertising posters at bus stops.

Marketing Manager

You love promoting services in any way possible, and the more imaginative and unusual, the better. You especially favour events such as stands at trade fairs or sponsoring a local sports team, but you are always happy to consider other ideas.

Sales Manager

Until now, visiting companies and architects has always been very successful, and you strongly believe in the personal touch. You would like the marketing budget to be spent on increasing the sales staff, who would be involved in direct selling, either by phone or by visiting potential customers.

3 Hold the meeting and make sure you reach agreement on how to promote your services.

4 Report back to the rest of the class on what you have decided to do.

A stand at a trade fair

Getting started

Work in pairs. Discuss these questions.

1 What is happening in the photos?
2 How can companies promote their products by having a stand at a trade fair?

The London Contemporary Design Show

Reading

1 Marcel Schaub works for Lucerne Design, a company which designs and manufactures furniture in Lucerne, Switzerland. The company's working language is English. Read the memo and the email below which he has received from his boss (ignoring the gaps) and answer these questions.

1 What is a memo?
2 How can you start and finish a memo?
3 How can you start and finish an email to someone in the same office?
4 What does Ulrike want Marcel to do? Why?

> **London Contemporary Design Show**
> The UK's first and leading contemporary design show is a key event in the international calendar.

Memo

> ## MEMO
>
> **From:** Ulrike Schütz
> **To:** All staff
> **Subject:** The London Contemporary Design Show
>
> ---
>
> Following conversations **1** ..with.. our distributors, I have decided that next year we will take a stand **2** .... the London Contemporary Design Show **3** .... September. The objective will be to expand our customer base and hopefully find new export markets **4** .... our products.
> Preparing **5** .... the exhibition and manning the stand will require quite a lot of extra work from staff, especially as this is the first time we have done this outside Switzerland, Germany or Austria. I shall be contacting individual members of staff to ask **6** .... their help **7** .... carrying out this new project successfully.
>
> US

Email

> **From:** Ulrike Schütz
> **To:** Marcel Schaub
> **Subject:** The London Contemporary Design Show
>
> Marcel
>
> Can you get in touch **8** .... the organisers of the Show and find **9** .... :
> • how much it will cost to have a stand at the exhibition
> • when we would need to book the space?
> This is their website:
> http://www.100percentdesign.co.uk.
>
> Thanks
> Ulrike

2 **Complete the memo and the email by writing the correct preposition in each gap.**

3 **Work alone. Write Marcel's email to the organisers. Try to write 40–50 words.**

> **Task tip**
> Make sure you cover all the points in the instructions.

Grammar workshop

Formal requests

1 Match the beginnings of these sentences (1–5) with their endings (a–e).

1 Can you please tell us how much   a about the exhibition.
2 We would appreciate it if you could send us details   b it will cost to exhibit at the show?
3 I would be very grateful if you could give me information   c the exhibition centre opens.
4 I wonder if you could tell me what time   d to reserve a space at the exhibition.
5 We would be pleased if you could inform us about how   e of your products.

2 Work in pairs. Answer these questions.

1 Which request ends with a question mark (?)? Why?

2 Which requests contain *would* and/or *could*?

3 Some requests use *I* and some use *we*. Which should you use when you are requesting information on behalf of your company?

4 Which prepositions follow *details* and *information*?

> page 43 Formal requests

Vocabulary

1 Business English students often confuse *find out, know, learn* and *teach*. Complete these sentences from the *CALD* (1–4) with the phrases below (a–d).

1 If you **know** something, you .... : *I know where the exhibition is.*

2 If you **find** something **out**, you .... : *I'll find out how much it costs.*

3 To **learn** is to .... : *I've learned a lot about computers since I started work here.*

4 When you **teach** someone, you .... : *She taught English to foreign students.*

a learn new information for the first time
b give them new knowledge or skills
c get new knowledge or skills
d already have the information

2 Complete these sentences with the right word or phrase in the correct form.

1 All staff have to attend the course so that they can .... how to reduce costs.

2 Could you phone the transport agency to .... where the order is?

3 On this course, we will .... you advanced programming skills.

4 I only .... about the problem that we have with our suppliers by accident.

5 He doesn't .... how the system works – we'll have to .... him.

6 Good sales techniques are something you .... with practice.

7 In this job, everyone has to .... how to handle customers tactfully from day one.

8 We're carrying out market research to .... exactly what our customers need.

Listening

1 Work in pairs. You are going to hear Tasha at 100percentdesign phoning Marcel. Before you listen, look at Marcel's notes and decide what type of information you need for each gap.

London Contemporary Design Show
22–25 September

Costs
• 1 .... : from £295 to £340 per square metre + VAT (Value Added Tax)
• 2 .... : £115
• Registration fee: £300
• Latest date for registration: 3 ....
• Will send 4 .... and floor plan by email
• Full amount to be paid one month before exhibition, otherwise space not 5 ....

2 ① 14 Listen to the conversation and complete Marcel's notes with one or two words in each gap.

3 Use the information from Marcel's notes to write his email to Ulrike Schütz, answering the questions in Ulrike's first email (page 34). When you have finished writing, compare your email with a partner's.

Preparing an exhibition stand

Writing 1

1 Work in pairs. Read Ulrike's next email to Marcel and discuss what information Marcel should include in his email.

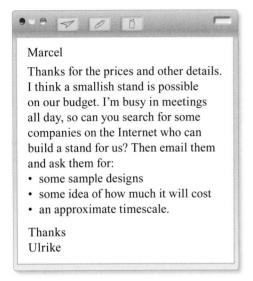

> Marcel
>
> Thanks for the prices and other details. I think a smallish stand is possible on our budget. I'm busy in meetings all day, so can you search for some companies on the Internet who can build a stand for us? Then email them and ask them for:
> * some sample designs
> * some idea of how much it will cost
> * an approximate timescale.
>
> Thanks
> Ulrike

2 Write Marcel's email to the companies which build stands. Try to write 40–50 words.

❯ page 117 Writing reference

Reading

1 Look at these questions and underline the key ideas.

Which builder:

1 can <u>keep costs down</u> by supplying you with <u>existing equipment</u>?
2 has wide international experience of exhibition stands?
3 promises to provide your stand on time?
4 will be more involved in your promotional activity than just providing the stand?
5 will provide you with a stand you know you can afford?
6 will supply stands which you needn't buy?
7 will try to ensure that as many people come to your stand as possible?

2 Read the publicity from three stand builders that Marcel found on the Internet and answer the questions in Exercise 1.

A

STAND the PACE

Do you want your company to stand out at business exhibitions and trade events? **Stand the Pace** can do this for you by supplying custom-built exhibition stands – for hire or for sale.

We guarantee to meet our clients' needs with our free computer design service. Our prices are keen and competitive due to our huge stocks of ready-made equipment.

We will take the work out of your hands by liaising with the exhibition organisers, transporting all equipment and associated publicity material to the event, setting up the stand, installing all the equipment and mounting all graphics. All you have to do is arrive, walk onto the stand and start promoting your products. What could be easier?

For more information, please contact James Steel, our Marketing Director.

B

HIGHSTAND DESIGN & DISPLAY

has the creativity, experience, skills and commitment to bring you a solution that will give you an edge over your competition.

Our stand will give your company the opportunity to make an impact. We ensure you make the very best of that opportunity by providing you with a solution that meets your brief and matches your budget.

We have delivered customised exhibition solutions worldwide and designed stands for almost every market you can name.

Our computerised designs provide you with a 3D view of your design. Our project-management skills ensure deadlines are met, costs controlled, and workshop and on-site construction monitored.

C

cutedisplay.co.uk

When you exhibit, it's all about customers – you want to impress your current clients and attract potential new ones.

So whatever your exhibition opportunity, cutedisplay.co.uk can offer you not just a great-looking stand, but creative designs with a commercial edge. We can provide a complete marketing solution for your project, including pre-event promotions, stand design and show activity. We'll not only design an attractive stand that grabs people's attention, we'll also work with you to maximise your visitor numbers.

You'll get an exhibition stand solution that enhances your products and services, impresses your customers and gives you that all-important marketing advantage. With over 18 years' experience in exhibitions, we know how to win you new business.

3 Read this reply to Marcel's email and choose the best word – A, B, C or D – for each gap.

INBOX   File | Edit | View | Favourites | Tools | Actions | Help   ✕

To: Marcel Schaub
Subject: Stand at London Contemporary Design Show

Dear Mr Schaub
Thank you for your **1** .... enquiry about a stand for the London Contemporary Design Show next September. For your interest, I'm **2** .... some photos of stands we have built to give you an **3** .... of the quality of our work.
There are a **4** .... of things we need to **5** .... before we can give you a quotation.
We would be **6** .... if you could tell us:
- **7** .... how much floor space your stand will **8** ....
- whether you **9** .... the stand to be open or closed
- how many shelves you would like for displaying products
- how many people you **10** .... to accommodate on the stand at any one time, **11** .... both staff and visitors.
If you would be so kind as to **12** .... us with this information, we will send you a **13** .... of draft designs for you to **14** .... from, with quotations for **15** .... of them.

Kind regards
James Steel

Task tip

The options for each gap will have similar meanings. Choose the word which exactly matches the meaning you need.

1 A latest	B last	C new	D recent
2 A enclosing	B attaching	C joining	D fixing
3 A idea	B impression	C opinion	D understanding
4 A number	B range	C choice	D variety
5 A learn	B know	C discover	D realise
6 A happy	B pleased	C grateful	D delighted
7 A specifically	B precisely	C exactly	D definitely
8 A take	B hold	C employ	D occupy
9 A hope	B require	C necessitate	D desire
10 A plan	B organise	C arrange	D foresee
11 A including	B involving	C adding	D combining
12 A give	B send	C offer	D supply
13 A choice	B selection	C collection	D quantity
14 A decide	B choose	C opt	D determine
15 A any	B every	C both	D each

Writing 2

1 Work in pairs. Imagine you are Marcel and Ulrike. Look at the photos on this page and decide which design you like best.

2 Decide what answers you should give to James Steel's email (you can invent them) and write an email in reply.

3 Now imagine you are Ulrike. Write a short memo to the sales staff.

- Inform them that the stand is being designed.
- Ask them what equipment they will need for the stand.
- Suggest they prepare graphics for the stand.

Use the memo on page 34 as a model.

Useful language
Replying to queries

Thank you for your .... (of .... [date]).
Here are the answers to the questions you raised: ...
In answer to your questions, ...
With reference to ...
Regarding ...

Being persuasive

Getting started

1   Work in small groups.

Achieving goals in business often depends on your ability to persuade. How can these things make you more persuasive?

- Looking good and dressing well
- Having good communication skills
- Being enthusiastic about what you do
- Knowing your job and your products well
- Understanding what other people need and how they feel
- Getting on well with the people you are working with

2   (1) 15 Listen to Karl (K), Adam (A), Rob (R) and Duncan (D) talking about what makes people persuasive in business. Complete the chart by ticking (✓) the things each of them mentions. One thing is mentioned by more than one person.

To be persuasive in business, you should:	K	A	R	D
1 be truthful.				
2 be persistent.	✓			
3 make sure your customers like you.				
4 pay attention to what your customers are saying.				
5 prepare your strategy carefully.				
6 know your customers' requirements.				
7 treat customers with respect.				
8 have confidence in your product.				

3   Work in small groups. Take turns to talk about a time when you persuaded someone to do something. What made you persuasive?

Breaking the ice

Speaking

1   Work in pairs. Imagine you are meeting some other business people for the first time at a trade fair. Here are some things you can talk about to 'break the ice'. What would you say in each case?

1   Say you like the stand. So this is your stand. Very smart!
2   Ask about the other person's journey.
3   Say how nice the city is.
4   Ask the other person about their hotel.
5   Offer to show your products.
6   Say how busy the fair is.
7   Offer refreshments.

2   (1) 16 Listen to a saleswoman talking to two buyers at a trade fair. What do they say for situations 1–7 in Exercise 1?

3   Look at the transcript of the conversation (Track 16) and underline the words and phrases which express positive feelings.

Example: Nice to meet you.

Role-play 1

Work in groups of four (Pair A + Pair B). Have conversations from the moment Pair A arrive at the office.

Pair A

You are visiting a company in a town or city you have not visited before. Think of two or three pleasant things you can say to start building a relationship with the people in the company you are visiting. You can use the conversation in Speaking Exercise 2 for ideas.

Pair B

You are working in a company. Think of two or three pleasant things you can say to your visitors to start building a relationship. You can use the conversation in Speaking Exercise 2 for ideas.

Role-play 2

1 Work in pairs. You are going to play the roles of buyers and sales reps at a trade fair. Each of you should take one of the roles below.

Student A: You are a buyer for a chain of stores visiting the stand. Read and prepare your role below. Then have the conversation for Product 1.

Student B: You are a salesperson working on a stand. Read and prepare your role on page 40. Then have the conversation for Product 1.

2 Change roles and talk about Product 2.

Student A: Buyer

Greet the salesperson, introduce yourselves, etc. Then ask questions about the product below, which you have seen on the stand, and complete the information.

**1 CorkPops™
Bottle opener**

Insert a long needle through the cork and into the bottle, then press a button ... POP! Your bottle is opened. It's simply the fastest, easiest way to open a bottle!
One cartridge can open
1 .... bottles.
Wholesale price: **2** ....
Recommended retail price: 3 ....
Availability: **4** ....

2 The Battery Peeler does all the work, so your hands won't ache.

Good news for arthritis sufferers. Now you can peel vegetables without worrying whether you will have enough hand strength.
Details
Length: **1** ....
Blade can be cleaned **2** ....
Weight: **3** ....
Requires **4** ....batteries (not included)
Wholesale price: **5** ....
Recommended retail price: 6 ....

The art of agreeing

Reading

1 Work in pairs. You are going to read extracts from an article about negotiating.

- Read the statements below and underline the key ideas.
- Discuss how you would express each underlined idea using other words.

1 Negotiators are <u>in a stronger position</u> if it's <u>not essential</u> for them <u>to reach agreement</u>.
They have more power if they can allow the negotiation to fail.

2 Negotiators can gain <u>confidence in each</u> other by exchanging information.
They can trust each other more if they share information

3 Negotiators should <u>always be in control of their feelings</u>.
They ought to keep their emotional reactions

④ Negotiators should try to acquire as much information as possible in advance.
They ought to be well informed for themselves

⑤ Negotiators should work out ways in which the other party can be flexible.
They should find how far they can go

6 Negotiators' main objective is not always financial gain.

⑦ Negotiators' non-verbal behaviour will influence the result.
BODY LANGUAGE

8 The negotiator who makes the opening proposal has an advantage.

2 Work in small groups. Which of the ideas in Exercise 1 do you agree with? Why? / Why not?

3 Which of these extracts (A–D) does each statement in Exercise 1 (1–8) refer to?

A

The better prepared you are with factual data before heading into a negotiation, the more effective you will be. After that, the most important requirement is to identify the real needs and goals. Though the most obviously stated need is money, it can be a proxy for other physical or more refined needs (shelter, reputation, self-esteem). In the case of a vendor/client, people are often simply seeking understanding and attention rather than money.

C

You can negotiate well only if you have the ability to walk away from an unfavourable agreement, and to do this, you should create a credible alternative to failure. A successful salesperson, for instance, can negotiate the best deals on his products if he has a potential back-up customer. You should also factor in the fall-back options for the other side. If you do this, it will be clear that the final agreement will necessarily fall between the back-up options of the parties concerned.

B

It is important to realise that your choice of words and your body language will have an impact on people and on the outcome of your negotiation. Listen with an open mind and focus on receiving and communicating with maximum clarity. While you are continuing to receive factual data, with both parties following the give-and-take principle, you are building trust gradually. It is important to respect each other to negotiate successfully.

D

Take time to help your client understand what he stands to gain from your offer. Listen carefully to make sure you understand what he really wants. Also remember never to lose your cool or emotions. Your friends may accept you as you are, but your clients could run scared. Try and be the first to make an offer. It will help anchor the client to your view, and the final agreement is more likely to end closer to your proposal.

adapted from *Business Today: The art of agreeing* by Devashish Chakravarty

Vocabulary

Find words or phrases in the extracts with these meanings.

1 substitute or replacement for something else (extract A) proxy
2 someone who is selling something (extract A) vendor
3 powerful effect that something, especially something new, has on a situation or person (extract B) impact
4 a result or effect of an action, situation, etc. (extract B) outcome

5 include something when you are doing a calculation, or when you are trying to understand something (extract C) factor in
6 describes a plan or position which can be used if other plans do not succeed or other things are not available (extract C) fall-back (plan b)
7 become angry or excited (extract D) To lose your cool

Student B: Sales rep

(Role-play, page 39)

Greet the buyer, introduce yourselves, etc. Then answer questions about the products.

1 CorkPops™
Bottle opener

Insert a long needle through the cork and into the bottle, then press a button … POP! Your bottle is opened. It's simply the fastest, easiest way to open a bottle! One cartridge can open 60 to 80 bottles.
Wholesale price: €12
Recommended retail price: €19.99
Availability: immediately

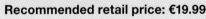

2 The Battery Peeler does all the work, so your hands won't ache.
Good news for arthritis sufferers. Now you can peel vegetables without worrying whether you will have enough hand strength.

Details:
Length: 21 cm
Blade can be cleaned in the dishwasher.
Weight: 85 g
Requires 2 AA batteries (not included)
Wholesale price: €6
Recommended retail price: €9.95

Speaking

Work in pairs. Prepare and make notes for a short presentation on this subject.

What is important when negotiating with a client?

Think about things such as preparation and strategy.

When you are ready, change partners and take turns to give your talks.

> **Task tip**
> Look at your partner when you give your talk. Use your notes just to remind yourself of what you want to say.

Listening

1   You are going to hear Helga (the sales rep) negotiating a deal for CorkPops with Jack and Susie (the buyers). Before you listen, complete these sentences by putting the verbs in brackets in the correct tense. Then decide whether Helga or Jack/Susie will say each sentence.

J   1   We've decided some of your products _could_ (can) interest us if the terms were right.

H   2   If you _took_ (take) 2,000, I'd take back whatever you couldn't sell after a year.

J/S 3   We'_ll accept_ (accept) that if we can agree on the other details.

S   4   If we bought the CorkPops at €12 each, we _wouldn't make_ (not make) any profit.

H   5   I can agree to €10 per unit if you'll _buy_ (buy) other products from us as well.

J   6   We could go to €9.50 if you _would give_ (give) us a discount of 5% on sales of over 2,000.

2   ①17 Listen and check your answers.

❯ **page 43** First and second conditionals

Writing

1   Without paying attention to the handwritten notes, complete Helga's email to Jack by writing a preposition in each gap.

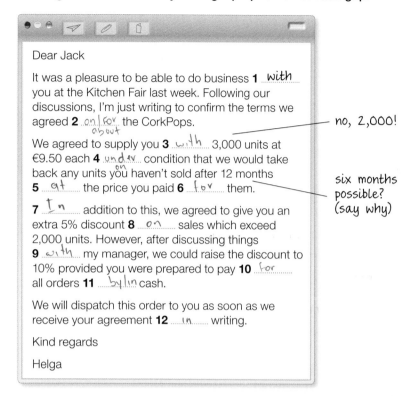

Dear Jack

It was a pleasure to be able to do business **1** _with_ you at the Kitchen Fair last week. Following our discussions, I'm just writing to confirm the terms we agreed **2** _on | for_ _about_ the CorkPops.

We agreed to supply you **3** _with_ 3,000 units at €9.50 each **4** _under_ condition that we would take back any units you haven't sold after 12 months **5** _at_ the price you paid **6** _for_ them.

7 _In_ addition to this, we agreed to give you an extra 5% discount **8** _on_ sales which exceed 2,000 units. However, after discussing things **9** _with_ my manager, we could raise the discount to 10% provided you were prepared to pay **10** _for_ all orders **11** _by|in_ cash.

We will dispatch this order to you as soon as we receive your agreement **12** _in_ writing.

Kind regards

Helga

— no, 2,000!

six months possible? (say why)

2   Read the email again and underline any words and phrases you think would be useful when you reply.

3   Write a reply to Helga's email using all the handwritten notes.

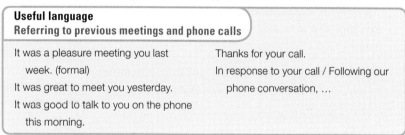

> **Useful language**
> **Referring to previous meetings and phone calls**
>
> It was a pleasure meeting you last week. (formal)
> It was great to meet you yesterday.
> It was good to talk to you on the phone this morning.
>
> Thanks for your call.
> In response to your call / Following our phone conversation, ...

Speaking and writing

1   Work in pairs. Your teacher will tell you whether you are buyers or sales reps. You are going to negotiate a deal for the Battery Peeler. Use the role cards from the Teacher's Resource Book that your teacher will give you and negotiate a deal.

2   Write an email confirming the terms of your deal. Use Helga's email above as a model.

Grammar workshop 2

Units 5–8

Infinitives and verb + -ing

We use **infinitives**

- to express purpose: *He borrowed money **to start** his own business.*
- after adjectives: *It's **great to talk** to you.*
- after *too* and *enough*: *He's **too busy to speak** to you at the moment.*
- after certain verbs, including: *agree, aim, appear, arrange, ask, decide, demand, expect, fail, help, hope, intend, manage, offer, plan, promise, refuse, threaten, want*: *I've **arranged to meet** the marketing manager at 11 o'clock.*

We use a verb + **-ing**

- after prepositions: *How **about running** a new advertising campaign?*
- as subjects of the sentence: ***Borrowing** money can be risky.*
- after certain verbs, including: *admit, appreciate, avoid, consider, delay, deny, enjoy, finish, imagine, involve, keep, mind, miss, postpone, prevent, recommend, report, risk, suggest*: *Running your own business **involves working** long hours.*

1 Complete the gaps with the correct form (infinitive or verb + -ing) of the verbs in brackets.

1 My company doesn't spend enough money on .... (*train*) staff.
2 My job involves .... (*deal*) with money.
3 I would be happy .... (*get*) a more responsible job.
4 .... (*advertise*) on television is too expensive for my company .... (*invest*) in.
5 You shouldn't consider .... (*develop*) a new product unless you know who your target customers are likely .... (*be*).
6 I wouldn't risk .... (*leave*) my job .... (*start*) up a business on my own.
7 If a member of my family had a good business idea, I would help them .... (*develop*) it by .... (*lend*) them money.
8 .... (*study*) for a business degree is a good idea if you want .... (*be*) successful in business.

2 ⊙ Business English students often make mistakes with infinitives and verbs + -ing. Choose the correct option in italics in each of these sentences.

1 I highly recommend *to choose / choosing* CTP Translations as our new translation agency.
2 I hope *to hear / hearing* from you soon.
3 To reduce our costs, we are considering *to close / closing* a store.
4 I suggest *to check / checking* all invoices from our suppliers in the future to avoid extra costs.
5 This report aims *to look / looking* into the reasons for the high staff turnover.
6 We look forward to *hearing / hear* from you.

Prepositions in phrases describing trends

- To say **what has changed**, we use a noun + *in* (*a change in, a rise in, a decrease in,* etc.): *There has been **a rise in** the amount of money spent on advertising.*
- To say **how much something changed**, we use
  - a noun + *of*: *There has been **an increase of** 25%.*
  - a verb + *by*: *The number of applicants **fell by** 30.*
  - a verb or noun + *from ... to*: *Our spending **rose from** $50,000 **to** $75,000.*
- To **express a level**, we use a verb + *at*: *In January, the price **stood at** $13.50.*
- To say **the level something reached**, we use a verb + *to*: *The number **rose to** 21,000.*

1 Study the table and complete the sentences below by writing a preposition in each gap.

	visitors	exhibitors
three years ago	70,000	450
two years ago	57,000	370
last year	140,000	515
this year	115,000	390

1 Three years ago, the number of visitors to the Beijing Tourism Fair stood .... 70,000.
2 Two years ago, the number of visitors fell .... 13,000 .... 57,000.

3   Last year, the numbers increased 57,000
    .... 140,000.
4   This year, they have decreased .... 25,000.

2   Write four sentences of your own about the number of exhibitors.

3   ⊙ Business English students often make mistakes with prepositions when describing trends. Complete these sentences by writing a preposition in each gap.

1   Customer satisfaction increased by 11% .... 83% last year.
2   In February, sales enquiries peaked .... 540.
3   Last year, our profits increased .... 10%.
4   This market is estimated .... 20,000 companies in France and 80,000 in the rest of Europe.
5   We have reduced our complaints .... 257 .... 230 thanks to the improvements.
6   We would like to increase our sales .... 13%.

Formal requests

Formal requests often contain *would* in the main clause and *would* or *could* in the *if* clause:
*We **would** be most grateful/pleased if you **would/could** send us the information as soon as possible.*
*We **would** appreciate it if you **would/could** participate in our survey.*
Other ways of making requests:
■   *Can/Could you please …?*
    ***Could you please** let us know what discount you are prepared to offer?*
■   *I wonder if you could …*
    ***I wonder if you could** phone him later today.*

1   ⊙ Business English students often make mistakes making formal requests. Correct the mistakes in each of these sentences.

1   We∧appreciate it if you could give us suggestions about how we can improve our performance.
    would
2   We would also appreciate it if you give us the name of your technical representative.
3   We would appreciate it if you let me know your final decision.
4   We would be very grateful if you can send us detailed information about the course.
5   We are very pleased if you could tell us what the price of a space at the exhibition is.

2   Write your own requests using the structure of the items in Exercise 1.

First and second conditionals

First conditional
If/Unless + present tense, future tense / modal verb (*may, can, should,* etc.) / imperative:
*If you **give** us a higher discount, we'**ll buy** more of the products.*
The first conditional is used to express a future condition the speaker thinks is possible or likely.

Second conditional
If/Unless + past tense, *would/could/might* + infinitive:
*If the flight **wasn't** so long, I'**d visit** my customers more often.*
The second conditional is used to express a present or future condition which is imaginary, contrary to the facts, impossible or improbable.
Instead of *if* or *unless*, we can use *on condition that, provided (that), providing (that)* or *as long as* to be more emphatic:
***Providing that** you deliver the goods on time, we'll pay the full price.*

1   ⊙ Business English students often make mistakes with tenses in conditional sentences. Choose the correct option in each of these sentences.

1   I can contact him directly if there *are / were* any problems afterwards.
2   If you *decide / decided* to choose one of them, please let me know.
3   If you *require / required* any further information, please do not hesitate to contact me.
4   It would be better if we *advertise / advertised* specifically in newspapers.
5   It would be much better if all extension numbers *contain / contained* five digits.
6   We can offer a 10% discount if you *book / booked* rooms with us for 18 months.
7   You say you require a minimum of six trainees, but would it be OK if there *are / were* five?

2   Complete these sentences with your own ideas.

1   We will offer you a contract provided that …
2   I'd be happy to join your team if …
3   If the offices weren't so far away, …
4   We'll give you a special price for the first six months on condition that …
5   They should finish on time providing …
6   Don't let anyone interrupt the meeting unless …
7   I wouldn't accept a contract to work overseas unless …
8   … as long as I can trust him.

Starting a business

Getting started

Work in pairs. Discuss these questions.

1 Why start your own business?
   (Think of as many reasons as you can.)
2 Would you like to run your own business?
   Why? / Why not?

Why start your own business?

Listening

1 Which of these seven reasons for starting a
   business did you mention in Getting started?

   a to give yourself more social status
   b to create employment for yourself
   c to achieve your ambition
   d to be your own boss
   e to become rich
   f to exploit a gap in the market
   g to do something more interesting

2 ① 18 Listen to three women being interviewed on a
   radio programme about people who have started
   their own businesses. Which of the reasons in
   Exercise 1 does each of them give for starting her
   business? Write one letter (a–h) for each name.

   1 Lisa 2 Naiara 3 Matylda

3 Work in pairs. Discuss these questions.

   1 Which woman do you think has the best reason
      for starting up her own business?
   2 When starting up a business, what are the
      advantages and disadvantages of buying into
      a franchise?

Grammar workshop

Prepositions in time phrases

⊙ ① 18 Business English students often make
mistakes with prepositions in time clauses. Complete
these sentences from the radio programme with a
preposition in each gap. Then listen again to check
your answers.

1 Anyway, I noticed that, in my home town, most
   specialist food shops had closed down .... the last
   few years …
2 … so, ... March 1st last year, I opened my own
   outlet.
3 I'd worked for an airline .... 20 years in
   marketing, that is, ... the end of last year, when I
   was made redundant.
4 So, ... the beginning of February, I bought into
   this franchise …
5 … my boss would say, 'Can you organise this meeting
   .... ten o'clock?' or 'Can you type up this report
   .... tomorrow?' …

❯ page 60 Prepositions in time clauses

An international franchise

Reading

1 Work in small groups.

   1 What international franchises can you name?
   2 What advantages do international franchises have
      when competing with local businesses?
   3 What do you think are the benefits and difficulties
      of extending franchises to other countries?

2 Work in pairs. Read the passage on page 45 quite
   quickly.

   1 What benefits of an international franchise are
      mentioned?
   2 What are the problems or dangers of having an
      international franchise?

Should you consider an international franchise?

BY RYAN UNDERWOOD

In Southern California, Jeffery Adler oversees three trendy, modern Dlush 'beverage joints' serving coffee, tea, and doughnuts. Things changed a few years ago, after the wealthy Alghanim family contacted Adler about developing the Dlush **concept** in Kuwait and other areas in the Gulf.

Adler found the proposal interesting: it would give Dlush an immediate cash infusion of several hundred thousand dollars, long-term income from a percentage of the **gross revenue**, and an immediate international presence. There are now seven Gulf Dlush stores, but it has proved more complex and more time-consuming than he first imagined.

In a recent survey of franchise businesses, more than 75 per cent of companies said they were planning new international projects. This is partly explained by basic economic trends, says Scott Lehr, Vice-President of Development for the International Franchise Association. As western businesses cope with tight lending markets and a weak economy, many emerging economies have strong consumer demand, as well as **investors** with plenty of **capital**. Lehr says increased international travel plus cheaper, easier communication technologies have facilitated international deals.

When a **lucrative** overseas deal suddenly emerges, it's important that company owners do not lose their heads, says William Edwards, CEO of Edwards Global Services. "You have to look at where it makes sense to go, not just where there's a deal," says Edwards. "Think of this as an investment, because you'll be spending **resources** in terms of time, support, and actual costs."

The first thing any company considering a foreign franchise agreement should do is secure the brand's **trademark**, says Edwards. Otherwise, a potential investor could soon turn into a troublesome copycat. Once an agreement is in place, business owners need to get heavily involved in helping the international franchisee accurately replicate the company's core concept. That includes helping the new franchise set up a **supply chain**, as well as laying out guidelines about product quality, the **retail** experience, and the prices. "The biggest challenge we see for small franchise businesses is to avoid losing control of their brand," Edwards says.

Adler worries that the fresh, youthful atmosphere of Dlush's southern California locations can't really be duplicated in the Middle East, where the culture is more conservative. "It really has to stay toned down," says Shady Badawi, Director of Operations for Dlush's Middle East franchises. "The brand has been well accepted here. It's young—it's fresh and trendy."

But Adler's main concern is that the Middle Eastern **outlets** have taken a lot of his time—and shifted his focus away from building the Dlush brand at home. When Adler meets with potential new investors, he says, they often find Dlush's international venture intriguing, but they ask, "What else could you have been doing in the U.S. with your time and attention?"

Still, for Adler the benefits of the franchise arrangement are clear, especially the solid revenue stream the Middle East stores have provided. Also, the Kuwait team developed a smaller kiosk version of the Dlush store that Adler hopes to eventually roll out to U.S. movie theaters, fitness centers, and college campuses. Adler says the experience has forced him to think about how to tailor the Dlush concept for areas beyond the West Coast.

adapted from Inc Magazine

---

3 **Read the text again and choose the best answer – A, B, C or D – for each question on this page and page 46.**

> **Task tip**
>
> Read the question and find the answer in the text **before** you read the four alternatives. Then choose the alternative which matches what you read.

1 Why was Adler interested in the Alghanims' offer?
   A It would subsidise his other operations.
   B It would bring benefits straightaway.
   C It would give him the opportunity to travel.
   D It would satisfy one of his long-term ambitions.

2 According to Scott Lehr, why do western franchises find emerging economies attractive?
   A Their costs are lower in emerging economies.
   B Their target customers tend to live in the main cities.
   C They provide a healthier business environment.
   D They can borrow money more easily for these investments.

3 What advice does William Edwards give company owners about overseas deals?
   A Avoid signing contracts with overseas investors.
   B Invest plenty of money in the new venture.
   C Appoint people you trust to run the venture.
   D Choose locations which suit your business.

4 According to Edwards, companies should secure trademarks in order to
   A prevent imitations.
   B protect the quality of their products.
   C support their franchisees.
   D ensure franchisees receive supplies.

5 What worries Adler about Dlush's brand identity in the Middle East?
   A It will be hard to attract the right customers.
   B It will conflict with the different way of life.
   C It will be difficult to build brand awareness.
   D It will be difficult to keep it the same.

6 What is Adler's main concern about opening outlets in the Middle East?
   A He may have to change the Dlush concept in the USA.
   B The outlets in the Middle East are too small.
   C Another company may take over the franchise.
   D He has been neglecting his American business.

Vocabulary

Find words or phrases in bold in the text which mean the following.

1 a large amount of money used for starting a new business
2 a name or a symbol which is put on a product to show that it is made by a particular producer and which cannot be legally used by any other producer
3 people who put money into something in order to make a profit or get an advantage
4 shops that are owned by a particular company and that sell the goods which the company has produced
5 an idea
6 producing a lot of money
7 the activity of selling goods to the public, usually in small quantities
8 the system of people and things that are involved in getting a product from the place where it is made to the person who buys it
9 the total income that a company receives regularly
10 useful or valuable possessions

Role-play

1 **Work in pairs. You are either Pair A or Pair B. Discuss what you will say.**

Pair A

Imagine some friends are considering buying into a franchise and have asked for your advice. Think of advice connected with:

• the type of franchise they should buy into
• estimating costs
• support from the franchising company
• researching the market
• anything else you think they need to know.

Pair B

You are thinking of buying into a franchise and have asked some friends for advice. Think of questions you would like to ask about:

• the type of franchise you should buy into
• how to ensure that you will make money
• what help to ask for from the franchising company
• any other issues.

2 **When you are ready, Pair A and Pair B should work together and discuss the issue.**

Useful language
Giving advice

You should …	Have you thought of …?
You ought to …	It might be a good idea to …
If I were you, I'd …	

Financial terms

Vocabulary

1 **Match these financial terms (1–8) with their definitions (a–h).**

1	profit	a	debt
2	turnover	b	money which is earned after paying the costs of producing and selling goods and services
3	asset	c	money paid to the government, which is based on your income or profits
4	liability	d	something valuable belonging to an organisation which can be used for the payment of debts
5	tax	e	a method of paying for goods or services at a later time, usually paying interest as well as the original money
6	costs	f	the amount that a bank charges on money that it lends
7	interest rate	g	the money you need to spend to keep an organisation functioning
8	credit	h	the total amount of money received from sales of goods and services

2 Complete this leaflet using the terms from Exercise 1.

PLANNING TO START YOUR OWN BUSINESS?

Before you start, there are a few things you should do.

- Research the market before you do anything and make a sales forecast: this way, you will know how much **1** .... to expect.
- Make an estimate of your **2** .... , for example what the rent will be on your premises, how much interest you will have to pay on your loan, your salary bill, etc.
- By subtracting your costs from turnover, you should be able to make a **3** .... forecast. The people who lend you money or invest in your business will want to know this.
- If you are going to ask for **4** .... from a bank, check the **5** .... – can you afford to pay back so much? Also, your bank will want some security on the money they lend you, so do you have a house or other **6** .... which you can use as a guarantee?
- Of course, the government will require you to pay **7** .... on your profits.
- Your main **8** .... will probably be your loan from the bank.

A letter to a franchiser

Reading

1 Work in pairs. What questions would you ask a franchiser before buying a franchise? Use some of the vocabulary from the previous exercise in your questions.

2 A friend of yours, Günther Ehlers, has written this letter to a franchiser and has asked you to check that there are no mistakes in the English. Read the letter: in most lines, there is one extra word. Find the extra words and write them in the gaps on the right. Some lines are correct. Mark them with a tick (✓).

Dear Sirs,

I am working a 28-year-old marketing specialist with a large multinational retail
company since I was graduated in 2010. I am interested in taking out a franchise
with your organisation in Austria.
I would be the most grateful if you could send me details of your franchises. I'd
like to know:
- what costs are involved in terms of start-up fees, and what is percentage of
  turnover I will have to pay for you each year
- how much more profit I can expect to make at the end of the first year
- if you offer credit facilities to cover the initial costs
- if you will be able to help me with finding my suitable premises
- how you can assist to me with marketing and credit facilities.
Many thanks in advance and I look forward to hearing from you.

Yours faithfully
Günther Ehlers

1 ....
2 ....
3 ....
4 ....
5 ....
6 ....
7 ....
8 ....
9 ....
10 ....
11 ....
12 ....

Writing

Write a letter of enquiry (about 150 words) to a franchiser which interests you. Include some of the questions you thought of. Use Günther's corrected letter as a model.

> **Useful language**
> **Requesting information**
>
> I'd be most grateful if you could tell us / give me information /
> send me details about …
> Could you also tell me …?
> I'd appreciate it if you could tell me …
> Many thanks in advance.

Financing a start-up

Getting started

Work in small groups. Look at the ways on the right of raising money for a new business activity.

1 Which are the most usual ways of raising money?
2 Which are the safest for the entrepreneur (the person starting the business)?
3 Which are the easiest to obtain?
4 Which are the cheapest / most expensive?
5 Which give the entrepreneur more/less control of the business?
6 Do you know any other ways of raising finance?

- a bank loan
- a mortgage (a loan normally used to buy a house)
- a government grant
- venture capital (investment from companies which specialise in high-risk new businesses)
- private equity (selling shares in the business, but not publicly on the stock market)
- personal savings
- going into partnership
- a loan from family or friends

Setting up a food consultancy

Listening

1 You are going to hear Jane Milton talking about her business. Before you listen, read these notes and decide what sort of information is needed for each gap.

Not Just Food

Jane Milton, cookery writer and expert, founded this food-development consultancy in 1996. She now heads a team of 60 people.

Task tip

The words in the notes are not exactly the same as the words in the recording, but you should write **words you hear** in the gaps.

- Company's activities: writing recipes, preparing food, organising 1 ....
- Before launching her company, she did a business 2 .... course.
- Her tutors insisted on a realistic 3 ....
- About half of the people she contacted when carrying out market research became 4 ....
- She is better at attracting new customers because she is 5 ....
- To cover overheads, at first she did a 6 .... job.
- Her advice for people starting new companies: Don't borrow more than you can afford to 7 ....

2 ①19 Listen and complete the notes in Exercise 1 with one or two words in each gap.

Raising finance

Vocabulary 1

1 Combine the verbs in Box A with the nouns/noun phrases in Box B to form collocations connected with starting companies. In some cases, more than one answer is possible.

Example: raise a loan, raise finance, raise money

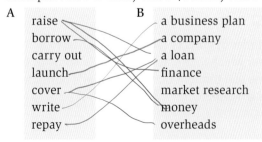

A
raise
borrow
carry out
launch
cover
write
repay

B
a business plan
a company
a loan
finance
market research
money
overheads

2 Use phrases you formed in Exercise 1 to complete this paragraph. Remember to put the verb into the correct form.

Before you start a business or **1** .... , it's a good idea to **2** .... to see if anyone will buy your product. If you don't have a lot of personal savings, it may be necessary to **3** .... This may involve taking out a mortgage or some other form of loan from a bank, in which case you will have to **4** .... This will show how you plan to set up and run your business. When you do this, you will have to forecast sales and profits, because the bank will want to be sure that you can **5** .... , as well as **6** .... such as the cost of electricity or social security.

Reading

1 Work in pairs. You are going to read four extracts about different ways of raising finance to start a business. First read these statements. Which statements give a) advice, and b) information?

1 As long as you can cover your debts, they are not worried about your ability to make money.
2 Do not accept their money without signing a formal contract.
3 Be ready to share information openly with them in order to get funding.
4 They may lend money in order to create employment.
5 They may lend money where other institutions might be afraid to do so.
6 You may pay less interest if you borrow money from them.
7 They will become owners or joint owners of the business.
8 You must have property to guarantee the loan.

2 Read these extracts (A–D). Which extract does each statement (1–8) in Exercise 1 refer to?

A
Banks like to use assets such as premises, motor vehicles or equipment as collateral (or security) against loans. Banks don't care whether or not your business has great profit potential. They are only interested in the business's ability to cover the principal and interest payments.

B
If your friends and family express an interest in helping you with your business financing, try to persuade them in a professional way. Make a presentation in exactly the same way as you would to a bank. Don't be embarrassed to show financial statements, tax returns or whatever else they want to see. Do anything to get that money! You should prepare a written agreement about any loans. If you don't, bitter arguments will damage the relationship eventually.

C
Venture capital is a general term to describe a range of ordinary and preference shares where the investing institution acquires a share in the business. Venture capital is intended for higher risks such as start-up situations and development capital for more mature investments. There are over 100 different venture capital funds in the UK, and some have geographical or industry preferences. There are also certain large industrial companies which have funds available to invest in growing businesses; this 'corporate venturing' is an additional source of equity finance.

D
Government, local authorities and local development agencies are the major sources of grants and soft loans. Grants are normally made to facilitate the purchase of assets and either the generation of jobs or the training of employees. Soft loans are normally subsidised by a third party so that the terms of interest and security levels are less than the market rate.

Vocabulary 2

Find words/phrases in the extracts on page 49 which mean the following.

1 things that are owned by a person, company or organisation, such as money, property or land (extract A)

2 property that someone borrowing money will give to the loan company if he or she cannot pay the debt (extract A)

3 documents in which income is reported each year so that income tax can be calculated (extract B)

4 shares of a company providing the owner with a right to vote at shareholder meetings and to receive a part of the company profits as a dividend (= part of the company's profit) (extract C)

5 shares in a company that give the owner the right to receive a dividend before dividends are paid to owners of ordinary shares (extract C)

6 the capital that a company gets from selling its shares rather than borrowing money (extract C)

7 loans with a low interest rate, often offered by the government of a country to another country or organisation (extract D)

8 the amount of money that something costs at a particular time (extract D)

Advice about starting a business

Role-play

Work in pairs. Your teacher will tell you whether you are Pair A or Pair B.

Pair A

You are business advisors. You will give advice to a pair of entrepreneurs about how to finance the small printing business they want to start.

Before talking to them, decide what types of finance might be suitable for them: a bank loan, a loan from family or friends, a mortgage or using personal savings.

You will need to ask them:

- about the type of business
- if they have done market research
- about their personal financial circumstances.

Prepare some questions and, when you are ready, meet the entrepreneurs, discuss their plans with them and give them your best advice.

Pair B

You are entrepreneurs who are thinking of starting a new business, but you need advice on how to finance it, so you are going to consult some business advisors.

Type of business: a photocopying and printing firm specialising in leaflets, small brochures, business cards, etc.

Your personal financial circumstances: between you, you have savings of €50,000

Financing requirements: approximately €70,000 if you are ready to use your personal savings. This extra money is for:

- equipment
- preparing your premises
- initial advertising
- materials, etc.

Work together and decide what questions to ask and what advice you need from the advisors.

When you are ready, explain your business idea to the business advisors, and get their advice on how best to finance your business.

Carter Bearings

> **Carter Manufacturing Limited**
> Specialist bearing supplier to aerospace and hi-tech industries

Listening

1 You are going to hear Karl Brundell talking about his company, Carter Bearings. Before you listen, read these questions and underline the key ideas.

1 <u>How</u> did Carter Bearings <u>start</u>?
  A Karl's father started it, then passed it to his son.
  B Karl's father had the idea, but Karl started it.
  C An agent from another company started it.

2 According to Karl, a new company is more likely to succeed against its competitors by
  A being better.
  B working harder.
  C being distinct.

3 Apart from using the Internet, what other way of finding clients does Karl mention?
  A placing advertisements
  B meeting them at conferences
  C phoning them   *calling them up*

4 In normal circumstances, Karl would give a European customer a discount when the
  A order is delivered late.
  B goods are paid for promptly.
  C customer negotiates a much lower price.

5 Karl thinks that written communication with customers works best with
  A online translation tools.
  B social media.
  C one well-written email.

6 What does Karl say is the advantage of buying from a distributor?
  A It's cheaper.   *s suport currency.*
  B You can pay in dollars.
  C You can buy larger quantities.

7 What sort of companies does Karl look for as suppliers?
  A companies who perform well in his area
  B companies with few sales in his area
  C companies who offer him good prices

8 Which does Karl mention as key to survival in difficult times?
  A concentrating on one market sector
  B using fewer services
  C keeping overheads down

Karl Brundell (right) and his colleague Martin Wakelin

2 (1) 20 Listen to Karl talking about Carter Bearings and choose the best answer – A, B or C – for each question in Exercise 1.

> **Task tip**
>
> You should not expect to understand every word the speaker says. You should try to understand the general meaning in order to choose the best answers.

Speaking

1 Work in pairs and discuss this question. While you are talking, take notes.

What is important when looking for finance to start up a business?

2 Change partners and take turns to talk for a minute to your new partner about what is important when starting up in business. When your partner is speaking, you should listen without interrupting, but when they finish, ask them a short question about some aspect of what they have said.

> **Useful language**
> **Some ways of starting questions**
>
> Can you tell me …?   What I wonder is …
> I'd like to know …   Something I'd like to know is …

Expanding into Europe

Getting started

1 Work in pairs. Read this email which Charles Langley, BioBok's CEO, sent to Alicia Flores, BioBok's Operations Manager in Europe, and discuss the questions below.

1 What extra information does Alicia need about BioBok's plans before she starts investigating?
2 What factors are important when choosing a location for a new operation?

2 Change partners and take turns to present the ideas you have just discussed.

To: Alicia Flores, Operations Manager, Europe
From: Charles Langley, CEO, Cape Town
cc:
Subject: Extending our European operations

Dear Alicia,
Following recent discussions with divisional heads, the board has taken the decision to open an R&D facility in Europe. We are interested in two locations where ground-breaking biotech work is taking place, one in Switzerland and the other in Germany. For obvious reasons, we would like the facility to be close to a major international airport. Please investigate and write a brief proposal for the board recommending which location we should choose and suggesting our next course of action.
I look forward to hearing from you by the end of next week.
Charles Langley
CEO
BioBok Cape Town

A new location in Europe

Listening

1 Work in pairs. Discuss what sort of information you will need to complete these notes.

New European venture

- Initial investment of ZAR 21m in laboratories, 1 _equipment_ and offices.
- Staff of ten, possibly rising to 2 _60_ .
- Staff to be recruited from other 3 _divisions_ and locally.
- Recruit 4 _manager_ for new operation internally.
- Check for availability of 5 _Government Grants_

2 ①21 Listen to Alicia phoning Charles and complete her notes in Exercise 1 with one or two words or a number in each gap.

Reading

1 Alicia has narrowed down the choice of locations for BioBok's European office to two options. Read the information on page 53 from Heidelberg Technology Park's website, which is Alicia's first option, and choose the best word – A, B, C or D – to fill each gap.

Task tip
Look at prepositions and other words before and after the gap to help you choose the right word.

	A	B	C	D
1	forms	consists	makes	sets
2	place	area	space	room
3	place	area	space	room
4	creation	origin	building	start
5	grown	risen	enlarged	widened
6	pushing	making	forcing	giving
7	help	backing	aid	support
8	nearly	strongly	closely	narrowly
9	possibility	opportunity	option	occasion
10	way	method	means	mode
11	optional	possible	accessible	available
12	brings	attracts	pulls	gains
13	pleased	delighted	glad	happy
14	same	alike	similar	both
15	arrival	journey	reach	trip

Heidelberg Technology Park

The Heidelberg Technology Park is a science park that **1**.............. up part of the Ruprecht-Karls University campus. Covering an extensive **2**.............. (nearly 50,000 m² of office and laboratory **3**..............) with more than 80 resident companies and nearly 1,600 employees, it is among the world's leading biotechnology sites.

Since its **4**.............., the Heidelberg Technology Park, with its mix of bio, medical, information, communication and environmental technologies, has **5**.............. into an important entity, **6**.............. fresh impetus to scientific research and business.

The Heidelberg Technology Park promotes the rapid expansion of this cutting-edge technology site through comprehensive **7**.............. services and by working **8**.............. with companies and research institutes.

Resident companies and associated members have the **9**.............. to take part in science, research and business training courses, seminars and conferences and in this **10**.............. have direct contact with new collaborators, customers and interested parties. Moreover, the Park is always there to help you with expert advice. You can use the Conference Centre for your training courses and presentations. Professional communications equipment is **11**.............. for use.

Heidelberg is without a doubt one of the most beautiful cities in Germany and famous for its cultural and artistic treasures and its long tradition as a centre of science and learning. The city **12**.............. 3.5 million visitors every year, 65 per cent of whom are business travellers, though doubtless they too are **13**.............. of the chance to let the old city and the famous castle work their magic. Heidelberg is also a very compact city, making it ideal for young and old **14**.............. and it is within easy **15**.............. of Frankfurt Airport.

adapted from www.technologiepark-hd.de

2 Read the page on the right from the website of Biopôle, Lausanne, which is Alicia's second option, and decide which website – Biopôle (B) or Heidelberg (H) – mentions the following.

1 efficient local transport systems B
2 what the country as a whole is known for
3 statistics for uptake of its facilities
4 ways in which the local organisation can assist
5 the opportunity to improve your staff's skills
6 the different disciplines within the park
7 help in finding new employees
8 figures for people coming to the area
9 where employees' children can study

3 Work in small groups. Discuss the situation and decide:

• which information is most important when deciding where BioBok should locate its premises
• which option would be more suitable.

Biopôle, Lausanne

Biopôle will make your arrival on its site as easy as possible. Do you have tax questions? Do you need work permits? Do you need to recruit staff, deal with the media, find architects, elaborate a business plan? Step across the threshold, and we will help you with pleasure.

Biopôle is the owner of the land on which the site is located and issues leases to interested investors. Investors award construction contracts themselves.

The Biopôle site is superbly served by metro, rail, motorway and air, making communication here in Europe as easy as possible, and the Lausanne campus is in the heart of a region which has seen its activities in the field of the life sciences expand hugely in recent years. The Geneva Lake Region in general is home to industry leaders in their sector and research groups at the cutting edge of their discipline.

The region has a high-quality public school system, plus a wide range of international-level private schools, and therefore offers a serious and viable alternative for the families of company staff located there. Various studies demonstrate that the educational system is ranked highest in Europe and in second position on a world scale. The same goes for the level of science teaching in schools.

Switzerland enjoys a world reputation for the quality of its services, its security, professionalism and reliability. It is often ranked among the world leaders with respect to development, maintenance, efficiency and distribution of its infrastructures.

adapted from www.biopole.ch

Vocabulary

1 Business English students often confuse these words: *place*, *space* and *room*; *opportunity*, *possibility* and *option*. Complete these Cambridge Dictionary entries (1–6) with the correct definition (a–f) in each gap.

1 **place**: .... *Trade fairs and exhibitions remain a common meeting **place** for retail buyers and suppliers.*
2 **space**: .... *There is greater demand for downtown office **space**.*
3 **room**: .... *Is there enough **room** for all of us in your car?*
4 **possibility**: .... (*Possibility cannot be followed by an infinitive*): *Is there any **possibility** of changing this ticket?*
5 **opportunity**: .... *There will be an **opportunity** to discuss the matter again next week.*
6 **option**: .... *You need to think very carefully about the various **options**.*

a space for things to fit into
b one of a number of choices or decisions you can make
c an occasion or situation that makes it possible to do something that you want to do or have to do
d an empty area that is available to be used
e an area, building, room, etc. that is used for a particular purpose
f a chance that something may happen or be true

A proposal

Reading

1 Complete Alicia's proposal by writing one word in each gap.

2 (1) 21 **Complete these extracts from the conversation between Charles and Alicia by writing one of the words from Exercise 1 in the correct form in each gap. Then check your answers by listening again.**

Charles: … we'll build up to about 60 people, so the **1** .... you find must have **2** .... for expansion.
Alicia: OK, I'll look for somewhere with plenty of office **3** ....
Charles: … can you suggest some people, so we have, say, two or three **4** .... to choose from? It'll be a great **5** .... for someone ambitious … I hear that in some regions in Europe, they offer government grants … Can you check the **6** .... and see what's going?

3 **Choose the correct option in italics in each of these sentences.**

1 Do we have *room / place* for another desk in this office?
2 We need to keep some parking *room / place / space* for visitors in the company car park.
3 We're thinking of moving our offices to a new *room / place / space*.
4 This new job is a great *possibility / opportunity / option* to get experience.
5 I think Hangzhou is the best *possibility / opportunity / option* for our new office.
6 The *possibility / opportunity / option* of getting the contract is very good.

Task tip

If you're not sure what word to write, decide what type of word you need first (preposition, pronoun, etc.).

Proposal for location of new facilities in Europe

INTRODUCTION
The purpose of this proposal is **1** *to* compare Lausanne and Heidelberg **2** .... possible locations for BioBok's new R&D facility in Central Europe and to recommend **3** .... option we should choose.

WORKFORCE
Although Heidelberg has a large, dynamic pool of labour already involved in life sciences, we shall be bringing a number of our **4** .... employees from other operations **5** .... the world. Lausanne will attract them with excellent educational facilities for **6** .... children. *Moreover*, Biopôle offers to help with the recruitment of local staff.

PREMISES AND LOCATION
Both locations are near major international airports and offer purpose-built facilities tailored to our requirements. *Also*, they are **7** .... surrounded by high-tech industries offering many opportunities for business and cross-fertilisation of ideas. *However*, Lausanne has more space available for expansion.

LIFESTYLE
Heidelberg is a dynamic, exciting university city with many cultural events. *On the other hand*, Lausanne also enjoys a high quality of life and is situated near **8** .... of Europe's **9** .... spectacular scenery. **10** .... will help us to attract staff to live and work **11** ....

RECOMMENDATIONS
On balance, I recommend that we choose Lausanne **12** .... the reasons given above, *although* Heidelberg is a strong second choice. Our next step should be to contact Biopôle in order to find a suitable building. I suggest that, at a later stage, we ask them to help us find the staff we require.

2 Underline phrases in the proposal in Exercise 1 which introduce recommendations.

3 Write other recommendations using these ideas.

1 premises / close / airport
2 commission / architect / design / building
3 contact Lausanne University
4 advertise / staff / science magazines

4 Which words/phrases in italics in the proposal ...

1 contrast two ideas?
2 mean *in addition*?
3 mean *after thinking about all the different facts or opinions*?

▶ page 60 Linking ideas

Writing

1 Work in pairs. You work as assistants in a software company which is planning to open an office in Poland. You have been asked to prepare a short proposal for the Operations Manager about the location. Look at the information below on which you have already made some handwritten notes.

1 Discuss what ideas you can use to complete the handwritten notes.
2 Look at Alicia's proposal on page 54. Then decide what sections you need for this proposal.

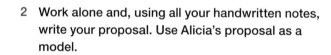

good location because ...

necessary for ...

Gdansk Technology Park
• Gdansk University of Technology: 26,000 students
• 13 other IT companies in park
• grants available

Wroclaw Technology Park
• Wroclaw University of Technology: 32,000 students
• major international IT companies with offices in park
• near Berlin and Prague
• business and legal advice available.

all very small, so ...

useful – say why!

Good to have so many students because ...

2 Work alone and, using all your handwritten notes, write your proposal. Use Alicia's proposal as a model.

Task tip

Avoid just copying words and phrases from the task. Use your own words and ideas as far as possible.

Presenting your business idea

Getting started

1 Work in small groups. Which of these things do you think are important when giving a presentation? Why? / Why not?

1 having a PowerPoint slideshow
2 giving the audience handouts
3 making one or two jokes
4 making eye contact with your audience
5 keeping your presentation short
6 letting people interrupt with questions
7 dressing smartly
8 looking confident

2 Add two more ideas of your own to the list.

3 Change groups and take turns to say what is important when giving a business presentation.

Structuring a presentation

Speaking

> When you give a business presentation, it is important that your presentation has a clear structure which your audience can follow easily. It is also helpful to repeat the important points several times.

Work in pairs. Look at these stages in a typical presentation (a–g). Write the phrases in the correct order in the chart on the right.

a Conclude and invite questions.
b Give the main part of your talk.
c Greet audience and thank them for coming. ✓
d Introduce your talk.
e Introduce yourself (and your colleague(s)).
f Outline what you are going to say in your talk and suggest people leave their questions to the end.
g Summarise the main points you have made.

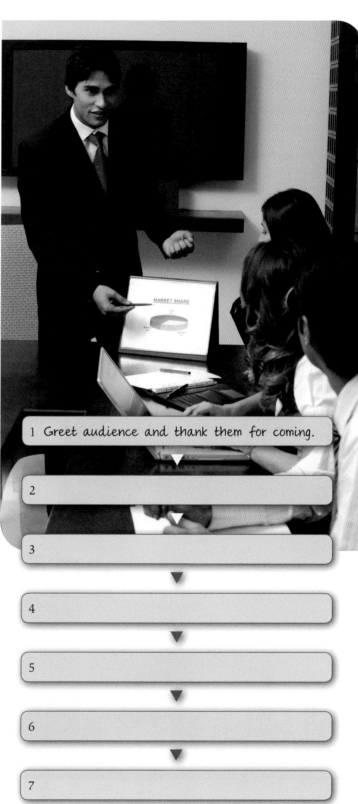

1 Greet audience and thank them for coming.

2

3

4

5

6

7

Signalling the parts of a presentation

Listening

> Good presenters make it easy for their audience to know where they are in the presentation. Handouts and slides can help you to do this, but it's also important to use phrases which signal where you are in the presentation.

1 **Look at these extracts from a presentation (a–k). In which part of the presentation (1–7 on page 56) would you use each of them?**

a I think that just about covers the market research, so let's deal with the third part of my presentation, which is to explain our financial requirements and plans.

b Good morning, and welcome to the Adelphi Hotel.

c In my presentation, I aim to do three things. First, I'll … Then I'll tell you … and finally I'll …

d Now, to move on to my second point: market research.

e If you have any questions you'd like to ask, I'll be happy to answer them at the end of the talk.

f Now, if I can just summarise the main points again, they're as follows: first, …

g So, finally, I'd like to finish off by saying that it's been a pleasure talking to you all and thank you for your patience and interest in listening to me. Now, if you have any questions, please feel free to ask them.

h So let me introduce myself: my name's … and this is my partner, …

i Let's start with my first point – our main business idea …

j Thank you all very much for coming; some of you have travelled a long way to hear us today …

k The purpose of this presentation […] is to explain our business plans to you …

2 (1) 22 **Listen to Peter Furlong giving a presentation of his business ideas and check your answers.**

3 (1) 22 **Listen again and complete these notes by writing one or two words or a number in each gap.**

Name of company
Clock Options Express
Business idea
- Information and 1 .... display panels.
- Will provide information for 2 .... and other travellers.
- Information on time, 3 ...., parking and public transport.
- Will be placed at 4 .... accesses to the city.
- Income from 5 .... space for advertisements.
Market research
- Interviewed more than 6 .... motorists and other travellers.
- Advertisers will pay 7 .... for space on panels.
Financial requirements
First year: 8 .... pounds

A
> Present the company or organisation you work for. You can say:
> - what the company or organisation does
> - how it started
> - what it will do in the future.

B
> Present a product or service you know well. You can say:
> - what the product is
> - what the advantages of buying it are
> - how it is marketed.

C
> Present the town you live in to a business person who is thinking of starting a business there. You can say:
> - what industries there are in your town
> - what facilities there are for new businesses
> - what the advantages of opening a business in your town are.

Speaking

Work in pairs. Choose one of the topics on the right (A–C) and prepare a brief presentation of about two or three minutes.

- Follow the seven steps of the presentation structure.
- Do not write exactly what you are going to say; just make brief notes.
- Change partners and take turns to give your presentations to each other.
- Listen to your new partner's presentation and ask two or three questions at the end.
- Give your partner feedback on what he/she did well and what could be improved.

Making the most of presentations

Reading

1 Work in pairs. Read the advice below about giving presentations (1–8) and say if you think each piece of advice is:

a excellent   **b** quite useful   **c** not very useful.

Give reasons for your answers.

1 Do a course on presentation skills.
2 Speak at a suitable speed.
3 Improve your speaking skills by filming yourself.
4 Look directly at your listeners when speaking.
5 Plan your presentation carefully.
6 Practise in order to reduce nervousness.
7 Prepare for possible questions.
8 Use photocopies for anything too long and complex.

2 Read these paragraphs (A–D), ignoring the options in italics. Which paragraph does each piece of advice in Exercise 1 (1–8) refer to?

A

The fear of speaking is considered by many business people as their number-one fear. They may even avoid speaking opportunities that **1** *can / could* advance their career. While there are many effective methods of relaxation that **2** *can / could* help reduce the fear of speaking, for most people it is not something they **3** *can / could* simply get up and do effectively without having at least some basic training. Rehearsing the presentation will greatly reduce anxiety. The more familiar the material, the more credible the speaker will sound.

B

The first step in making a really effective presentation is to prepare. As the saying goes, 'failing to prepare is preparing to fail'. You will need to spend some time thinking about the material you want to cover, brainstorming all the things it might be possible to include, and then ranking them according to which topics you must include, which topics it might be nice to include if time allows, and which things it is worth knowing about in case anybody asks you about them.

C

Nothing will improve your presentation more than seeing yourself on screen. You will notice mannerisms that you never noticed before. And you will instantly begin to make changes. Recording and listening to yourself is another tool to use when you rehearse your presentations. You'll immediately know if you are speaking clearly or if some words **4** *can / could* be difficult to understand. You will hear mistakes in grammar and inappropriate 'ums' and 'ahs'.

D

- Enthusiasm is essential. Try to smile, and make eye contact with members of the audience as often as possible.
- Remember to speak slowly and clearly. Pause regularly to allow the audience to digest what you have said.
- Short words and simple sentences will have more impact than long and complicated sentences. Avoid technical language, too.
- If you are worried about drying up, then use notes. These should be prompts only – don't read straight from your notes.
- Convert statistics into charts and graphs wherever you **5** *can / could*, and put any lengthy detail into a handout which people **6** *can / could* read at their leisure.

3 Work in small groups. What advice would you give about using PowerPoint in presentations? Why?

Grammar workshop

Can and could

⊙ Business English students often make mistakes with *can* and *could*. Choose the correct options (1–6) in the paragraphs on page 58.

❯ page 61 *Can* and *could*

Presenting your business idea

Role-play

Situation

You have an idea for a new business start-up, but you need to raise finance in order to make your dream a reality (it might be one of the ideas in the photos). One possibility is to get financial support from an 'angel investor' – a private investor who specialises in putting money into new enterprises.

A group of angels is meeting at a hotel in your area to listen to presentations from would-be entrepreneurs like yourselves.

Work in pairs. Your job is to prepare a presentation, rehearse it and give it to the angels. Use one of the ideas in the photos if you want to. Otherwise use your own idea.

1 Decide what your business idea is, i.e. what kind of company you want to start up, your product, the size of the company to start with, your location and the premises you need.
2 Imagine you have carried out some market research and invent some results to present to the investors.
3 Decide how much money you need from your investors. Invent a few financial details, such as your sales and profit forecasts, your projected return on investment, etc.
4 Prepare the presentation which you are going to give together. Write notes to work from. Decide which of you is going to give each part of the presentation.
5 Rehearse your presentation together.
6 Imagine that the other members of your class are the angel investors. Give your presentation to them.
7 While you are listening to other people's presentations, think of one or two questions you would like to ask them at the end.

Grammar workshop 3

Units 9–12

Prepositions in time clauses

We use *at* for
- exact moments of time: *He phoned **at** four o'clock.*
- the beginning/end: *We'll pay you **at** the beginning of next month.*

We use *in* for
- parts of the day: *The meeting is **in** the afternoon.*
- months and years: ***in** April, **in** 2013*
- part of a period of time: *We haven't had a single visit from head office **in** the last three years.*

We use *on* for days/dates:
*We signed the contract **on** Monday, July 22nd.*

We use *for*
- + a number of hours/days/years, etc. to say how long something has been happening:
*He's been in the meeting **for** three hours.*
- to say what time something is needed:
*Can you arrange the meeting **for** 3.30?*

We use *during* to say a period of time when something happens, but not how long (for this we use *for*):
*Please switch off your mobile phones **during** the meeting.*

We use *since* + a time in the past to say when something started which is still happening now:
*Kurt has been on the phone **since** nine o'clock this morning.*

We use *from ... to* for the beginning and end of a period of time:
*Aziz worked for us **from** 2008 **to** 2011.*

We use *until* to say 'up to that time':
*I'll be in the office **until** six o'clock.*

We use *by* to say when something must be completed:
*The goods must arrive **by** 13th August.*

1 **Complete these sentences by writing a preposition in each gap. In some cases, more than one answer is possible.**

1 Could you book a table at the restaurant .... eight o'clock this evening?
2 Francine has been working on the report non-stop .... the last three days.
3 I'll be out of the office .... Friday morning.

4 They managed to complete the contract .... just under three months.
5 We got through all our work .... the morning and went out to lunch .... 1.30.
6 We've had offices in Warsaw .... 1987.
7 You must leave your desk tidy .... the end of each working day.
8 The meeting will last .... exactly two hours, ... ten .... 12.
9 I can stay in the meeting .... 3.30, but then I have to go and meet a client.
10 Applications for the post must be submitted .... December 31st at the latest.
11 Bruno finished writing the proposal .... his summer holiday, so his family were not pleased.
12 We've organised the tour of the factory .... three o'clock.

2 ⊘ **Business English students often make mistakes with prepositions in time phrases. Find and correct the mistake in each of these sentences.**

1 Could you please give me this information until Monday at the latest?
2 For the last two years, she has only taken sick leave once.
3 I'm afraid we can't manage it because we are holding a conference at that day.
4 Our company has been using their service since many years.
5 Susan worked for us since 2001 to 2012 as a sales representative.
6 The meeting was originally scheduled on 1st June.

Linking ideas

To contrast two ideas, we can use *although, even though, however* and *on the other hand.*
- *Although* and *even though* join two sentences. They can be placed at the beginning of a sentence with a comma [,] or in the middle of a sentence without a comma:
***Although** he left school at 16, he was a millionaire by the age of 30.*
*She left the company **even though** they had offered her a managerial post.*
Even though expresses a stronger contrast than *although.*

- *However* and *on the other hand* are adverbs. They normally start new sentences and are followed by a comma:
  He was a lazy student. **However,** *he became a hard-working and successful businessman.*

To add more ideas or information, we can use *also*, *in addition* and *moreover*.

To say we are finishing, we can use *on balance*, *in conclusion*, *to sum up* or *in summary* at the beginning of the sentence.

- We use *on balance* to show we have thought about all the facts and arguments.
- We use *in conclusion* to say 'These are the final things I want to say'.
- We use *to sum up* and *in summary* to express the most important facts or ideas again briefly.

1 Complete each of these sentences with a linking word/phrase. In some sentences, more than one answer is possible.

1 She took out a loan .... interest rates were high.
2 Manuel is an excellent local manager. .... , he does not speak English. .... , Silvia speaks fluent English and German, so .... , I think we should offer her the job.
3 .... we met our sales targets, my manager was not satisfied.
4 The premises are rather expensive for a new business. .... , they are not in the best part of town. .... , I suggest we continue searching for a better location.
5 Everyone is complaining about the economy. .... , it doesn't seem to have affected us.
6 He has original ideas. .... , he's bad at putting them into practice.
7 .... the meeting lasted three hours, they were unable to reach a decision.

2 Complete these sentences about yourself. Then compare your answers with a partner.

1 I've made progress learning English, although …
2 Although I enjoy some aspects of my work, …
3 In spite of working hard, I …
4 Money is important to me. On the other hand, …

Can and could

We use **can** to express …
- an ability in the present:
  *I **can** make a meeting at four o'clock, but it will be difficult to get there any earlier.*

- permission:
  *You **can** use my mobile if your phone isn't working.*
- a general possibility:
  *It **can** be very embarrassing to miss a meeting.*

We use **could**
- to express a general ability in the past:
  *Thirty years ago, you **could** phone, but you **couldn't** send an email.*
- in second conditionals, including requests using a second conditional (see pages 35 and 43):
  *We'd appreciate it if you **could** send the information as soon as possible.*
- to make a suggestion:
  *We **could** ask for a bigger discount.*
- to express a possibility (like *might*):
  *Ian **could** be late because the traffic is bad.*

We use **can** or **could** to
- make requests:
  Can/Could *you print this email out for me?*
- offer to do something:
  *We **can/could** send the order by special delivery.*

1 Complete these sentences by writing *can* or *could* in each gap.

1 Five years ago, you .... get a loan to start a new business quite easily.
2 I'd be grateful if you .... order the parts as soon as possible.
3 If you want a quiet place to work, you .... use my office.
4 We'll ask Marga to do it because she .... type faster than anyone else in the office.
5 We .... offer free parking – that might attract more clients.
6 There's a lot to discuss, so this meeting .... go on for several hours.

2 ⊙ Business English students often confuse *can* and *could*. Choose the correct option in italics in each of these sentences.

1 I would be grateful if you *can / could* provide more information.
2 It would be best for us if you *can / could* run the courses at our company's office.
3 The company delivers everywhere, and that *can / could* be important for us when deciding whether to use them or not.
4 The range of products on display *can / could* be wider, as 38% of customers are unhappy with the product range displayed.
5 We hope you *can / could* give us further details regarding the cost for each course.

Arranging business travel

Getting started

Work in small groups.

- Why do business people need to travel? Think of as many reasons as you can.
- Do you think communication technologies such as video conferencing can replace business travel? Why? / Why not?
- Would you enjoy a job which involves a lot of travelling? Why? / Why not?

Vocabulary

1   Business English students often confuse *travel, journey* and *trip*. Read this extract from the *CALD* and write the correct word (*travel, journey* or *trip*) in the examples (1–3) below.

> The noun **travel** [U] is a general word which means 'the activity of travelling'.
> Use **journey** [C] to talk about when you travel from one place to another.
> A **trip** [C] is a journey in which you visit a place for a short time and come back again.

1   He's just back from a business ....
2   He fell asleep during the train ....
3   Air .... has become much cheaper.

2   Complete these sentences by writing *travel, journey* or *trip* in the correct form in the gaps. In some cases, two answers are possible.

1   Business .... account(s) for a large part of the airline's profits.

2   I've just been on a .... to Turkey to look into sourcing from a new supplier.
3   Unfortunately, I'm going on a business .... , so I won't be able to be present.
4   The reason is that our CEO will not be back from his .... to China before 5th June.
5   If we want to reduce hotel costs, we could begin our .... during the night.
6   Members of staff are obliged to make some long-distance .... to visit customers.

A company meeting

Speaking

1   **Work in pairs. Your company is considering changing its policy on business travel, and you have been invited to a meeting about it. Discuss this question and make some notes on your ideas.**

What is important when deciding whether to travel on business or stay in the office? Think about: meeting clients, expanding your business, meeting colleagues from different offices, etc.

2 **① 23** Listen to Dimitri, a sales manager, talking about business travel.

1 What does he say about each of the points in Exercise 1?

2 Complete each of these phrases, which Dimitri uses to organise his information, with one word.
a First, and by far the most .... is ...
b Secondly, and also ....
c Finally, and also absolutely .... in today's global workplace ...

3 What phrase does he use to introduce his conclusion? Can you think of other phrases you could use instead?

3 Change partners and take turns to answer the question from Exercise 1 with your own ideas, but using phrases from Exercise 2.

4 Work in pairs. You have been asked to make another short presentation at the meeting. Choose one of these questions and work together for a minute or two to make notes for your presentation.

- What is important when choosing a hotel to stay at? Think about location, facilities, etc.
- What is important when preparing for a trip abroad? Think about local customs, local working hours, etc.
- What is important when choosing an airline to fly with? Think about prices, schedules, etc.

5 Change partners and take turns to give your presentations. You should each speak for about one minute. When you have finished, your partner should:

- say if there is anything they disagree with, and why
- ask you a question about what they have heard.

Arranging to travel

Writing

1 You work in the sales department of an international company. Complete this email you received from your team leader, Dimitri, by writing one word in each gap.

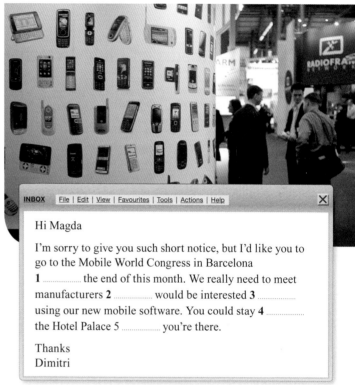

INBOX   File | Edit | View | Favourites | Tools | Actions | Help   ✕

Hi Magda

I'm sorry to give you such short notice, but I'd like you to go to the Mobile World Congress in Barcelona **1** .... the end of this month. We really need to meet manufacturers **2** .... would be interested **3** .... using our new mobile software. You could stay **4** .... the Hotel Palace **5** .... you're there.

Thanks
Dimitri

2 Read Dimitri's email again. What words does he use to:

1 apologise?   2 instruct?   3 suggest?

3 Imagine you are Magda. Reply to Dimitri's email.

- Agree to his request.
- Suggest a colleague to go with you and say why.
- Explain how long you'll be away.

4 Write an email to your personal assistant.

- Explain where you are going.
- Instruct him/her to book your trip.
- Ask him/her about places for entertaining customers.

Useful language Instructing
I'd like / I want you to ...
Could/Would you please ...?
I'd be grateful if you would ...
I'd appreciate it if you would ...

Useful language Agreeing to do something
I'd be happy/glad to ...
Yes, certainly. I'll do that right away / as soon as I have a moment.
Sure, no problem.

How business travel is changing

Reading

1 Work in pairs. You are going to read an article about business travel. Before you read, discuss this question.

How do you think business travel is changing?

2 Read the article quite quickly, ignoring the gaps. In what ways is business travel changing?

How social media and mobile technologies are changing business travel

Hotels are upgrading their technology strategy for **1**............ customers. Advertising and **2**............ discounted rates are no longer enough, as customers turn increasingly to social media and mobile technology.

In last year's travel survey, TripAdvisor, a travel website, reported that only 39% of travellers are faithful to one hotel brand, down from 59% a year ago. Customers are becoming more aware of their options, and **3**............ limits mean that travellers are looking for cheaper accommodation.

With **4**............ to competing online deals, guests care less about brand loyalty and more about **5**............ for money. Hotels have to make more **6**............ to meet their guests' demands and create loyalty programmes which will retain interest and bring repeat visits.

For many years, search engines were the main **7**............ of finding hotels and conference venues, but things are changing with the emergence of social networks. Using hotel-review websites like TripAdvisor, people can now select a hotel **8**............ on previous guests' comments. With Facebook, they can find reviews on their Friend list. Another new service called *Room77* goes even further by **9**............ users submit reviews of individual rooms in hotels. With the **10**............ of such services, selecting a hotel and even a specific room is getting easier for the traveller.

The **11**............ of mobile travel research and booking has changed consumers' behaviour. Travellers are booking hotels on tablets and other mobile devices while they are in **12**............ , shortening the time between the booking and arrival date. Hotels with mobile-optimised websites are cashing in on this **13**............ . Mobile apps allow business travellers to **14**............ a flight's status, book a hotel and check in while still on the road. With fast-changing social media and mobile technology, travellers' behaviour will continue to **15**............ .

adapted from www.hotelhub.com

3 Choose the best word – A, B, C or D – for each gap.

	A	B	C	D
1	attracting	appealing	bringing	catching
2	providing	asking	offering	suggesting
3	allowance	budget	finance	resource
4	entry	approach	reach	access
5	worth	value	benefit	profit
6	effort	work	force	trouble
7	possibility	chance	manner	way
8	depending	based	focused	arising
9	helping	assisting	aiding	supporting
10	implementation	extension	progress	growth
11	facility	readiness	ease	usefulness
12	transfer	transport	translation	transit
13	possibility	occasion	opportunity	chance
14	check	control	supervise	oversee
15	develop	adjust	evolve	advance

Speaking

Work in small groups. Discuss these questions.

1 Do social media and internet reviews affect the decisions you make and the way you spend money? How?

2 What things do you use mobile communication technology to do? Does it affect the way you travel?

Task tip

When you answer these questions, think of several different areas you can talk about, not just one.

Conference problems

Listening

1 **Work in pairs. Read this list of things (A–I) which could go wrong at a conference and discuss what the problem could be in each case.**

A the access   F the conference rooms
B the accommodation   G the programme
C the dates   H the staff
D the keynote speaker   I the technology
E the location

2 ①24 **You are going to hear five colleagues in a meeting complaining about things which went wrong in different conferences they attended. Listen and choose the problem from Exercise 1 (A–I) that each speaker is complaining about.**

1 Candice   2 Igor   3 Paula   4 Harry   5 Susan

3 ①24 **Listen again and complete these sentences from the conversation.**

1 They .... us to South America or the Far East or something.

2 She had a PowerPoint presentation prepared, but she couldn't make it work ... She really .... a bit beforehand.

3 They .... one of those purpose-built conference centres.

4 **Work in small groups. Discuss what the organisers could/should have done to avoid the problems mentioned.**

❯ **page 78** Modal verbs: perfect forms

Planning a business trip

Speaking

Work in small groups. You work for an international company. Your manager has decided that several people from your company should travel to the United States to meet people who work in your offices there. You have been asked to plan the trip.

Discuss the situation together and decide:

• why it would be useful to make this trip
• which members of staff would benefit most from the visit
• how long they should go for.

Task tip

Make sure that you take turns in the discussion: listen carefully to your partners and react to what they say. Ask them for their ideas and opinions.

Business conferences

Getting started

Work in small groups.

1 Why do business people go to conferences?
2 What aspects of conferences does each of the photos show?

Arranging conference facilities

Listening

1 You are going to hear two telephone conversations with Sally McBride, who is organising a conference for the South Pacific Tourism Organisation. Before you listen, read Sally's notes carefully. What type of information do you need for each gap?

Conversation 1

South Pacific Tourism Organisation Annual Conference
- Number of delegates: 550 plus
  1 .... (numbers to be emailed)
- Also: eight **2** ....
- **3** .... : traditional dance
- Gala dinner with fireworks – Air New Zealand's **4** .... on programme

Conversation 2

South Pacific Tourism Organisation Annual Conference
Equipment available:
- In main conference room: screen, projector and **5** ....
- Guest speakers should bring **6** ....
- Meeting rooms: screens and projectors; sound equipment available **7** ....
- Stands for exhibitors in **8** ....
- **9** .... available at all times.

Task tip

Make sure that you spell your answers correctly.

2 ① 25–26 Listen to the two conversations and write one or two words in each of the gaps in Exercise 1.

3 Work in pairs. Read this message which Sally wrote to her assistant. What instructions does Sally give, and what reasons does she give for them?

> Safia
> I'm afraid I've had to go to an urgent meeting with a client, so can you phone the National Auditorium for me and tell them we need a cinema projector to show the new promotional film? Tell them it needs to be in the main auditorium as part of the opening session.
> Thanks, S

4 Imagine you work in an English-speaking office and you are organising a conference. Write an email to your assistant.

- Explain why you are out.
- Ask him/her to book some equipment for the conference.
- Say when and why the equipment is needed.

> **Useful language**
> **Explaining why you can't do something**
>
> I'm afraid I have (an urgent meeting), which means I can't …
> Unfortunately, I have to ……… so …
> I'm afraid I'm unable to / can't ……… because …

5 Work in pairs.

- Would you enjoy organising a conference or other business event? Why? / Why not?
- What are the problems of organising events with large numbers of people?

Making the most of business conferences

Reading

1 Work in pairs. You are going to read some advice about going to business conferences. Before you read, look at these statements. Which do you think are the best *three* pieces of advice? Why?

1 You needn't attend each session.
2 Be flexible about how you use conferences.
3 Get one useful idea from each session.
4 Highlight the points you want to act on later.
5 Organise meetings before you arrive.
6 Think how the things you hear relate to your work.
7 Try to meet people who are valued by your colleagues.

2 Read sections A–D quite quickly. What is the main idea of each section?

A I realised that I had never read my notes from the last conference. However, the Action Steps that I had come up with during the conference had fortunately been noted separately and dealt with after the conference. I had recorded these Action Steps with a star next to each, making it easier to distinguish them from other notes. There were people I planned to follow up with and a few ideas for improving one of our products.

B Every presenter at a conference has his or her own style. Some people tell a story, sometimes there is a video or set of images, and sometimes there is a full slide presentation. Given our short memories and the great amount of stimuli, it is important to distil each presentation down to a central point. After each presentation, ask yourself what struck you, what did you learn? Perhaps there was a specific tip that you could adapt when you get back to your office – or some piece of counter-intuitive advice that is worth additional consideration upon your return to real life.

C How should you spend your time at a conference? Should you cut off a great conversation with a fellow attendee to make the next session? Don't assume that you should go to every event. The greatest benefits of a conference are often circumstantial, outside the organised events – a chance conversation in the coffee line could make all the difference. A great conference is especially fertile ground for collaboration. So don't feel pressured by the structure.

D Conferences are more than just the programming, they are an assembly of like-minded people. How often do you get uninterrupted time to discuss matters of interest with industry peers from around the world? Many frequent conference-goers claim that their greatest conference experiences happened during the 'downtime'. Don't leave these benefits up to chance. Reach out to your contacts in advance and suggest grabbing an early breakfast together, lunch or dinner during the conference. Encourage each person to invite one or two people that they deeply respect, thus broadening the potential of the meeting.

adapted from *5 Tips for Making the Most of a Conference* by Scott Belsky

3 Which section (A, B, C or D) does each statement from Exercise 1 (1–7) refer to?

4 Work in pairs.

1 What other advice would you give to people attending a conference?
2 Which conference activities do you / would you enjoy most: the sessions, the networking, or the meals and entertainment? Why?

Speaking

Work in pairs. This year, your company has decided to send a small number of staff to an international conference for your industry being held in Guangzhou, China. You have been asked to make recommendations.

Discuss the situation and decide:

1 how staff should be selected to go to this conference
2 what sort of follow-up there should be when the staff return.

> **Task tip**
>
> Quickly think of some selection criteria and some ideas for follow up before you start speaking.

Networking at a conference

Listening

1 **Match each of the phrases (1–8) with one of the functions (a–h).**

1 He's a great manager, isn't he? Really gets things moving.
2 How about having lunch together the next time you're in Zurich?
3 I thought it was very persuasive. I wish we'd had the same idea ourselves.
4 It's unfortunate. You see, what happened was this …
5 Look, if you like, I could drop her an email and …
6 No, we'd be really happy if you people did it for us. Would it interest you?
7 Great to meet you at last. I've heard about you from various friends, so this really is a stroke of luck.
8 You know, if I were you I'd try B&H. They're really the best people for this sort of thing.

a Arranging to meet
b Congratulating someone
c Explaining a problem
d Offering a contract
e Offering to contact someone
f Recommending an organisation
g Talking about a colleague
h Greeting someone

2 🔘 27 **You are going to hear five short conversations in which people are networking during a break at a conference. Listen and, for each conversation, decide what the main speaker is doing. Choose from the options (a–h) in Exercise 1. (Note: the speakers will not use exactly the same phrases as those in Exercise 1.)**

Conversation 1: ....   Conversation 4: ....

Conversation 2: ....   Conversation 5: ....

Conversation 3: ....

3 **Look at the transcript of the conversations (Track 27) and underline the phrases which gave you the answers.**

Role-play

Work in pairs. You are at a conference. You have never met before, but you have a mutual business friend, Patrick Wu. Before you start speaking, study your role and think about some of the things you can say.

Student A

- Introduce yourself.
- Say how you know Patrick Wu (you used to work together).
- Ask Student B how he/she knows Patrick.
- Tell Student B you are interested in talking to someone who can find places for your company to advertise on the Internet.
- Respond to Student B's suggestions.

Student B

- When Student A introduces him/herself, say you've heard about him/her from Patrick Wu.
- Say how you know Patrick Wu (one of your best customers).
- Ask if Student A is enjoying the conference.
- You have a lot of contacts in the advertising industry, and one of your specialities is web-based advertising.
- Suggest a meeting somewhere else at another time to organise the advertising.

A destination management company (DMC)

Listening

1 **Work in pairs. You are going to hear Charlotte Weston talking about the company she works for, Pacific World. Before you listen, discuss this question.**

What are the advantages for an organisation of employing a specialist company to organise their travel for them?

2 **①28 Listen and choose the correct answer – A, B or C – for each question.**

1 What does Pacific World do?
   A It sells package holidays.
   B It organises journeys to specific destinations.
   C It prepares the trip at the destination.

2 Event-management agencies use DMCs because they
   A employ more creative staff.
   B know the area better.
   C can reduce costs.

3 Who are typical clients for Pacific World?
   A marketing agencies
   B pharmaceutical companies
   C IT companies

4 Why are DMCs essential for organising conferences in China?
   A They can handle phone calls and correspondence.
   B They know how to do business there.
   C They speak Chinese.

5 Why is Shanghai a good place to hold a large conference?
   A It is more fashionable than Hong Kong.
   B It offers competitive rates.
   C It has suitable venues.

6 The finance company has chosen Shanghai for their conference in order to
   A motivate their staff.
   B develop their business in China.
   C teach staff about Chinese finance.

Speaking

1 **Work in pairs. Discuss these questions.**

1 What factors are important when choosing a conference destination?
   You can consider:
   - the conference centre
   - hotels
   - the atmosphere of the destination
   - accessibility, etc.

2 Which places in the world would you most like to go to for a conference?

2 **Work in small groups. Your company has decided to hold a two-day conference for people from your company, and you have been asked to help plan it. Discuss the situation together and decide:**

- what kinds of activities should be organised for the main part of the conference
- what entertainment could also be provided
- where the conference should be held.

UNIT 15

Business meetings

Getting started

1 Work in pairs. Match the words from the first column (1–8) with words from the second column (a–h) to make reasons for holding different types of business meeting. (Although different combinations may be possible, you should use each letter only once.)

Meetings can be held in order to …

1 produce action a creativity.
2 exchange or b decisions.
 pass on
3 build c ideas.
4 motivate d information.
5 solve e plans.
6 brainstorm f problems.
7 stimulate g sales staff.
8 take h teams.

2 Work in pairs. Discuss these questions.

1 Do you attend any of these types of meeting?
2 Which do you think are the most enjoyable? And the least?

3 Read these statements and decide whether you agree or disagree with them. Then compare your opinions with other pairs.

1 Every meeting should have an agenda.
2 The agenda should be circulated in advance.
3 The chair is responsible for the success of a meeting.
4 In every meeting, there should be someone taking the minutes.
5 At the end of meetings, the participants should agree a list of action points.
6 All meetings should be for a fixed length of time.
7 If people are going to attend meetings, they should always prepare beforehand.
8 Everyone should have a chance to speak at meetings.

Talking about meetings

Listening

1 Match these verbs (1–7) with their definitions (a–g).

1 **set up** a meeting a cancel
2 **chair** a meeting b disturb
3 **call off** a meeting c lead or supervise
4 **put off** a meeting d not attend
5 **adjourn** a meeting e organise
6 **skip** a meeting f postpone
7 **interrupt** a meeting g stop temporarily

2 (1) 29 You are going to hear four people talking about meetings. Listen and decide which of the things in Exercise 1 (1–7) each of them had to do. Write one number by each speaker.

1 Martyna   2 Sasha   3 Mei Lin   4 Paul

A survey of meetings

Speaking

1 Work in pairs. A recent survey of companies revealed the information in the charts on page 71. Prepare to present the information using your own words where possible.

2 Change partners.

1 Take turns to present the information.
2 Discuss the advantages and disadvantages of in-person meetings, face-to-face meetings and virtual meetings using technology.

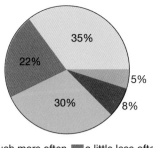

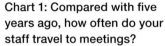

much more often ■ a little less often
a little more often ■ much less often
the same

Chart 1: Compared with five years ago, how often do your staff travel to meetings?

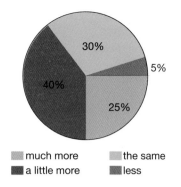

■ much more ■ the same
■ a little more ■ less

Chart 2: Compared with five years ago, how much do you use technology for meetings?

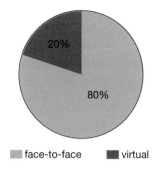

■ face-to-face ■ virtual

Chart 3: Which type of meeting do your staff prefer?

> **Useful language**
> **Expressing statistics**
>
> Thirty per cent of companies said that …
> We found that 35% of business people …
> The survey shows that 40% of business people …

> **Useful language**
> **Expressing contrasts and comparisons**
>
> While/Whereas 25% of companies use much more technology, 30% hadn't made any change.
> In contrast / By comparison, only 5% used less.

Reading

1 Read this article quite quickly. What advantages of face-to-face meetings are mentioned?

The new face of face-to-face meetings

BY JOE MULLICH

Recent surveys suggest companies are putting greater emphasis on making sure their meetings achieve quantifiable results. There is a growing mandate to measure their outcomes and identify the practices that directly lead to greater learning or increased sales.
5 Instead of looking at video conferencing as an alternative to meetings held offsite, many companies are now combining the two, as well as using social networking tools as a powerful follow-up to face-to-face connections.

Psychologists and behavioral scientists have long known that facial
10 expressions, hand gestures, and voice tone provide more clues to listeners than the words themselves.

"It's harder to follow cues such as expressions on people's faces in two dimensions," says Dr. Carlos Ferran, D.B.A., Assistant Professor of Management Information Systems at Pennsylvania State University,
15 who specializes in research that develops a better understanding of how technology-mediated communications differ from face-to-face communications.

Conference calls, email, texting, video conferences, social networks, and other forms of communication are all crucial elements
20 in building and maintaining business relationships. However, none of them captures the impact of meeting someone face to face. In-person business meetings let attendees develop transparency and trust in ways that are not always possible with other forms of communication. One member of a corporate team wrote in an online forum that although
25 her team had held many virtual meetings and work sessions, she only felt truly comfortable with the other team members after finally meeting them face-to-face. She said her deadlines now take on greater importance for her, because the project is no longer just a voice on Skype or a person writing an email—but a friend and colleague who
30 is now real to her. Thom Singer, author of The ABCs of Networking, points out that "it's easy to replace a vendor you've never met, but

people think twice before firing a colleague or friend that they respect on a personal level."

In a survey of its customers, a leading New York-based organization
35 that provides meeting-management technology, found that the majority considered the capability to host a hybrid meeting—one which incorporates remote attendees into a face-to-face gathering—as "somewhat" or "very" important. More and more, companies don't see a black-and-white divide between face-to-face meetings and
40 virtual ones. Both are complementing each other.

This emerging practice is demonstrated by Sprint-Nextel. The communications giant has always stressed in-person meetings for its sales force, especially in the business-to-business space where solutions need to be tailored based on the business's size, location, and need.
45 "You can't beat face-to-face meetings for opening the relationship or closing the decision," says Tom Shaughnessy, who runs their small-business segment. Instead of eliminating face-to-face meetings, Sprint reduced the number of its people who attend them. In past times, the company might have had a team of account and technical personnel at
50 a key meeting. Now, they might send two people in person and have the rest participate through video conferencing. As a result, Sprint trims meeting costs, while still giving customers a true face-to-face experience.

Experts say companies must strategically determine how to
55 integrate face-to-face meetings and new technology based on specific objectives. For example, many companies are using technology for preliminary discussions or training, followed by in-person meetings to build relationships, present critical information and move forward on a project. In addition to this, use of social media is also gaining
60 momentum. "Social networking is important, because companies can keep the dialogue going with their customers," says Fay Beauchine, president of the National Business Travel Association Foundation. But getting it started depends on being face to face.

adapted from the *Wall Street Journal*

2 Work in pairs. Understanding pronouns and other ways of referencing such as *this, ones, each other,* etc. helps you to follow the argument of a text. Look at the underlined words in the text and say what each of them refers to.

Example: 'their' in line 3 refers to 'meetings'.

❯ **page 78** Referencing

3 Choose the correct answer – A, B, C or D – for each question.

Task tip

When different people are named in the questions, quickly scan the text to find the names. Then read what they say carefully.

1 In the first paragraph, how does the writer say in-person meetings have changed?
A They have become more effective.
B They have become more frequent.
C They make greater use of technology.
D Fewer of them happen offsite.

2 What point does Dr Ferran make about meetings?
A Some information is easier to obtain face-to-face.
B Business people have difficulty interpreting certain visual signs.
C Technology can distract listeners in meetings.
D Some people find it difficult to operate technology in meetings.

3 What point does the writer make about the effect of face-to-face meetings in paragraph 3?
A People generally finish their work more punctually.
B People stay in the same jobs for longer.
C Most face-to-face meetings can be replaced by technology.
D After face-to-face meetings, colleagues feel more committed to each other.

4 What finding did the New York-based organisation make about companies?
A They prefer meetings to be held face to face.
B They increasingly need to combine in-person and virtual meetings.
C They require increasingly sophisticated meetings technology.
D They find it impossible for everyone to attend meetings.

5 The effect of Sprint-Nextel's change to its meeting practices has been to
A improve customer relations.
B decide things more efficiently.
C lower its expenditure on meetings.
D deal with problems more effectively.

6 The writer's final point is that face to face meetings are essential for
A getting new employees started.
B starting to use social media.
C starting off new projects.
D starting customer relationships.

4 Work in small groups.

1 How do you use remote-meetings technologies in your work or studies?
2 When you use these technologies, do you give the meetings your full attention? What other activities do you do at the same time?

Vocabulary

Match these words/phrases (1–5) with their definitions from the *CBD* (a–e).

1 practice (line 4)   a extremely important to the progress or success of something
2 follow-up (line 7)   b make something else seem better or more attractive when combining with it
3 complement (line 40)   c reduce the amount or size of something
4 trim (line 53)   d something that is done to finish a previous action or make it more successful
5 critical (line 58)   e the way of doing things in a particular business, industry, etc.

Looking for solutions

Listening

1 The phrases below (1–10) are typically said at meetings. Classify them according to whether they:

| a agree | c ask someone's opinion |
| b disagree | d introduce your own opinion |

1 ... don't you think?
2 Frankly, I think that ...
3 I'm not sure.
4 That's right.
5 Well, I think ...

6 Personally, I feel that ...
7 That's true.
8 What do you think?
9 Yes, and ...
10 Yes, but ...

2 ①30 You are going to hear part of a business meeting at a company which produces watches and clocks. The Export Manager, Barry, is discussing with colleagues how to break into the Chinese market. Listen and tick (✓) the phrases in Exercise 1 as you hear them.

Writing

Imagine you are Sandra or Mark. Write a short email to Barry in which you:

- agree to go to China to investigate
- suggest dates
- say what promotional literature and samples you will need
- request details of expenses the company is prepared to pay for your trip.

❯ **page 117** Writing reference

A meeting at a medical equipment company

Role-play

Work in groups of four. Study the background and instructions below. Each of you should take one of the roles. Study your role for a few minutes and decide what you will say at the meeting. Then hold a meeting to discuss the problem.

Background

You work for a large company which specialises in manufacturing and supplying high-tech medical equipment to hospitals and patients in a number of countries in your region.

Last year, the sales department's budget for travel (for example, for sales personnel to visit hospitals, health authorities, etc.) was $2m. The finance department has asked whether it would be possible to save money on this, and an initial meeting has been called to discuss the problem.

In this meeting, you will have to exchange ideas and opinions, but you do not need to reach a firm decision.

A Finance Director

You think:
- significant savings could be made by using email and video conferencing to talk with customers, especially for routine visits by sales staff to existing customers.
- sales staff should use economy class and low-cost airlines where possible. This could reduce travelling costs by up to 50%.
- sales staff should go for one day only, instead of staying in a hotel overnight.

B Sales Director

You think:
- face-to-face meetings are essential, both to meet new customers and to show existing customers new products and innovations.
- it is difficult to get high-quality sales staff who know the very specialised products which you sell, and it is important to treat them well, for example, by allowing them to fly business class.
- your staff try to make several visits to different customers when they are in a different city, and this may involve a stay of several days.

C Marketing Director

You think:
- new technology (video conferencing, etc.) could replace some visits by sales staff – many routine visits do not result in increased sales.
- it should be possible to reach agreements with certain airlines and hotels to arrange discounts for sales staff.
- sales staff should state the objectives of each visit before they make them, so that managers can decide whether the visit is worth the cost.

D Senior Sales Manager

You think:
- your clients (doctors, hospital managers, etc.) are very busy people, and unless you visit them, they don't have time to look at your products.
- you spend a lot of time travelling – at least 150 days a year – and it's important to do so in comfort.
- you work in a very competitive sector where you know sales people from other companies visit your clients regularly.
- the products you sell are highly technical and very expensive. Sales staff have to make high-quality presentations and answer technical questions, so face-to-face meetings are essential.

Spending the sales budget

Getting started

Work in small groups.

1 In a non-retail business, which of the following do you think are more important for sales staff? Why?

 a visiting existing customers or potential customers?

 b the right personality, expert knowledge, or good sales techniques?

2 What sales techniques do you know about which are particularly effective?

Useful language
Giving opinions

As far as I'm concerned, …

Personally, I think …

I feel quite strongly that …

In my view, …

There's no doubt in my mind that …

Spanish sales

Listening

1 **Work in pairs. You are going to hear Adam Evans, a promotions manager, talking about sales in Spain. Before you listen, look at these notes and decide what type of information you need for each gap.**

2 **(2) 01 Listen and complete the notes with one word or a number.**

3 **(2) 01 Listen again. Which do you think is Adam's priority: visiting existing customers or potential new customers? Why?**

Meeting customers

- The key to successful sales is
  1 ....

- Each member of his team competes with approximately
  2 .... other sales reps.

- The sales reps decide how to achieve their sales in
  3 ....

- They make a 4 .... of customers and centres to visit.

- The reps' knowledge of their 5 .... allows them to build a better customer 6 ....

- Reps visit customers 7 .... to 8 .... times a year.

- The team is able to compete on 9 .... rather than numbers.

DF Software

Reading

1 DF Software specialises in software for clinics and hospitals. Work in small groups. Look at the charts below from their sales department and discuss these questions.

1 How have national and international sales evolved over the last three years?
2 What about the company's total sales?
3 How has the sales reps' travel budget changed over the three years?
4 Can you see a correlation between the first and second charts?
5 What does the third chart show about how attention to customers has changed over the period?
6 Based on the information in these charts, what recommendations would you make to the Sales Director regarding travel and visits?

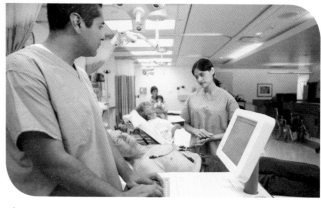

1 DF Software: national and international sales

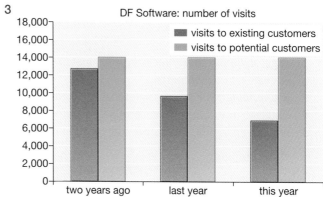

3 DF Software: number of visits

2

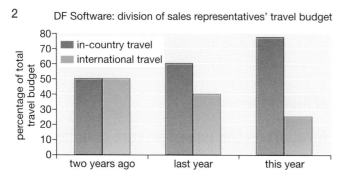

DF Software: division of sales representatives' travel budget

2 Complete this report for the Sales Director by writing one word in each gap.

Task tip

Don't leave any gaps blank. If you can't answer a question, make a guess. When you've finished, read the complete text again to check your answers.

3 Match the answers you gave to the questions in Exercise 1 with the information given in the report. Are there any differences?

DF Software sales report

Introduction
The purpose of **1** _this_ report is to summarise DF Software's sales over the **2** _____ three years and **3** _____ recommendations for our future sales strategy.

Sales
4 _____ the charts show, national sales have increased from €14 million to €16 million. **5** _____ , the international sales have decreased from €27 million to €13 million over the same **6** _____ . Our total sales have fallen **7** _____ €12 million.

Sales travel and visits
Last year, it was decided that the international travel budget should be reduced. Sales staff were encouraged to maintain contact **8** _____ overseas customers by means of video conferencing, as **9** _____ was thought to be equally effective. Meanwhile, national travel was given a higher share of the budget, on the basis that this was expected to be a **10** _____ lucrative market. Our poor sales performance can be put down to the fact that we paid less attention **11** _____ existing customers.

Recommendations
Since it is clear customers prefer to meet sales staff face to face, I strongly recommend increasing our international travel budget by reducing the budget for the annual sales conference. At the **12** _____ time, I suggest that more time is **13** _____ visiting existing customers so that we do not lose **14** _____ .

4 Read the report again and answer these questions.

1 What reason is given for:
   a using video conferencing?
   b increasing the budget for national travel?
   c poor sales performance?
   d increasing the international travel budget?
   e suggesting that more time is spent visiting existing customers?

2 What words/phrases are used to introduce each of these reasons (e.g. *because*)?

3 In what way were staff expected to keep in touch with overseas clients?

4 In what way will the company be able to raise its travel budget?

5 Which words/phrases are used to introduce each of the ways of doing things referred to in questions 3 and 4 above?

5 Look at the recommendations in the report and the phrases in the Useful language box, then write recommendations using these prompts.

1 recommend / use / low-cost airlines / business travel / possible
2 suggest / more time / meeting customers / instead / writing reports
3 recommend / incentivise sales staff / award prizes
4 suggest / training course / product knowledge
5 recommend / hire local staff / international markets

> **Useful language**
> **Making recommendations**
>
> I would like to make the following recommendations/ suggestions: first, we should …
> I would like to suggest/recommend that we (should) open …
> I (strongly) suggest/recommend that the branch (should) be closed.

6 ☉ Work in pairs. Business English students often make mistakes when expressing or introducing recommendations. Choose the correct option in italics in each of these sentences.

1 At the meeting, you will be able to *make / give* suggestions about how to cut the budget.
2 I am submitting this report to *propose / suggest* which taxi firm our company should use.
3 The aim of this report is to *make / give* a recommendation on how to solve the problem.
4 I am writing to *propose / suggest* you buy the new IT solutions equipment.
5 We recommend that all employees *use / must use* email to send documents.

Grammar workshop

Using the passive to express opinions and ideas

1 Read these passive sentences from the report. Why do you think the writer used the passive for these sentences?

1 Last year, it was decided that the international travel budget should be reduced.
2 Sales staff were encouraged to maintain contact with overseas customers by means of video conferencing, as this was thought to be equally effective.
3 Meanwhile, national travel was given a higher share of the budget, on the basis that this was expected to be a more lucrative market.

2 Rewrite these active sentences using the passive. Use the sentences in Exercise 1 as models.

1 At a recent board meeting, the board decided to increase the number of sales staff.
2 The company is encouraging its front-office staff to write emails to customers instead of phoning, as they think this will save money.
3 Managers have implemented an incentive scheme, as they expect this to encourage staff.

❯ **page 79 Passives**

A report on the use of private company jets

Listening

1 Work in pairs.

What do you think the advantages of using a private company jet for business trips instead of a normal commercial flight might be? List as many advantages as you can.

2 Compare the list you made in Exercise 1 with this list (A–G). Did you think of the same reasons? Did you think of other reasons which are not given on this list?

A You are not distracted by other passengers.
B You can discuss business matters during trip.
C It impresses potential customers.
D It saves on journey time.
E You can deal with customer problems quickly.
F It is more comfortable than commercial aircraft.
G It offers more flexibility.

3 (2)02 You are going to hear three executives from Florentino International being interviewed about why they prefer using the company jet instead of a normal commercial flight. Listen and, for each person, decide what their main reason is. Choose from the list (A–G) in Exercise 1.

1 Gustav Bremitz
2 Pascuala Fernández
3 Patrykcja Krawiec

Writing

1 Work in pairs. Look at this writing task and discuss the questions (1–3) in the next column.

> You work for Florentino International.
> - You have been asked to write a report on how the company aircraft are used by departmental directors and make recommendations for changes.
> - Look at the graphs below and use all the handwritten notes to write your report for the CEO.

Chart 1
Average number of flights by departmental directors and above

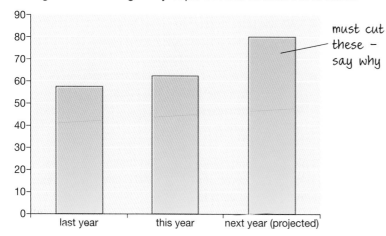

must cut these – say why

Chart 2
Reasons for flights

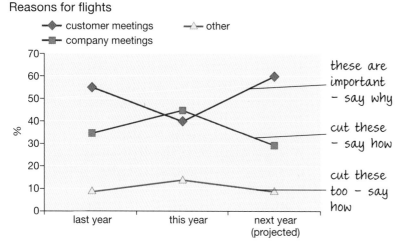

these are important – say why

cut these – say how

cut these too – say how

1 What does each chart show?
2 What can you say for each of the handwritten notes?
3 What sections can you put in your report?

2 Work alone. Write the report.

- Use the report on page 75 as a model.
- Use phrases from the model to express reasons and ways of doing things.
- Use the passive where appropriate.

> **Useful language**
> **Explaining the purpose of the report**
>
> The purpose/aim/intention of this report is to …
> The reason for writing this report is to …
> In addition, I shall …
> I also intend to …

Task tips
- Quickly write a plan before you start writing. When you write, follow your plan.
- Include some statistics from the charts in your report.

Grammar workshop 4

Units 13–16

Modal verbs: perfect forms

- When we want to criticise people for past mistakes, we can use *should have* or *ought to have* + past participle:
  *They **should have planned** the conference better. It **ought to have been** held in a more interesting place.*
- When we want to say that something was possible, but it didn't happen, we can use *could have* + past participle:
  *They **could have held** the conference in Shanghai, but they didn't because it was too expensive.*
- When we want to say that perhaps something happened in the past, we can use *may have, might have* or *could have* + past participle:
  *The accident **may have happened** because the workers didn't follow safety procedures. They **might have been** smoking in a non-smoking area.*

Complete this paragraph with *should have, could have* or *might have* and the correct form of the verbs in brackets.

My boss really irritates me. For example, he **1** .... (*ask*) me which was the best hotel to stay at, but he didn't, because he doesn't like asking for advice. So we found ourselves staying at a noisy, ugly hotel by the motorway when we **2** .... (*stay*) at the luxurious lakeside hotel where all top managers go. If we had stayed there, we **3** .... (*rest*) between meetings, but as it was, the noise was so great that we couldn't relax at all. I don't know why he chose that hotel. It **4** .... (*be*) because he has already spent all the travel budget when he went to that conference in Singapore. Or he **5** .... (*make*) a mistake – after all, they're next to each other in the telephone book. He **6** .... (*just dial*) the wrong number. Still, he **7** .... (*tell*) me to make the booking. After all, I am his PA, and that's what I'm paid to do!

Referencing

- We use *he, she, they*, etc. to refer to people. We use *they/them* for people in the singular when talking in general about males and females, or it is unspecified: *When **a client** gets angry with you, **they** will often tell your other clients why **they** are angry.*
- We use *this, that* or *it* to refer to things last mentioned:
  *Costs have been rising. **This** means our profit margins are smaller.*
- We use *that* to refer to a reason:
  *Many of our staff have a long journey to work. **That** is why they arrive at the office feeling stressed.*
- We use *one* to refer to singular countable nouns from a group:
  *There were several good candidates for the job, but I particularly liked the **one** from China.*
- We use *ones* to refer to plural nouns:
  *These are our offices: you'll see the **ones** on the top floor have an excellent view.*
- We use *each other* to show that each person in a group does something to the others:
  *Our team is successful because the team members help **each other**.*

Replace the underlined words in these sentences with a pronoun to avoid repetition and make any necessary changes to the verb forms.

1 I find many meetings frustrating, especially <u>meetings</u> [*ones*] which are badly planned.
2 The new computer program should increase productivity, but staff will need training to use <u>the new program</u> [*it*]. <u>The fact that they need training</u> [*that*] is why I've called this meeting.
3 There has been a lot of bad weather across Europe, and <u>the bad weather</u> [*this*] will lead to delays in deliveries.
4 We've been experiencing problems paying some of our suppliers and <u>the problems</u> [*that has*] have meant that <u>the suppliers</u> [*they*] are not sending us components.
5 When a member of staff has their annual interview, I always ask <u>the member of staff</u> what training <u>the member of staff</u> [*them*] needs.
6 When I've been negotiating with a client, <u>I usually email the client and the client usually emails me</u> [*we usually / they / need / email each other*] to summarise what we've agreed.

Passives

We use the passive when:

- we want to emphasise what happened to something, not who did it. Compare:

  Apple launched the iPad in 2010. (Active: you are emphasising Apple, who did it.)

  *The iPad **was launched** in 2010.* (Passive: you are emphasising what happened to the iPad.)

- the agent (the person/thing doing the action) is not important, or we don't want to mention who did it, or we don't know who did it:

  *The consignment **was sent** last week.* (I don't know who sent it, or it's not important.)

  *€2m of goods **were stolen** from our warehouse last weekend.* (We don't know who did it.)

- we want to use a more formal style. Compare:

  We pay salaries on the 28th of each month.

  *Salaries **are paid** on the 28th of each month.*

Here are two common passive structures:

- | X is/was | believed | + infinitive with *to* |
	reported	
	said	
	considered	
	expected	
	thought	

  *His personal fortune **is believed to exceed** €500 million.*

- | It is/was/has been | agreed | + *that* + clause |
	announced	
	believed	
	considered	
	decided	
	expected	
	explained	
	hoped	
	reported	
	said	
	suggested	
	thought	

  *It **was agreed that** we should implement the new measures at the end of the financial year.*

- We use these structures when we:
  - want to use a more formal style
  - don't know, or don't want to say, who thinks or said the thing.

1 **Rewrite these statements to make them more formal by using the passive.**

1 We've sent your application to head office.
   Your application ...
2 The Minister for Industry will open the conference.
   The conference ...
3 You must submit your application by 19 March.
   Your application ...
4 The Board of Directors has taken a number of important decisions this morning.
   A number of important decisions ...
5 They're interviewing candidates for the job at the moment.
   Candidates ...
6 In our manufacturing process, we reject 9% of finished articles as substandard.
   In our manufacturing process, 9% ...
7 Unfortunately, we opened the envelope by mistake.
   Unfortunately, the envelope ...
8 You must always keep the computer codes in a locked safe.
   The computer codes ...

2 **Complete the second sentence of each pair so that it means the same as the first.**

1 We expect that turnover will fall next year due to increased competition.
   Turnover is expected ...
2 We expect prices of raw materials will rise by 50% in the next six months.
   Prices of raw materials ...
3 According to the announcement, profits have reached record levels.
   It has ...
4 It is reported that Sunshine Cruises Ltd is losing money.
   Sunshine Cruises Ltd is ...
5 Most people consider that he is an excellent human resources manager.
   He is considered ...
6 We expect the project will meet its deadlines.
   The project is expected ...
7 According to reports, Samsung are bringing out a new smartphone.
   Samsung are reported ...
8 Someone suggested that we should replace certain items in our product range.
   It was suggested that certain ...

Social media and business

Getting started

Work in small groups.

1 Which of these social media have you used?
2 How can social media help:
   - people in their jobs?
   - people to find work?
   - businesses?

Social media and customers

Listening

1 **Work in pairs. You are going to hear Felicity Bannerman, a marketing consultant, talking about social media. Before you listen, look at these notes and decide what information you will need to fill the gaps. Can you predict any of the answers?**

- Benefits of social media: websites are **1** .... to use + many people have accounts, so great for reaching **2** .... in particular.
- Companies should avoid using media to communicate their **3** .... – people annoyed by this.
- Train staff to see media as a **4** .... between company and customers.
- Coca-Cola took on two **5** .... to organise their social media presence – they now have approximately **6** .... followers.
- Small businesses tell customers about a new product or a **7** .... by sending customers 'tweets' to their mobile devices.

---

2 (2) 03 **Listen and complete the notes by writing one or two words or a number in each gap.**

3 **Work in small groups.**

   1 What other companies do you know which use social media to communicate with customers?
   2 How successful are they at doing this?

Vocabulary

1 **Complete these extracts from the interview with Felicity by writing a verb in the correct form in each gap to form a verb–noun collocation. Then note the verb–noun collocations in your notebooks.**

   1 This is an opportunity which is too good to ....
   2 Using social media is a change they can .... which won't hurt their budgets.
   3 The most common mistake that companies .... is to treat the social media as if it was somewhere to advertise.
   4 One of the recommendations I .... to companies is that they need to train their staff to listen to customers and potential customers.
   5 According to research which the company .... , the page itself has a phenomenal number of followers.

2   ⊙ **Business English students often make mistakes with verb–noun collocations. Choose the correct option in italics in each of these sentences.**

1   Would it be possible for your trainers to *take / run* both the courses for our staff on the same day?

2   We cannot *hold / do* a meeting on this date, as we'll be at a trade fair.

3   If we *make / place* an order this month, we will be given an early settlement discount of 20%.

4   Some modifications must be *made / done* to the network.

5   This report is on the recent customer survey *conducted / made* at our store.

6   We have to *do / make* these cuts due to our financial situation.

7   The deadline for *making / giving* suggestions is next Friday.

3   **Match the verbs (1–12) with the nouns (a–d) to form more common business collocations. You can use more than one verb with each noun.**

1   arrange   a   a deadline
2   attend   b   a survey / research
3   carry out   c   changes
4   conduct   d   a meeting
5   do
6   hold
7   implement
8   make
9   meet
10 miss
11 schedule
12 set

4   **Complete this email from a manager to her assistant by writing a verb in each gap to form a verb–noun collocation. In some cases, more than one answer is possible.**

5   **Imagine you are Sasha. Write a short email to managers.**

• Explain the reason for the meeting.
• Say where it will take place.
• Ask them to suggest a time.

INBOX   File | Edit | View | Favourites | Tools | Actions | Help   ✕

Sasha,

Last month, we decided we needed to **1** .... some changes to the way we communicate with customers, and I commissioned a consultant, Felicity Bannerman, to **2** .... some research into how we could use social media. We have now received the results of her research and we need to **3** .... a meeting with heads of departments to decide how we are going to **4** .... the changes she suggests and **5** .... deadlines for completing them.

Can you please **6** .... the meeting for later this week and make sure that as many managers as possible can **7** .... it?

Thanks
Petra

Some ways of using social media

Reading

1   **Work in small groups. You are going to read extracts from an article about social media in business. Before you read, look at the words and phrases in bold in these issues and think of synonyms for each of them.**

1   The importance of admitting **errors**
2   Using social media to ensure **staff** work towards the same **ends**
3   The effectiveness of word of mouth on the **Web**
4   The need to combine your knowledge of your **clients** with your company's **goals**
5   The need to use a range of **training** techniques
6   A description of persuasive people **outside** the **company**
7   The need to **pay attention to** current conversations in the social media
8   **Employing** social media across all departments of the company

2 Now read these extracts, ignoring the gaps. For each issue (1–8) in Exercise 1, decide which extract – A, B, C or D – it refers to. You will need to use some letters more than once.

A

1 _____ – Business people are still not sure how to handle social media. **2** _The_ technology you use has to tie in with **3** _____ business objectives of **4** _____ company you work for. Your social strategy should include an element of listening to what is already being said in the space. You have to really listen and focus on how to get the company engaged with **5** _____ right customers. Your strategy can then be to marry your business objectives with your insights into your customers. Your competitive advantage lies in really understanding what you know about them that no one else does.

B

One of the areas where Thomson Reuters, with over 50,000 employees worldwide, really differentiate themselves is how they use social media within their global organisation to align all their employees to their overall business objectives. This requires extensive employee training and education and use of social tools across all business functions, from PR to marketing to customer service.

C

Getting the people who work for you to understand some basic principles of social media such as 'acknowledge your mistakes' or 'listen to your customers' is in itself a big win. Going beyond that, you can help them by providing everything from hands-on classroom work to virtual instruction, from written guides to recorded video and webinar-style sessions. These efforts will make a huge difference to how the company and its employees view social media.

D

One of **6** _____ ways for a business to succeed is by making use of external influencers in the marketplace. These people have three characteristics: they like to try **7** _____ new things because they are new, they are intrinsically motivated, and they share stories with **8** _____ friends. They do this because they are excited or interested, not because they want to sell their friends something. **9** _____ Research published by Proctor and Gamble stated that an influencer's story spreads up to one million times within their social network on **10** _____ Internet within one year.

adapted from www.forbes.com

3 Which words in the extracts are synonyms for the words in bold in Exercise 1?

4 Work in small groups.

1 How are social media changing the way organisations and clients relate to each other?
2 What are the advantages and disadvantages of companies using social media in:
   • marketing?
   • recruitment?
   • communication between employees?
3 How can customers use social media to influence the way companies and other organisations behave?

Grammar workshop

When to use *the*

Complete Extracts A and D in Exercise 2 above by writing *the* in the gap or leaving it blank (–).

page 96 The definite article

An email enquiry

Speaking

Work in small groups. You work for a chain of restaurants. Your manager has suggested using social media to build customer relationships. Discuss the situation and decide:

• how social media can be used to build relationships
• which members of staff should be involved
• what your next steps should be.

Useful language
Talking about steps

I think the first/next thing we should do is …
We could/should start off by …
After that, we could/should …
At the same time, we can …

82 Social media and business

Writing

1 Work in pairs. Your manager, Bill, has sent your colleague, Katrin, the email below on which Katrin has made some handwritten notes.

  1 Underline the things Katrin must deal with in her email.

  2 Write a plan for the email Katrin should write: how many paragraphs does the email need, and what should each contain?

Katrin
A friend told me this firm was good.

Lang Consulting Group

We can advise you on how to give your company a presence in the social media and reap the benefits. ← *Introduce our company*

Contact: Moira Lang mlang@langconsulting.com ← *Say why we want to use social media*

Can you send Moira Lang an email to find out if she can help and how much she charges?

Thanks

Bill

2 Read Katrin's email.

  1 Was her plan the same as or different from your plan? In what ways?

  2 In most of the numbered lines, there is one extra word. It is either grammatically incorrect or does not fit in with the meaning of the text. Some lines, however, are correct. Find the extra words.

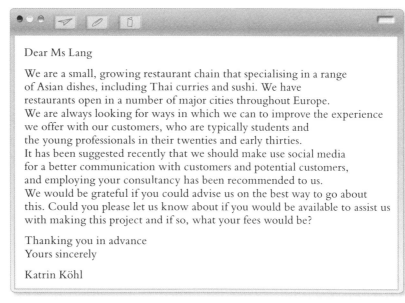

Dear Ms Lang

We are a small, growing restaurant chain that specialising in a range of Asian dishes, including Thai curries and sushi. We have restaurants open in a number of major cities throughout Europe. We are always looking for ways in which we can to improve the experience we offer with our customers, who are typically students and the young professionals in their twenties and early thirties. It has been suggested recently that we should make use social media for a better communication with customers and potential customers, and employing your consultancy has been recommended to us. We would be grateful if you could advise us on the best way to go about this. Could you please let us know about if you would be available to assist us with making this project and if so, what your fees would be?

Thanking you in advance
Yours sincerely

Katrin Köhl

1 ....
2 ....
3 ....
4 ....
5 ....
6 ....
7 ....
8 ....
9 ....
10 ....
11 ....
12 ....

3 Look at Bill's and Katrin's emails again.

  1 What differences can you see between the vocabulary Bill and Katrin have used to express the same ideas?

  2 Why have they used different vocabulary?

4 Now imagine your manager has sent you the same instructions. Write an email introducing your company (or a company you know about) and asking for information from Moira Lang. Write 120–140 words.

Business and the environment

Getting started

1 Work in pairs. Make a list of six things offices can do to be more environmentally friendly, e.g. use less heating / air conditioning.

2 Work with another pair and compare your lists.

• Which are the best ideas?
• Which of these things does your company or school do?

Making the office **greener**

ue to climate change, few business people can fail to realise the importance of the environmental issues that now affect all parts of our day-to-day lives. All businesses, no matter what size, can help to save resources. **1** ......G...... In practice, it only takes a few steps to achieve considerable environmental savings, and these need not impact upon the effectiveness of the business.

If you take a look around your workplace, you are bound to have any number of computers and other equipment in use. Of course, computer equipment consumes electricity. Most people will start up their computer in the morning and only switch it off at night, leaving it on all day, often wasting power. **2** .... Yes, it may take a while for the PC to boot up in the morning, but think of the energy saved.

Modern operating systems have a feature so that if a PC is left idle for a pre-determined time, it will automatically enter standby mode, switching off the monitor and hard disk, effectively sending the PC to sleep. **3** .... The benefit of using standby mode is that the PC will restart a lot quicker than from 'cold', but remember it will still be consuming some power.

Twenty years ago, computer vendors were foretelling the death of the printer as we entered the age of the paperless office. **4** .... Accepting that printers will be with us for the foreseeable future, there are some steps we can take to reduce the cost of printing.

Recycling printer cartridges is an obvious measure, as is using recycled paper or maybe a paper of less thickness or weight. Double-

The green office

Reading

1 Work in pairs. You are going to read an article about making offices more environmentally friendly. Before you read, decide whether you think these statements are true (T) or false (F), and give reasons for your opinions.

a Environmentally friendly offices have higher costs.
b It's hard to make an office environmentally friendly.
c Environmentally friendly offices are more efficient places to work.

2 Now read the article quite quickly, ignoring the gaps. Which of the statements in Exercise 1 does the passage suggest are true, and which are false?

sided printing is also a great way of saving money, as is encouraging printing only when it is absolutely necessary. **5** .... If it is blank on one side and not confidential in nature, then use the blank side as note paper, so at least you are maximising the use of the paper.

Most computers are under-utilised. **6** .... Unfortunately, the energy a computer consumes is pretty much the same if it is busy or quiet, due to the fact that it still needs cooling and the monitor still needs powering. To deal with this issue, many companies are changing their working methods and asking staff to share computers, so that fewer computers are used. This saves money, space and energy.

adapted from eSkills UK

3 Read the article again and note the subject of each paragraph in a few words.

Example: 1 *All businesses can save resources.*

4 Six sentences have been removed from the article. Read these sentences and underline the words and phrases which refer to something in the article.

A <u>Their</u> hard disks are often half empty, and <u>their</u> central processor is only active for a small fraction of the working day.

B Once you have finished with the documents, recycle the paper appropriately.

C A few minutes taken to set this up on each PC can start to save money from day one.

D Get staff involved in these measures, perhaps by holding a short brainstorming session one morning.

E Clearly this is not the case, as we simple humans are often better at interpreting data from a piece of paper than we are on a screen.

F An obvious solution would be to power it down when you go out for lunch and certainly when you leave the office at night.

G In addition, by reducing waste, a business can save money and establish itself as a socially responsible employer.

5 Now choose the best sentence (A–G) above to fill each of the gaps. Do not use any letter more than once. There is one sentence you will not need. The first one has been done as an example.

Vocabulary

Quickly find these words and phrases (1–8) in the article. Then match them with their definitions from Cambridge dictionaries (a–h).

1 issues
2 impact upon
3 idle
4 foretelling
5 foreseeable
6 confidential
7 maximising
8 appropriately

a can be known about or guessed before it happens
b have an influence on something
c in a suitable or right way for a particular situation or occasion
d making something as big in amount, size or importance as possible
e not operating or not being used
f private and intended to be kept secret
g stating what is going to happen in the future
h subjects or problems that people think or talk about, or need to deal with

Speaking

1 Work in pairs. You are going to give a short presentation on this subject.

What is important when making a workplace environmentally friendly? (You can mention: cost savings, efficiency, staff involvement and any other ideas you wish to.)
- Work together and make notes for your presentation.
- Look back at the article you have just read and underline any vocabulary that would be useful when you speak.
- When you are ready, change partners and take turns to give your presentations.

2 Work in small groups. Discuss these two questions using the ideas below.

1 Apart from being environmentally friendly, what else can a business do to establish itself as being socially responsible?
2 Why is it important for companies to be socially responsible?

You can think about:
- working conditions and treatment of employees
- products and services
- treatment of and relationship with customers
- the company's place in the community
- how the company spends its profits or invests money
- ethical standards and honesty.

Grammar workshop

Expressing causes

1 Complete these sentences from the article by writing *due to* or *due to the fact that* in each gap.

1 .... climate change, few business people can fail to realise the importance of the environmental issues that now affect all parts of our day-to-day lives.
2 Unfortunately, the energy a computer consumes is pretty much the same if it is busy or quiet, ... it still needs cooling …

2 Which of these words/phrases are like (a) *due to*, and which are like (b) *due to the fact that*?

1 because
2 because of
3 owing to
4 owing to the fact that

3 Complete these sentences by writing one of the words/phrases from Exercises 1 and 2 in the gap. In all cases, more than one answer is possible.

1 .... the new legislation, many companies are reducing their carbon emissions.
2 Our annual profits have fallen .... poor export sales.
3 We need to get permission for the new building, ... it's a legal requirement.
4 Our production process has become more efficient, ... we invested in new machinery.
5 .... criticism in the newspapers, the company's reputation was damaged.

4 Look at these words/phrases which also express causes. Then complete each of the sentences below with one of the phrases in the correct form.

- cause + noun (+ infinitive):
  Our new process **causes less pollution**.
  The bad economic situation **caused the factory to close**.
- result in + noun/verb + -ing:
  New laws have **resulted in changes** to our production process.
  The scandal **resulted in** the CEO **resigning**.
- the reason why … is/was:
  The reason why people don't shut down their computers **is** laziness.

1 .... companies lose customers .... often poor service.
2 Strict anti-pollution laws sometimes .... companies to lose money.
3 Failure to observe clean-air legislation may .... legal action against the company.
4 .... the company lost business .... the damage to their public image.
5 The late delivery .... by a breakdown in the system.
6 Printing both sides will .... a lot less paper being used.

Reducing waste

Vocabulary

1 Business English students often confuse *method* and *way*. Complete these extracts from the article on page 84 with the correct form of *method* or *way*.

1 Double-sided printing is also a great .... of saving money.
2 Many companies are changing their working .... and asking staff to share computers.

2 Read these explanations. Then complete the sentences below with *way* or *method*.

---

way or method?
- *Way* is used on its own or followed by *to (do something)* or *of + -ing*.
  *You can pay in a number of **ways**.*
  *What's the best **way to pay**?*
  *What's the best **way of paying**?*
- Use *method of* before a noun.
  *Debit cards are many people's preferred **method of payment**.*
- *Method* is used for more complex techniques: *working methods, teaching method*

---

1 His sales .... are extremely unusual, but very efficient.
2 However ambitious you are, you'll find there's no easy .... to get to the top.
3 Many people find that reading on-screen is not the easiest .... to read documents.
4 The course teaches the most effective and reliable .... of staff appraisal.
5 The quickest .... to send us the translation would be by email.
6 We have advertised job vacancies many times and as a .... of recruitment, it has proved to be effective.
7 We were not impressed by the .... the company treats its employees.

Writing

1 Read this memo and choose the best options in italics.

MEMO

Dear colleagues

1 *Because of / Due* rising fuel bills, we need to reduce the **2** *volume / amount* of electricity we use in this office. I'd be **3** *grateful / pleased* for any ideas you have on the best **4** *methods / ways* to do this. I'll **5** *give / provide* a box of chocolates for the best idea.

Isabel Mengual
Office Manager

2 Work in pairs. Do you think reducing electricity consumption is a good way to reduce costs? Why? / Why not?

3 Work in pairs. Imagine you are administrative assistants in a large international company. Your manager has complained about the amount of waste in the office. She has asked you to email your colleagues in the office to:

- explain why it is necessary to reduce waste
- ask them to suggest how to reduce waste
- offer a prize for the best suggestion.

Discuss what you can say for each of the points above.

4 Work alone. Write the email in about 40–50 words. When you have finished, compare your email with your partner's.

5 Exchange your email with a different partner and write a brief reply to the email you have received.

- Suggest how waste can be reduced.
- Explain what benefits this will have.
- Explain how it will affect staff.

An environmental consultant

Listening

1 Work in pairs. You are going to hear Harriet Barber, an environmental consultant who works for Arup in London, talking about her job. Before you listen, discuss these questions.

1 What do you think is the role of an environmental consultant in a large company?
2 What subjects would it be best to study at university to get a job as an environmental consultant?

> **Arup**
> An independent firm of designers, planners, engineers, consultants and technical specialists offering a broad range of professional services

2 (2)04 Listen to the interview. Note down Harriet's answers to the questions in Exercise 1.

3 (2)04 Listen again and choose the correct answer – A, B or C – for each question.

1 What does Harriet's job consist of?
   A designing environmentally friendly systems for new buildings
   B obtaining permission for the construction of new buildings
   C assessing the effect of new buildings on the environment

2 What does Harriet recommend companies to do about their environmental impact?
   A gather information before taking action
   B allow inspections of their premises
   C prevent all pollution from their premises

3 According to Harriet, how can large companies make their environmental policy more effective?
   A by making employees aware of it
   B by recycling paper
   C by making one person responsible for it

4 Why did Harriet decide not to work in scientific research?
   A There were few projects to be involved in.
   B There is less variety in research work.
   C She lacked suitable skills.

5 Which of these reasons does Harriet mention for more people working from home in the future?
   A Employees will be more productive working at home.
   B Employees would prefer to spend more time with their families.
   C Companies will look for ways to reduce their costs.

6 Harriet says offices will be used in the future for …
   A running large projects.
   B meetings.
   C completing large amounts of work.

4 Work in small groups.

1 Harriet says that, in the future, more people will work remotely from home. Do you agree?
2 What other changes to the ways people work do you think will happen in the future? Why?

> **Useful language**
> **Talking about the future possibilities**
>
> It's quite likely that …
> There's a chance that …
> People are bound to / may well / will almost certainly …
> People are likely/unlikely to …
> They may possibly …
> They will probably … / They probably won't …

A staff survey

Getting started

Work in pairs. You work for the human resources department of a precision engineering company. You have been considering changes in the way staff work. Recently, you carried out a survey of staff opinions. Read the results on the right and answer the questions below them.

> **Useful language**
> **Talking about consequences and benefits**
>
> This change would mean staff could …
>
> The change would lead to …
>
> The change might/would/will result in …
>
> One benefit would be that …
>
> Staff would also benefit from .... because …

Staff reactions

Listening

1 Work in pairs. You are going to hear members of staff talking about the benefits of the changes. Before you listen, discuss what each of these phrases means.

   A higher productivity
   B better work–life balance
   C lower staff turnover
   D lower costs
   E an opportunity to do other things
   F reduced stress
   G more motivated staff
   H lower absenteeism

2 ②⁰⁵ Listen to the five members of staff and decide which benefit from Exercise 1 (A–H) each one mentions.

   1 Linda
   2 Konstantin
   3 Oliwia
   4 Chung
   5 Martin

RESULTS OF STAFF SURVEY	Would be interested	Not interested	No opinion
Flexible working hours	76%	13%	11%
Career breaks	29%	37%	34%
Optional part-time working	17%	48%	35%

Additional staff request: Nursery facilities for small children

1 Which change would give staff the option of choosing:
   a to work a shorter week?
   b to take time away from work, e.g. to travel or study?
   c when to start and stop work?
2 What would be the benefits of the changes?

Reading a report

Reading

1 Read the report on page 89 based on the survey. Choose the best word below it – A, B, C or D – for each gap.

REPORT ON STAFF SURVEY

Introduction

The aim of this report is to summarise points which have **1** .... from our recent staff survey about changes in working **2** ....

Reasons for changes

Staff **3** .... represents a major cost in our company. It involves **4** .... recruitment processes and staff training. We hope that by **5** .... these changes, we will increase staff retention, motivation and efficiency.

Opinions of staff

A large **6** .... of our staff (three-quarters) asked for flexible working hours. Several people complained about their journey to work. They stated that they **7** .... commuting at **8** .... times stressful and time-consuming.

A **9** .... number of our employees (29%) told me that career breaks would be attractive for them. One **10** .... of staff explained to me that he had always wanted to travel round the world, and that he would like to return to his job **11** ....

A smaller percentage have **12** .... optional part-time working. These are generally people with young children. Several employees asked me if we could **13** .... their pre-school children with on-site nursery care.

Recommendations

I believe we should go **14** .... with these changes because staff generally agree with them and because employees can choose whether to **15** .... advantage of the changes or not.

1	A	arisen	B	raised	C	rose	D	risen
2	A	ways	B	routines	C	practices	D	approaches
3	A	renewal	B	turnover	C	changeover	D	switchover
4	A	pricey	B	valuable	C	extravagant	D	costly
5	A	introducing	B	causing	C	doing	D	adding
6	A	variety	B	quantity	C	proportion	D	range
7	A	suffered	B	experienced	C	found	D	discovered
8	A	top	B	high	C	key	D	peak
9	A	big	B	significant	C	important	D	minority
10	A	worker	B	member	C	colleague	D	partner
11	A	next	B	after	C	following	D	afterwards
12	A	required	B	requested	C	asked	D	claimed
13	A	offer	B	give	C	provide	D	cater
14	A	on	B	up	C	ahead	D	into
15	A	take	B	make	C	do	D	get

2 Read the report again and answer these questions.

1 What is the purpose of the report?
2 Does the report contain all the figures from the results table on page 88? Why? / Why not?
3 Does the report contain all the opinions from the table on page 88?
4 What action does the writer say should be taken? Where is this in the report?
5 Does the writer give reasons for his/her opinions? Where?

Vocabulary

1 Look at these phrases from the report that express numbers.

a   a large proportion
b   a significant number
c   a smaller percentage

Which means:

1 less than the number already mentioned?
2 most people?
3 not a majority, but a number which is worth taking into consideration?

2 Match these phrases (1–7) with their meanings (a–g).

1 a tiny minority of staff
2 growing numbers of staff
3 a substantial majority of staff
4 a limited number of staff
5 around half the staff
6 just over half the staff
7 the vast majority of staff

a   approximately 50% of staff
b   slightly more than 50% of staff
c   not many staff
d   nearly all staff
e   much more than 50% of staff
f   an increasing number of staff
g   a very small number of staff

Grammar workshop

Reporting verbs and reported speech

1 ⊙ Business English students often need to use these reporting verbs: *agree, ask, complain, explain* and *tell*. Complete these sentences by writing one word in each gap. Then check your answers by looking at the report.

1 A significant number of staff asked .... better food in the staff canteen.
2 Several staff complained .... the lighting in their offices.
3 A substantial majority of staff agreed .... our suggestions.
4 A few staff told .... that they needed childcare facilities while at work.
5 One member of staff explained .... me that he needed time off for a distance-learning course.

Some common reporting verbs

- *agree to* do something / *agree with* an idea or a plan:
  *My boss **agreed to increase** my salary by 5%.*
  *I **agree with** the recommendations in the report.*
- *announce/explain/report/say/state* + (*to* + noun/pronoun) (+ *that*):
  *The company **has announced that** they are moving their offices to Slovakia.*
  *Maria **explained to us that** she had arrived late for the meeting because of the traffic.*
- *ask/tell* + infinitive with *to* for requests or orders:
  *She **asked** me **to work** late last night.*
- *ask for* something (request):
  *Staff **have** all **asked for** offices with natural light.*
- *complain about*:
  *Pascual **complains about** the hours he has to work.*
- *discuss* + verb + -ing:
  *Management **discussed changing** working hours.*
- *invite* someone to something / to do something:
  *He **invited me to** the meeting.*
  *He **invited me to make** a presentation at the meeting.*
- *promise* + infinitive with *to*:
  *They **promised to send** the spare parts straight away.*
- *recommend* (+ *that*) / *recommend* + verb + -ing:
  *I **recommend that** we improve the office furniture.*
  *I **recommend improving** the office furniture.*
- *suggest* (+ *that*) / *suggest* + verb + -ing:
  *He **suggested that** they should change suppliers.*
  *He **suggested changing** suppliers.*
- *tell* + noun/pronoun (+ *that*):
  *He **told her that** new equipment was being installed.*

---

2 ⊙ Business English students often make mistakes with reporting verbs. Correct the mistake in each of these sentences.

1 A lot of customers also complaint about their products arriving in poor condition.
2 I also would like to ask you more information about the training course.
3 I am very sorry to tell that we have to reduce our research team by five people.
4 I have invited the senior staff for a meeting next Thursday.
5 I'm writing to you to tell about our employees' training in the area of health and safety.
6 Most of the team agreed to my reasons for wanting to change our working methods.
7 We can't agree with the proposed date for the installation.

▶ page 96 Tense changes in reported speech

Calls to HR

Listening

1 Work in pairs. You are going to hear three telephone conversations with Katrin Reiner in the human resources department of your company. Before you listen, look at the notes below and decide what information you need for each gap.

2 ②06–08 Listen and complete the gaps with one or two words or a number.

Conversation 1

From: Lee Chen (1 .... department)
- complaint: slow 2 ....
- needs to 3 .... in real time
- his suggestion: change 4 ....

Conversation 2

From: Stepan Vasiliev
Invitation: lunch in 5 ....
Reason for meeting: to discuss 6 ....
Other people present: 7 .... managers
Want to suggest improvements for calculating 8 ....

Conversation 3

From: Manuela Ferrer
Agrees with most 9 .... in staff survey
Wants to be member of 10 ....
Suggested:
- 11 .... from each department
- get extra input by using 12 .... website

3 Work in pairs. Complete Katrin's notes to report what the three callers said to her. If necessary, refer to the transcript for Tracks 6–8.

1 Lee Chen complained
  about the slow internet connection.

2 Chen explained that ....

3 He suggested ....

4 Stepan Vasiliev invited me ....

5 He told me that the reason for ....

6 He would like to suggest ....

7 Manuela Ferrer told me she agreed ....

8 She wants ....

9 She suggested ....

Working conditions and social activities

Speaking

1 Work in pairs. Choose either Task A or Task B.

Task A
You work in a large company on the outskirts of your city. Your manager has asked you to take part in a working party to improve staff working conditions.
Discuss the situation together and decide:
• why it is important for employees to have good working conditions
• how working conditions can be improved without increasing costs for the company.

Task B
You work for a large company on the outskirts of your city. Your manager has asked you to take part in a working party to set up a social programme with events for members of staff.
Discuss the situation together and decide:
• how the staff and the company might benefit from staff socialising together
• what social activities and events staff might enjoy participating in.

2 Work with someone who did the other task. Take turns to present the ideas you discussed when doing your tasks.

A survey report

Writing

1 Work in pairs. Your company's offices were built 30 years ago and they are urgently in need of modernisation. You and a colleague were asked to carry out a staff survey to get suggestions for changes, then write a report for the Board of Directors. Your colleague prepared these charts which reflect staff opinions. Discuss what the charts show, ignoring the handwritten notes for the moment.

Chart 1
How should we change our offices?

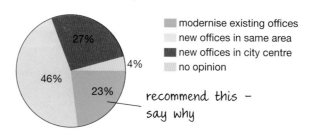

recommend this – say why

Chart 2
What do you think is the best layout for the offices?

not the managers – they want ... (say why)

Chart 3
Do you mind working in artificial light?

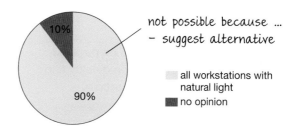

not possible because ... – suggest alternative

2 Write four or five sentences about the charts using phrases from the Vocabulary exercise on page 89.

3 Work in pairs. Decide what section headings the report should have, and what ideas you can include to deal with your handwritten notes.

4 Work alone. Using all your handwritten notes, write your report.

Offshoring and outsourcing

Getting started

- **Offshoring** is when a company moves part of its activities, for example its factories or call centre, to another country.
- **Outsourcing** involves employing a different company or someone outside your company to do part of the work your company needs, such as your accounting, advertising or part of the production process.

Work in small groups.

1 What do you think are the advantages of outsourcing and offshoring for companies?

2 What are the disadvantages?

You can talk about:

- costs and prices
- customer services
- flexibility
- security
- employment
- management
- efficiency

> **Task tip**
>
> Give general answers to the questions, but support them with examples from your experience or what you have read about or studied.

When should we outsource?

Reading

1 Read this article about outsourcing and offshoring quite quickly. What advantages of outsourcing are mentioned in the article?

2 Now read Questions 1–6 in Exercise 3 on page 93 and underline the names in them. Then quickly find and underline the same names in the article.

When to outsource

by Amy Reinink

Michele Hanson-O'Reggio, founder of the small-business outsourcing and consulting firm Biz Success Partner, says that small-business owners tend to assume they can and should handle all business functions in-house rather than pay to outsource those functions. But, she says, it can save even the smallest businesses time and money. In fact, Hanson-O'Reggio recommends entrepreneurs outsource non-essential functions almost immediately upon launching a business to let them focus on the functions they specialize in. "The expected return is greater than the investment," she says. She also says it's important to consider the financial gains associated with spending time netting new clients rather than doing the bookkeeping or replying to emails.

The first layer of cost savings in outsourcing comes from payroll taxes, insurance and benefits paid to full-time employees. Mark Loschiavo, Executive Director of Drexel University's Baiada Center for Entrepreneurship, says entrepreneurs should expect to pay roughly 30 per cent of an employee's salary in addition to the salary itself for these overhead costs, but that lunch breaks, doctor appointments and other gaps in working hours bring the actual cost of a full-time employee to nearly double their base salary.

Increasingly, owners of small businesses in a wide variety of fields are outsourcing executive-level positions such as Chief Financial Officer and Chief Marketing Officer, seeking overall strategy solutions rather than single functions such as bookkeeping or graphic design. Entrepreneur David Walsh, author of *Source Control*, an e-book on outsourcing for small businesses, says entrepreneurs are learning that "outsourcing your CFO might mean a light monthly retainer with a retired CFO in the Midwest, or that outsourcing your legal

3 Choose the correct option – A, B, C or D – for each of these questions.

1 According to Michele Hanson-O'Reggio, small-business owners should outsource because they:
A can concentrate on their areas of expertise.
B cannot manage routine business functions.
C will be surprised how much money they save.
D will have more money available to invest.

2 According to Mark Loschiavo, how much more do employees cost in addition to their salary?
A about a quarter more
B about a third more
C almost 50 per cent more
D almost 100 per cent more

3 According to David Walsh, small businesses should outsource executive posts because they:
A will find more highly qualified people.
B can employ people in different places.
C have to meet fewer legal requirements.
D can pay people for fewer hours.

Task tip

Underline the words in the article which give you the answers: this will help you to confirm that you have chosen the correct option.

might mean a bi-weekly teleconference with an attorney you couldn't possibly afford to hire full-time."

Experts say the CFO position is especially ripe for outsourcing, as many entrepreneurs don't feel comfortable handling high-level financials on their own. Paul R. Shackford, founder of B2B CFO, which provides CFO services to businesses nationwide, says entrepreneurs often come to his firm when they find they can't answer banks' questions about issues such as cashflow projections. Shackford says outsourcing a CFO position can save an entrepreneur 20 per cent to 30 per cent compared with a full-time employee.

Cost savings vary greatly from one small business to another. For example, Business Network Consulting, an IT consulting firm, calculates that a company with ten employees that needs a "modest amount" of IT help and has a single one-year-old server could save more than $6,000 annually by outsourcing IT functions. "Your potential cost savings are totally tied to the type of industry you're in and the complexity of what you're trying to do," says Joe Kelly, CEO of BNC. "If you're a 100-user company that only needs file sharing and email, you may have the same costs as a ten-person company that offers financial advice and needs a redundant site and a lot of support."

Advances in technology make it easy for even small businesses to connect with offshore programers, and they're likely to realize cost savings by doing so, says Steve Mezak, CEO of Accelerance, which connects small companies with teams of contract programers worldwide. But Mezak says offshore contractors may require more time to manage thanks to differences in time zones, language, and culture.

adapted from *Entrepreneur Magazine*

4 According to Paul R. Shackford, companies use his services when they:
A need to reduce their overheads.
B lack the necessary expertise.
C wish to operate throughout the country.
D cannot find a full-time member of staff.

5 What does Joe Kelly say about outsourcing IT?
A There are more benefits for small companies than large companies.
B The more complicated the activities, the greater the savings.
C The newer the equipment, the greater the need to outsource.
D There may be security problems for some companies.

6 What does Steve Mezak say about offshoring?
A It is not a viable option for small businesses.
B Offshoring is cheaper than outsourcing in the same country.
C Extra problems may arise when dealing with offshore contractors.
D Small businesses need help finding the right contractors.

Speaking

1 **Work in pairs. You have been asked to give a talk at a business seminar on this subject:**

What is important when deciding what business activities to outsource?

Work together and make notes for your talk. You can look at the article you have just read for ideas and vocabulary.

2 **Change partners and take turns to give your talks.**

Useful language
Starting a talk

I'm going to talk about …

I'm going to start my talk by saying / telling you about …

The first thing I want to say is …

Let me start off by saying …

There are three main points I want to make. First, …

Useful language
Rounding off a talk

In conclusion / Finally, I'd like to say …

As a final point, …

I'd like to round off by saying …

Thank you.

Outsourcing IT

Listening

> **The jm group**
> Provides information technology (IT) recruitment services in the UK and the rest of Europe

1 Work in small groups. You are going to hear Duncan Mackintosh, a sales manager with the jm group, talking about jobs in IT and outsourcing IT. Before you listen, discuss these questions.

   1 How has IT been changing in recent years? What trends have you heard about?
   2 What do you think students should study if they want a job in IT in your country?
   3 What personal qualities do you think a person needs to be successful in IT?

2 **(2) 09** Listen and take notes on Duncan's answers to the questions in Exercise 1.

3 Work in pairs. Read these questions. Which ones can you answer already?

   1 Which of these reasons does Duncan give for needing more people in IT?
      A The industry is evolving fast.
      B The work is growing more varied and difficult.
      C Many people have left IT to join management.
   2 What tasks does he say are being offshored?
      A producing software
      B managing IT
      C production of computers
   3 What reason does Duncan mention for a company to outsource IT?
      A The company's computer equipment is too old.
      B Computer security is no longer a problem.
      C IT is not the company's main activity.
   4 According to Duncan, what do people need to get to the top in IT?
      A a university degree in computer science
      B an ability to work hard in highly technical work
      C a combination of technical knowledge and people skills
   5 For university students wanting to work in IT who are not studying computer science, which of these activities does Duncan suggest?
      A develop a website
      B write a good CV
      C get a Master's degree

4 **(2) 09** Listen again and complete or check your answers.

5 Work in pairs.

   1 Would a career in IT interest you? Why? / Why not?
   2 Were you surprised by any of Duncan's ideas? Which ones?

Outsourcing and offshoring – the pros and cons

Speaking

Work in small groups.

You work for a small company which manufactures electrical appliances. The company produces many of the components for the appliances; it manufactures and markets the tools; it has its own transport and distribution department; it owns several warehouses in different countries to aid storage and distribution of its products; and it has a large customer-service department, including after-sales service.

With competition from abroad becoming increasingly fierce, your Board of Directors has decided that your company should consider outsourcing some of its activities.

You have been asked to prepare a report about the situation and to suggest which activities should be outsourced. Discuss the situation together, and decide:
- how outsourcing could reduce your costs
- which parts of your company could be outsourced
- how outsourcing will secure your company's future.

A proposal for outsourcing

Writing

1 Work in pairs. You work as assistants to a director of an advertising agency. The Board has decided to outsource some of the agency's IT work, and you have been asked to look at possible contractors to do this work and prepare a proposal. Look at the information below and your notes.

1 Which contractor do you think you should choose? Why?
2 What sections do you think you should have in this proposal, and what headings will you give them?

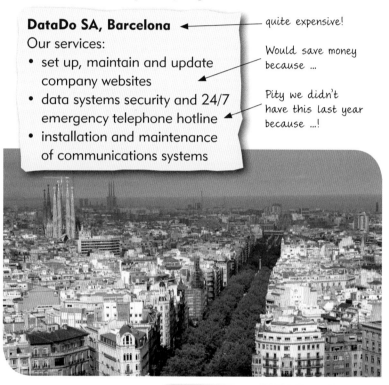

DataDo SA, Barcelona ◄ —— *quite expensive!*
Our services:
- set up, maintain and update company websites —— *Would save money because ...*
- data systems security and 24/7 emergency telephone hotline ◄ —— *Pity we didn't have this last year because ...!*
- installation and maintenance of communications systems

cheaper, but ...

Too late! Staff given this last year, so ...

But we need web design ...

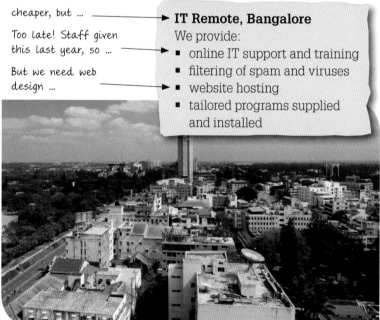

IT Remote, Bangalore
We provide:
- online IT support and training
- filtering of spam and viruses
- website hosting
- tailored programs supplied and installed

2 Look at these two pairs of sentences expressing the ideas in the handwritten notes in Exercise 2. In each case, which do you think is more suitable for the proposal? Why?

1 a DataDo's services are pretty expensive, but they can save us money by looking after our website.
   b Although DataDo's charges are comparatively high, their website services would offset the cost.

2 a What a pity we weren't using DataDo last year! If we had used them, we wouldn't have lost all that info from a virus.
   b If we had contracted DataDo's services last year, we might not have lost vital data due to a virus infection.

3 Look at the conditional form in sentences 2a and 2b in Exercise 2.

1 Does this conditional talk about present or past time?
2 Which of these (a or b) describes the form of this conditional?
   a *If + had done/been*, etc., *would have + done/been*, etc.
   b *If + did/was*, etc., *would do/be*, etc.

4 Complete these sentences by putting the verbs in brackets into the correct form.

1 If we had outsourced our IT services, we .... (*save*) money.
2 We would not have lost so much data if our computers .... (*not be infected*) with a virus.
3 If our server .... (*not break down*), we .... (*complete*) the order last week.
4 We .... (*deliver*) the goods on time if the weather .... (*be*) better in the last few days.

❯ page 97 Third conditional

5 Work in pairs. Express the other handwritten notes in Exercise 1 using your own words and ideas.

6 Work alone. Write the proposal in Exercise 1 for the Board of Directors.

Grammar workshop 5

Units 17–20

The definite article

We use *the*:
- with things we have already mentioned, or when it's clear who/what we are referring to:
  *Sonia bought a laptop from a department store. **The** store assistant told her **the** laptop had a three-year guarantee.*
- with things which are unique:
  ***the** Internet, **the** world*
- when the noun is followed by *of*:
  ***the** introduction of new technology*
- when the noun is followed by a defining relative clause:
  ***The** program we find most useful is Excel.*
- with adjectives to express groups:
  ***the** unemployed, **the** rich*
- with superlatives: ***the** best, **the** longest*

We do not use *the* when:
- talking in general:
  ***Business people** prefer **luxury hotels**.*
- using abstract nouns:
  ***Technology** has changed the way we do **business**.*

1 Complete this article by writing *the* or – in each gap.

1 ___–___ Businesses need to work out how to use
2 _the_ power of social media to encourage co-operation from both **3** _____ employees and customers, to get **4** _____ best results.
   A clear example is **5** _____ growing trend of forward-thinking companies to use their community of customers to help **6** _____ other customers who have a problem with a product, rather than use **7** _____ call centres.
   What is more, not enough companies are using **8** _____ social tools to motivate their own employees. Internet tools such as these can help **9** _____ companies solve **10** _____ problems. Take, for example, **11** _____ case of a car manufacturer. Some of **12** _____ company's cars were not performing well in **13** _____ most challenging environments, such as **14** _____ deserts. By using a social network on **15** _____ Internet, **16** _____ business got employees from different parts of **17** _____ world to look at **18** _____ problem and collectively collaborate on **19** _____ solution. A solution was found in weeks, when before it would have taken around a year to find **20** _____ answer.

adapted from the *Daily Telegraph*

2 ⊙ Business English students often make mistakes with the definite article. Find and correct the mistakes in these sentences. One sentence is correct.

1 I am sorry to inform you that there has been a delay setting up ~~a~~ new computer system I told you about. ~~the~~
2 I am writing with reference to your letter you sent me last week.
3 I'm writing to tell you that we are changing the date of a marketing meeting that was previously scheduled for next Friday.
4 Photocopy all documents we have about our export market.
5 Remember that our new product we want to launch is a soft drink for teenagers.
6 A fall in the company's sales last year happened as a result of the competition from other companies.
7 This report aims to explain why the company's sales have dropped.
8 We would like both courses to be held on a same day in September.

Tense changes in reported speech

These are some of the changes we make when putting direct speech into reported speech.
- present simple → past simple:
  *'I **work** for Ford.'* → *She said (that) she **worked** for Ford.*
- present continuous → past continuous:
  *'I**'m doing** the accounts.'* → *He said (that) he **was doing** the accounts.*
- present perfect → past perfect:
  *'I**'ve written** the report.'* → *She said (that) she **had written** the report.*
- past simple → past perfect:
  *'I **missed** the meeting.'* → *He told me (that) he **had missed** the meeting.*
- *will* → *would*:
  *'Profits **will** rise.'* → *She predicted (that) profits **would** rise.*

These modal verbs also change:

- can → could:
  'I **can** see you at ten o'clock.' → She said (that) she **could** see me at ten o'clock.
- may → might:
  'Costs **may** fluctuate.' → He stated (that) costs **might** fluctuate.

Would and must do not normally change:
'I **would** prefer to work in London.' → She said (that) she **would** prefer to work in London.

1 Look at these things which people said when they were interviewed for a staff survey. Put them into reported speech.

1 'I find travelling to work at peak times stressful and time-consuming.'
One worker complained that ....

2 'If the new scheme is introduced, I hope I'll be able to take a career break.'
The accountant explained that if ....

3 'I have always wanted to travel round the world.'
One employee said that she ....

4 'Can you provide on-site nursery care for pre-school children?'
Several members of staff asked if ....

5 'In my last job, we used flexitime, and it was very successful.'
One person told me that ....

6 'If you introduce these changes, I may decide to work part time.'
One of the secretaries said that if ....

2 Business English students often make mistakes with the tenses of verbs in reported speech. Complete these sentences using the verbs in brackets in the correct tense. In some cases, there is more than one correct answer.

1 I am told that he .... (arrive) late for work at least three times a week.

2 Last week, she said she .... (sell) ten cars and she did.

3 My line manager has asked her if she .... (want) to take a posting in South Africa for six months.

4 We agreed that your company .... (install) a new telephone switchboard at our offices.

5 We asked her to stop work and go home, but she said that she .... (go) until she .... (finish).

6 We had frequent complaints from our customers who said that they .... (send) back the goods with defects.

7 You told us that the work .... (be) finished very soon, but it still hasn't been completed.

Third conditional

- The third conditional is formed using If + past perfect tense, would/might/could have + (done/been/opened, etc.):
  If you **had reminded** me yesterday, I **would have gone** to the meeting.
  If the exchange rate **had been** better, we **could have exported** more.
- We use the third conditional to talk about something which did not happen in the past and its imaginary results:
  If we had outsourced our finance section last year (something which did not happen – we didn't outsource the finance section), we would have saved several thousand euros. (an imaginary consequence because we didn't save several thousand euros)

1 Complete these sentences using the verbs in brackets in the correct tense.

1 If you had asked me, I .... (rearrange) yesterday's meeting for later in the week.

2 The company would have based its operations in this region if the government .... (give) it a grant, but in fact they set up a factory in Scotland.

3 We .... (sign) the contract with you last year if the conditions .... (be) right, but we felt you were just asking too much.

4 What a pity they didn't increase her salary. If they .... (raise) her salary, she .... (stay) with the company instead of leaving and going with a competitor.

5 They didn't offer us a long enough guarantee.
If they .... (offer) a five-year guarantee, we .... (buy) the machine.

6 The equipment .... (not break down) if you .... (follow) the maintenance schedule, but you didn't.

2 Complete these sentences in any way you like.

1 If my company had been able to borrow the money it needed, ...

2 Our computers wouldn't have been infected with a virus if ...

3 We might have achieved our sales targets if ...

4 If our suppliers had been more efficient, ...

Customer satisfaction and loyalty

Getting started

Work in small groups.

1 What are the statistics for dissatisfied customers? Complete the sentences below by writing a number from the box in each gap.

> about 85%   25   4 to 100   68%
> 8 to 16   91%   thousands

- For every dissatisfied customer who complains, there are at least **1** .... who do not.
- Dissatisfied customers will tell **2** .... others about their dissatisfaction by word of mouth. On the Web, some are now telling **3** ....
- **4** .... of dissatisfied customers never purchase goods or services from the company again. A prompt effort to resolve a dissatisfied customer's issue will result in **5** .... of them returning as repeat customers.
- Depending upon the business, new customer sales may cost **6** .... times that of a sale to an existing customer.
- **7** .... of lost customers are due to one cause: employee attitude.

adapted from www.adamssixsigma.com

2 Check your answers by looking at the bottom of page 100, then discuss what conclusions you can draw from the statistics.

> **Useful language**
> **Expressing conclusions**
>
> One of the conclusions we can draw from the information/ statistics is that …
> The information shows/tells us that …
> We can infer from this information/these statistics that …
> There's no/little doubt that …

3 Have you ever been a dissatisfied customer? Why, and how did you react?

From **satisfaction** to **loyalty**

Just how do you make satisfied customers into loyal customers? Dr Jodi Simco and Dr Mark Royal of Hay Group, a global management consulting firm, explain about the link they've found between business culture, employee loyalty, customer loyalty and revenue growth.

'First, it's important to ask ourselves just what our definition of customer loyalty is,' Simco says. 'And based on our research, we've found that it's when your customers have a strong bond with you and come back to you time and time again. They view you as the provider of choice. So they're not just looking for the lowest-cost vendor. They're going to come back to your company and not only use your current products and services, but they maybe start using some new ones which they then recommend to others.'

Simco identifies two factors that decide whether satisfied customers will become loyal ones: the outcome that customers experience and the process by which they receive it. 'We've all bought cars, and the car might be the most wonderful car, so the outcome was positive,' Simco says. 'But we might decide not to go back to the car dealership because they were annoying to work with. In this case, the process was negative.' People, in the form of employees, are part of that process, she explains, and 'people are your key competitive advantage. It's your people who developed those relationships with your customers, and you really need to focus on them.'

Furthermore, when it comes to convincing people in your organisation of the impact that customer loyalty can have

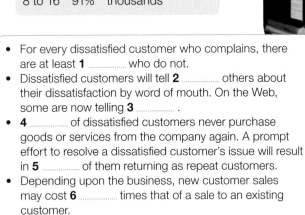

From satisfaction to loyalty

Reading

> **Hay Group**
> Hay Group is a global management consulting firm with 84 offices in 48 countries.

1 Work in small groups. You are going to read an article about customer satisfaction and customer loyalty. Before you read, discuss these questions.

  1 What do you think is the difference between the two?
  2 What can companies do to encourage
    a) satisfaction, and b) loyalty?

2 Read the article quite quickly. Which of the ideas you discussed does it contain?

on your bottom line, the business case for building loyalty is quite simple. 'None of us is surprised that loyal customers are going to repurchase at two to four times the rate of just purely satisfied customers,' she says. 'And they're going to enthusiastically recommend your company to others. So they can serve as your best marketer. Loyal customers are also willing to pay more for your services.'

Hay Group has identified a few primary factors about a company that can make the difference between customer satisfaction and customer loyalty. 'The top factor is value: "Is this company's product or service having a positive impact on my business? Do I have a strong return on investment?" Ease of doing business is a big thing, too,' says Simco. 'Are you easy to do business with, or are you problematic? Finally, your people are important, in terms of whether they show responsiveness, integrity, trust and professionalism.'

'In today's marketplace, where most organisations are facing global competitors and a rapid flow of information, it's hard to be different from your rivals because best practices spread across an industry very rapidly,' Royal says. 'But it's much harder for your competitors to duplicate a successful organisation that consists of a lot of highly motivated, highly engaged people who are focused on the customer, and this provides real opportunities for competitive advantage.'

For employees to deliver excellent customer service, Royal says, there are three key ingredients. 'First, there needs to be a strong focus on teamwork. We find that in organisations where employees perceive strong levels of teamwork, there tends to be a much higher level of customer satisfaction. The second ingredient is training: if we want people to drive high levels of customer satisfaction, we have to make sure they have the skills to deliver them. And the third ingredient is empowerment, which means that organisations need to empower employees to make decisions and take risks in carrying out their job roles.'

adapted from *Resource* © LOMA

3 Read the article again and choose the best answer – A, B, C or D – for these questions.

1 What produces customer loyalty, according to Simco in paragraph 2?
  A the price of the product
  B the quality of the product
  C the relationship with the supplier
  D the recommendation of friends

2 What, according to Simco in paragraph 3, is the key factor in making a company better than its rivals?
  A a superior product
  B good-quality staff
  C good value for money
  D good procedures for dealing with customers

3 In paragraph 4, what is given as the main benefit of having loyal customers?
  A It improves the company's image.
  B It increases profits.
  C It is easier than finding new ones.
  D They will accept higher prices.

4 What, according to Hay Group, is the main factor which changes customer satisfaction to customer loyalty?
  A Your customer does not have problems doing business with you.
  B Your customer gets what he asks for.
  C Your customer has confidence in you.
  D Your customer's own business becomes more profitable.

5 Why does Royal believe it is difficult for companies to be different from their competitors?
  A Their competitors can quickly imitate them.
  B Their competitors are spread all over the world.
  C Employees in different companies are equally hard-working.
  D Most companies nowadays are customer-centred.

6 Which of these does Royal say is an essential characteristic of a good employee?
  A They enjoy working alone.
  B They are naturally good at dealing with customers.
  C They consult their superiors before taking decisions.
  D They take responsibility for their actions.

Vocabulary

Match these words/phrases (1–8) from the article with their definitions from Cambridge dictionaries (a–h).

1 revenue

    a the conditions that make a business more successful than the businesses it is competing with, or a particular thing that makes it more successful

2 outcome

    b a working method, or set of working methods, which is officially accepted as being the best to use in a particular business or industry

3 bottom line

    c continue buying

4 repurchase

    d the final line in the accounts of a company or organisation, which states the total profit or loss that has been made

5 return on investment

6 best practice

    e giving someone official authority or the freedom to do something

7 competitive advantage

    f the income that a government or company receives regularly

8 empowerment

    g profit made from something you have bought

    h a result or effect of an action, situation, etc.

Grammar workshop

Relative clauses

Look at these sentences from the article and complete them with *who*, *which*, *where* or *that*, or leave the gap blank if you think no relative pronoun is needed. There is more than one possible answer in most cases.

1 Dr Jodi Simco and Dr Mark Royal [...] explain about the link .... they've found between business culture, employee loyalty, customer loyalty and revenue growth.

2 ... but they maybe start using some new ones .... they then recommend to others.

3 Simco identifies two factors .... decide whether satisfied customers will become loyal ones: the outcome that customers experience and the process by .... they receive it.

4 It's your people .... developed those relationships with your customers ...

5 ... the impact .... customer loyalty can have on your bottom line ...

6 Hay Group has identified a few primary factors about a company .... can make the difference between customer satisfaction and customer loyalty.

7 In today's marketplace, ... most organisations are facing global competitors and a rapid flow of information, it's hard to be different from your rivals ...

8 ... it's much harder for your competitors to duplicate a successful organisation .... consists of a lot of highly motivated, highly engaged people .... are focused on the customer ...

❯ **page 114** Relative clauses

> **Useful language**
> **Some verb/adjective/noun collocations**
>
> to have/produce a(n) successful/satisfactory/positive/
>   unexpected outcome
> to give/provide a(n) good/excellent/disappointing/unsatisfactory
>   return on investment
> to bring in/produce a(n) annual/expected/overall/total revenue
>   of ...

Speaking

Work in small groups. Discuss these questions.

1 Simco and Royal think what makes the difference when dealing with customers is the quality of a company's employees. Do you agree? Why? / Why not?

2 Which do you think they would value most highly in a customer-service employee: efficiency or the ability to form a friendly relationship? Which do you think is more important?

3 To what extent do you think technology can replace people in the relationship with customers?

> **Useful language**
> **Talking about the extent to which you agree/disagree**
>
> I think technology can replace people ...
> ... only to a very small / tiny extent.
> ... to a certain/large/considerable/great extent.
> ... in certain cases/circumstances.
> ... up/only to the point where ...

> **Answers to *Getting started***
> **1** 25   **2** 8 to 16   **3** thousands   **4** 91%   **5** about 85%
> **6** 4 to 100   **7** 68%

Encouraging customer loyalty

Listening

1 (2) 10 Listen to Christina Bunt talking about Tesco's relations with its customers. Complete the notes on the right with one or two words in each gap.

2 Work in pairs. Talk about a large shop or supermarket you know well. How do they go about building customer relationships?

Customer complaints
- Usually solved by staff on customer 1 ....
- More serious complaints put on customer 2 ....

Building relationships with customers
- Tesco Clubcard: a 3 .... with vouchers
- Visits to 4 .... and other groups
- Free transport to store from 5 ....
- Vouchers for schools to obtain 6 ....

Measuring customer satisfaction
- 'Mystery shopper' does a 7 .... every four weeks + report from Head Office
- Accompany customers in store – note down comments about their 8 ....

A staff meeting

Writing and speaking

1 You work in a medium-sized travel company. You have just received this memo. Complete it by writing one word in each gap or leaving it blank if no word is needed. In some cases, more than one answer is possible.

Memo

To: All staff
From: Customer Services Director
Subject: Customer loyalty

Market research which we have carried 1 .... recently has shown a high level of customer satisfaction with 2 .... services we provide. However, we are looking for ways in 3 .... we can convert our customers' satisfaction into loyalty. There will therefore be a meeting on Friday afternoon at 2 p.m. 4 .... all staff should attend and 5 .... we would welcome ideas from all of you on any of the following questions:

- What do customers want in terms of service?
- What is important when dealing with customers?
- What is important when organising staff to provide better service?

The member of staff 6 .... gives the best suggestions will receive a prize of dinner for two at the Brasserie.

Please attend the meeting punctually.
Simone

2 Unfortunately, you are going to be slightly late for the meeting. Write a short email to Simone.

- Apologise for being late.
- Give a reason.
- Say when you expect to arrive.

Useful language
Apologising and saying when you can do something

I'm afraid / I regret that I won't be able to make it / the meeting until …
Unfortunately, I have another appointment/meeting, etc. at ...., so …
I expect to arrive / I should be able to make it / get there by …
Apologies/Sorry for any inconvenience.

3 You have decided to give your ideas at the meeting.

- Choose one of the questions from Simone's memo and take two or three minutes to prepare what you are going to say. Prepare to speak on your subject for at least one minute.
- Hold the meeting and listen to everyone's ideas.
- Discuss whose ideas were the best (and therefore should get the dinner for two).

Communication with customers

Getting started

Work in small groups. You work for an international logistics company which is making a number of changes to its organisation. How should the company communicate the changes below to existing and potential customers? You can choose from options in the box.

an advertisement	a social media website
an email bulletin	a leaflet an operative at a call centre
visit from a sales rep	the company's website

- the company has opened a new operation in East Asia
- a price increase
- a survey of customers' opinions
- the company is moving its headquarters from Paris to Frankfurt
- dealing with an individual customer's problem
- giving general information about a range of products or services

Training in customer communication skills

Reading

1   Work in pairs. You have been asked to investigate customer-care courses for staff in your organisation. Discuss these questions.

   1   Why is customer care vital for companies?
   2   What would you expect trainees to learn on a customer-care course?

2   Underline the key idea in each of these statements.

   1   Satisfying your customers' requirements by understanding how they are thinking
   2   Getting your customers to tell other people about your company
   3   Using writing skills successfully
   4   Becoming more certain of your professional abilities
   5   Understanding how your body language affects clients
   6   Learning suitable ways of dealing with difficult clients
   7   Giving a better service than the customers thought they would receive
   8   Using some increasingly popular media for dealing with customers

3   You have found these four courses (A–D) on the Internet. Which course does each
    statement from Exercise 2 (1–8) refer to?

A

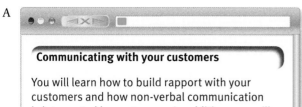

Communicating with your customers

You will learn how to build rapport with your
customers and how non-verbal communication
is interpreted by customers. In addition, you will
be trained in telephone skills, including how to
project professionalism and how to provide quality
customer service over the telephone. Finally, you
will learn how email can be used for effective
communication with your customers and to build a
good reputation.

C

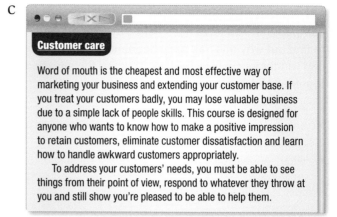

Customer care

Word of mouth is the cheapest and most effective way of
marketing your business and extending your customer base. If
you treat your customers badly, you may lose valuable business
due to a simple lack of people skills. This course is designed for
anyone who wants to know how to make a positive impression
to retain customers, eliminate customer dissatisfaction and learn
how to handle awkward customers appropriately.

To address your customers' needs, you must be able to see
things from their point of view, respond to whatever they throw at
you and still show you're pleased to be able to help them.

B

A FIRST-CLASS SERVICE

Providing first-class customer service and creating
the right impression first time is a must for front-line
staff. To be successful at customer care requires an
understanding of customer expectations and the skills to
exceed that expectation. This practical and interactive
course provides a wide range of personal and professional
skills for staff who are often the first point of contact for
customers. Throughout the course, delegates will have the
opportunity to practise customer-handling skills with role-
play and in discussion groups, enabling a confident return
to the workplace.

D

Telephone skills and customer-care training course

Large numbers of companies have set up helplines as the
quickest and most convenient way of managing customer
contacts. Call centres and internet sales are the fastest-
growing operational departments for many organisations. It
is essential that all employees represent their organisation
in a professional and friendly way. Clear and effective
communication is essential to ensure that the business is
not lost. Failure to train your staff properly in telephone skills
may result in fewer customers.

Vocabulary

1   ⊙ Business English students often use adjectives with nouns which are not collocations.
    Choose the correct adjective in italics in the sentences below. Then check your answers
    by looking at the course details you have just read.

    1   The company has a *good / high* reputation for making innovative and reliable products.
    2   A *big / large* number of people have visited our website in the last few days.
    3   We offer a *big / wide* range of services to customers worldwide.

2   Cross out the adjective / adjectival phrase in each group which does *not* form a collocation
    with the noun in bold.

    1   Our customers don't buy the product in ~~big~~ / *huge / large* **quantities**, so we deliver quite small
        consignments to each of our outlets.
    2   They're one of our *biggest / most significant / most important* **customers**, so we need to
        concentrate on taking care of them.
    3   Thank you all for the *big / great / tremendous* **effort** you have made to get the new operation
        up and running.
    4   This campaign is expected to draw the attention of a(n) *important / large / significant* **part**
        of the population.
    5   I read your advertisement with *big / considerable / great* **interest**.
    6   TS is an old taxi firm and enjoys a(n) *excellent / good / high* **reputation**.
    7   We distribute a(n) *big / extensive / wide* **range** of products.
    8   We've been experiencing *big / important / serious* **problems** with our server.
    9   We have chosen to advertise on the radio because of the *big / large / vast* **number** of people
        we can reach.

Speaking

Work in pairs or groups of three. The company you work for has been losing important customers to your competitors. You have been asked by your manager to find out why this has been happening and how you can win these customers back. Discuss the situation together and decide:

- why, in general, companies lose customers
- how you can find out why customers are leaving your company
- what actions you can take to win back the lost customers.

Customer communication at Not Just Food

Listening

1 You are going to hear Jane Milton from Not Just Food talking about her customers. Read questions 1–5 below and underline the key ideas.

1 Jane normally <u>approaches</u> <u>potential clients</u> by
   A calling them first.
   B sending company literature, then calling.
   C visiting the client.
2 The original purpose of her website was to
   A attract new clients.
   B show potential clients the type of work they do.
   C help existing clients to keep in contact.
3 Her company demonstrates its commitment to clients by
   A always quoting the correct price for a job.
   B doing more work than her clients expect.
   C reducing the price if the work doesn't take as long as she quoted.

4 Why does her company take trouble with small clients?
   A They often grow into bigger clients.
   B They are easy to deal with.
   C They improve the reputation of the company.
5 Jane has avoided having dissatisfied customers by
   A always exceeding customers' expectations.
   B working from written instructions.
   C continually speaking with the client while the job is being done.

2 (2)11 Listen and choose the best answer – A, B or C – for each question in Exercise 1.

3 Work in pairs.

1 How does Jane Milton exceed customers' expectations?
2 What does she do to build long-term relationships with clients?

Turning complaints to your advantage

Reading

1 Work in pairs. You are going to read an article from a management magazine about customer care. Before you read, discuss these questions.

1 How should businesses deal with comments or feedback from customers?
2 What procedures have you seen for dealing with complaints?

2   Read this article, ignoring the options in italics. Why, according to the writer, should businesses welcome complaints from customers?

Handling complaints – a boss's view

Whenever customers make complaints, **1** *it / that* is an opportunity to build a stronger, more profitable relationship with them. **2** *It / This* is because complaints that are handled properly can be converted into increased loyalty, extra business and recommendations.

In my company, when a customer made a complaint in the past, **3** *it / this* was often ignored by staff. However, over the years, listening to customers has helped us to improve our services, so that now those services are better and faster, resulting in greater customer loyalty.

4 *This / That* is what you should do: firstly, at the point of purchase, you should provide comment forms and an email link or phone number to you, the manager, personally. In many companies, complaints are dealt with by junior members of staff and **5** *it / that* is why they lose customers: junior members of staff are not in a position to put things right. Secondly, answer all of them and put your personal signature on each response to show you are taking a personal interest. Thirdly, create a customer-user group and pay attention to what they tell you. Finally, the golden rule is **6** *this / that*: when customers give you valuable feedback, make sure they're rewarded in some special way. **7** *It / This* can be done by sending them a handwritten thank-you note, a free gift or a unique discount, and the result of **8** *it / this* may be that they become loyal customers who feel their input is valuable.

3   Business English students often confuse *it*, *this* and *that*. Choose the best options in italics in the article.

> **page 115** Which pronoun: *it*, *this* or *that*?

Speaking

1   Work in small groups to prepare a presentation on this subject.

In a B2B (business to business) situation, what's important when complaining about a service or to a supplier in order to get satisfaction?

Use these questions to help you.

• When is it better to write a letter than to complain in person?
• When should you insist on seeing the manager?
• Should you show you are angry, or should you keep calm?
• When should you use a lawyer?

2   Work in pairs with someone from another group and take turns to give your presentations.

> **Useful language**
> **Talking about factors to consider**
>
> You have to consider …
> One thing you must bear in mind is …
> Another thing to take into consideration/ account is …
> You should also remember that …

Corresponding with customers

Getting started

1 Work in pairs. Look at the two leaflets and discuss these questions.

1 What services do the companies offer?
2 If they were going to extend their services, what new services could they offer?
3 What sort of things can go wrong with services like these and cause customers to complain?

2 Work in small groups. Discuss these questions.

1 When your company launches its latest product or service, who would you send information to first: existing customers or potential new customers? Why?
2 Why are dissatisfied customers dangerous for a business? How much should you do to make them happy?

TopTen Leasing Equipment

leasing to the construction industry

BDD Couriers

express courier delivery

anywhere in the UK within 24 hours

Vocabulary

1 Business English students often confuse *last* and *latest*. Look at this question from *Getting started*. Does the word in bold mean 'most recent' or 'final'?

When your company launches its **latest** product or service, who would you send the information to first?

2 Read the extracts from the *CALD* on the right. Then complete these sentences by writing *last* or *latest* in each gap.

1 We are pleased to present our .... car.
2 The .... research shows that the market for tablet PCs is increasing.
3 This is your .... chance to buy the product before we raise the price.
4 It's the .... technology.
5 I didn't get on with my .... boss – she had no sense of humour.
6 She worked so late at the office that she missed the .... train home.

> **the latest:** the newest or most recent or modern: *the latest fashions*
> Note: with *the latest*, we understand there will be more in the future.
>
> **the last:**
> 1 (the person or thing) after everyone or everything else: [+ *to* infinitive] *I hate being the last one to arrive at a meeting.*
> 2 the only one or part that is left: *I'm down to my last 50p – could I borrow some money for lunch?*
> 3 the most recent or the one before the present one: *My last office had no natural light.*

3 Would you expect to use *the last* or *the latest* with each of these nouns / noun phrases?

1 .... gadget
2 .... meeting I went to
3 .... line manager/boss/teacher I had
4 .... news
5 .... job I had / course I did
6 .... shop I bought something in

4 Work in pairs. Take turns to tell each other about each of the things (1–6) in Exercise 3.

Example: *The shop in Pushkin Square has all the latest gadgets.*

A letter about a new service

Reading

1 Read this letter telling an existing customer about a new service and choose the best word below – A, B, C or D – to fill each gap.

Dear Mr Müller,

New services from BDD

I'm delighted to be able to inform you, as a valued **1** .... client of BDD Ltd, that from 1 April of this year, our Budget Document Delivery service is going global, with express deliveries worldwide. This **2** .... we shall be offering the same **3** .... of service that you have come to **4** .... from our European operations. It includes a 24-hour door-to-door pick-up and delivery service, document delivery within 36 hours at the **5** .... anywhere in the world, and prices on average less than 30% of prices **6** .... by our main competitors. I enclose a leaflet detailing our new service.

If you would like to know more about this, our **7** .... innovation, or if there is any other **8** .... in which we can help you to **9** .... trouble-free business with maximum efficiency, please do not **10** .... to contact me personally.

Yours sincerely,

Mohamed Sarawi

Mohamed Sarawi
Managing Director

---

1 A permanent	B long-standing	C lasting	D lengthy
2 A supposes	B involves	C means	D suggests
3 A height	B amount	C quantity	D level
4 A hope	B wish	C expect	D want
5 A last	B latest	C least	D longest
6 A placed	B demanded	C required	D charged
7 A last	B latest	C recent	D final
8 A way	B method	C manner	D means
9 A do	B perform	C make	D carry
10 A wait	B deliberate	C stop	D hesitate

2 Work in pairs. Read the letter again and answer these questions.

1 How will Mr Müller immediately know the subject of the letter?
2 Which word suggests that Mr Müller is an important client to BDD?
3 Which phrase implies that BDD's services are high quality?
4 Which words suggest that, by using BDD's services, Mr Müller will avoid problems?
5 Which phrase shows that Mr Müller will be given personalised treatment?

Writing

1 You work in the customer relations department of TopTen Leasing, a company which leases equipment to the construction industry. Your boss has asked you to write a letter to one of your most important clients, Mr Rodriguez of Rodriguez Construcciones S.A., to tell him about some new services which your company is offering. Look at this leaflet, on which your boss has written some notes, and write a plan for the letter. Divide your plan into paragraphs.

2 Write the letter. Use the letter on page 107 as a model.

3 When you have finished, compare your letter with a partner's.

TopTen Leasing
NEW SERVICES!

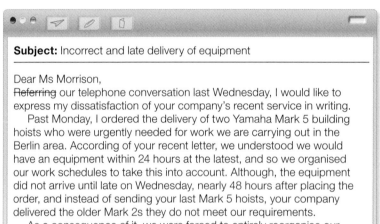

Tell Mr Rodriguez he's important to us

Just order the equipment you need by going to our website or by phone.
- Delivery guaranteed within 24 hours anywhere in Europe!
- For leases of 7 days, 1 free day.

Tell him about these two new features

AS USUAL
- All equipment delivered in perfect condition.
- No deposit required from premium customers.

Remind him of these

An email from a dissatisfied customer

Reading

1 Mr Rodriguez dictated this email to his iPad using a voice-recognition app. As a result, in most lines there is an incorrect word. Read the email carefully. Cross out the wrong words and write the correct words in the gaps provided. Put a tick (✓) beside lines that are correct.

> **Task tip**
>
> Think about the meaning of the email you are reading, not just whether it is grammatically accurate.

Subject: Incorrect and late delivery of equipment

Dear Ms Morrison,

~~Referring~~ our telephone conversation last Wednesday, I would like to express my dissatisfaction of your company's recent service in writing.

Past Monday, I ordered the delivery of two Yamaha Mark 5 building hoists who were urgently needed for work we are carrying out in the Berlin area. According of your recent letter, we understood we would have an equipment within 24 hours at the latest, and so we organised our work schedules to take this into account. Although, the equipment did not arrive until late on Wednesday, nearly 48 hours after placing the order, and instead of sending your last Mark 5 hoists, your company delivered the older Mark 2s they do not meet our requirements.

As a consequence of it, we were forced to entirely reorganise our construction teams and our building programmes until the correct equipment arrived. This meant a huge amount of more work and loss of time on projects where our costs have been calculated very exactly.

We have, in the years, been very happy with your service and we have recommended you to another companies working in the sector. A repetition of last week's incident would result in our having to look for other leasers, it is something we would prefer to avoid.

Yours sincerely,
Roberto Rodriguez
CEO

1 Following
2 ....
3 ....
4 ....
5 ....
6 ....
7 ....
8 ....
9 ....
10 ....
11 ....
12 ....
13 ....
14 ....
15 ....
16 ....
17 ....
18 ....

2 Work in pairs. Discuss which of these things a letter or email of complaint should contain.

1 Details of the problem which occurred
2 An explanation of the consequences of this problem
3 What action you want them to take
4 An explanation of why you chose their product or service in the first place
5 A threat about what you will do if they do not correct the problem
6 An explanation of how happy you have been with them in the past
7 A comparison of their product or service with their competitors' products or services.

3 Which of these things are in Roberto Rodriguez's email, and in which paragraphs?

Grammar workshop

Expressing results

Study these ways of expressing results (in italics). Three of them come from the email you have just read. Then complete the sentences below in any way you want.

A *As a consequence of this*, we were forced to entirely reorganise our construction teams and our building programmes …

B *This meant* a huge amount of extra work and loss of time …

C A repetition of last week's incident *would result in* our having to look for other leasers …

D *As a result*, we had to reschedule the shipment.

E *Consequently*, we lost about 250 man hours.

F Your late delivery *meant that* the production line had to stop for one hour.

1 You delivered the wrong model. As a consequence of this, …

2 Some of the goods were damaged. As a consequence of this, …

3 You were late sending the information. This meant …

4 There were several mistakes in the invoice. As a result, …

5 You sent the components to the wrong factory. This meant, …

6 Two of the pieces were broken. Consequently, …

❯ page 115 Expressing results

Preparing a letter or email of complaint

Listening

(2) 12 Your company recently used BDD to deliver some vital documents to a major client in Katowice. Unfortunately, they arrived late. Listen to Karl Müller talking to his assistant, Jolanta, and complete the handwritten notes with one or two words or a number.

Dear Mr Müller,

New services from BDD

I'm delighted to be able to inform you, as a valued long-standing client of BDD Ltd, that from 1 April of this year, our Budget Document Delivery service is going global, with express deliveries worldwide. This means we shall be offering the same level of service that you have come to expect from our European operations. It includes a 24-hour door-to-door pick-up and delivery service, document delivery within 36 hours at the latest anywhere in the world, and prices on average less than 30% of prices charged by our main competitors. I enclose a leaflet detailing our new service.

If you would like to know more about this, our latest innovation, or if there is any other way in which we can help you to do trouble-free business with maximum efficiency, please do not hesitate to contact me personally.

Yours sincerely,

Mohamed Sarawi
Mohamed Sarawi
Managing Director

1 .... of this!

It took 2 ....
Tell him what
3 .... of this
were.

We'll only continue
if deliveries are
4 ....

Writing

1 Work in pairs. Write a plan of the letter to BDD complaining about their service. Use the handwritten notes on BDD's letter (in the Listening exercise above).

2 Write your letter. Use the email on page 108 as a model.

Business across cultures

Getting started

Work in small groups.

1 Which of these are typical parts of business culture in your country?
- long business lunches where you get to know your customers
- giving presents to clients
- getting straight to the point in business meetings
- doing as much as possible face to face or over the phone
- working very long hours
- dressing formally
- using people's first names
- asking about your associates' family and free-time activities

2 What other behaviour is normal in your country's business culture?

Working in another culture

Reading

1 Work in pairs. You are going to read an article about working abroad. Before you read, discuss these questions.

1 What sort of people are best suited to working in foreign countries?
2 What skills are important for working abroad?
3 Do you think you would be good at doing your job, or the job you want to do, in a foreign country? Why? / Why not?

2 Read the article quite quickly and note in the margin the main idea of each paragraph.

3 Read the sentences before and after each gap and underline anything which might refer to the sentence which fits the gap.

Interculturally competent and considering a global business career?

MBAs need to prepare more for work abroad.

One of the biggest trends in the 21st-century business landscape is the need for more global business executives. Although many international MBA programs prepare students for business, they should also emphasize the cultural components for a successful global executive and successful expat assignments. The failure rate for global assignments is exponentially higher than for national assignments.

Many business professionals dream of working in glamorous, international destinations but are not sure how to even begin to qualify for global jobs. A licensed career counselor who specializes in global careers can help you create a "global career action plan." You may in addition need

4 Read these sentences and underline any words which may refer to something in the article.

A In these risk-averse times, they will look at your previous international track record before offering you a posting.

B Instead, most difficulties are due to intangible, cross-cultural misunderstandings.

C However, many business people, especially those who have never lived abroad before, refuse to see things this way.

D It will instead contain an exciting, often bewildering and steep learning curve.

E Only then will they be allowed to recruit an international worker.

F This is an essential global career skill.

G Choosing a country as a global destination should be a well-researched and well-reasoned choice, because not every country will be a match for you.

5 Now choose the best sentence to fill each gap. There is one sentence you will not need.

6 Work in pairs.

1 Are there many expatriate workers in your country?

2 What skills do they bring?

3 What problems do they have?

Speaking

1 Choose either Question 1 or Question 2 below to give a short presentation.

- Look back through the article you have just read and note down any words you would like to use when you give your presentation.
- Take a minute to make some notes and prepare. When you prepare, note down two or three main points and think of reasons and examples to support them.

> 1 What is important when going to work in a foreign country?
> - culture
> - language
> -

> 2 What is important when deciding whether to accept a job in another country?
> - personality
> - family situation
> -

industry-specific psychometric testing, aptitude testing, career focus testing, and also assessments of your preferred cultural style of conducting business. **1** ___G___ I strongly recommend informal or formal testing to determine your work style and business psychology style and the range of countries which you would be most suited for.

Often, problems with expat assignments are not about an executive's experience or intelligence. **2** _____ Thus, the choice of an expat assignment should not be taken lightly. It should be closely researched and matched with a particular candidate. Remember, that a global employer will typically have to pay three times as much to import a worker as to hire a local worker. In many socialized countries, the employer will need to formally post the position through local channels and gather evidence that there aren't any locals to fill the position. **3** _____ You will need to have some very unique skills or some fabulous business contacts to even pass this first hurdle.

Employers generally are very concerned that an expat or 'imported worker' will not be able to withstand the rigors of a foreign assignment and foreign culture. **4** _____ Successful previous experience is the best predictor of quick adjustment to new assignments.

Once you are on the job, learn how to navigate your new country, culture, and business environment in an inter-culturally sensitive way. **5** _____ What we may assume are standard business norms are often culture-bound constructs.

Working abroad will not be business as usual. **6** _____ Added to the complexity is any given individual's degree of adaptation to a new culture. Some global professionals may in fact be bi-cultural, speak several languages, and have more fluid business styles. However, for everyone, the initial adjustment to a new global location can be very challenging, but for most it is ultimately extremely rewarding.

2 (2) 13 Listen to Grazyna answering Question 1.

1 What three points does she make?
2 What reasons does she give to support each of them?
3 Which point does she support with an example?

3 Work in pairs. Read the transcript of Grazyna's answer (Track 13).

1 How does she rephrase the question using her own words?
2 What words/phrases does she use to:
   a introduce her three points?
   b introduce reasons?
   c introduce an example?
   d round off her answer?

4 Work in pairs. Take turns to give your presentations. When you speak, try to use words and phrases you looked at in Exercise 3.

Task tip

Use words and phrases to structure your talk so that your listeners know exactly what you are talking about at all times.

Grammar workshop

Phrases followed by a verb + -ing

1 (2) 13 Complete the sentences below from Grazyna's answer with a word from the box. Then check your answers by listening again.

> difficulty   good   point   problems   use   worth

1 It's no .... thinking that you're going to behave in exactly the same way at work as you did in your home country.
2 If you're a manager, it's no .... being autocratic in the United States.
3 It's .... learning the language well, both written and spoken.
4 If you don't, you'll have .... doing your job, however skilled you are.
5 There's no .... in telling people how you do things in your country all the time.
6 If you bear those things in mind, you'll have much less .... in achieving success.

2 Complete these sentences by writing a verb or phrase in each gap.

1 I decided it was definitely no good .... the bank for a loan when interest rates were so high.
2 It's just not worth .... for a job when there are 500 other candidates.
3 It's really no use .... meetings when no one has prepared for them.
4 You'll have serious problems .... your PowerPoint presentation if you use that old laptop.
5 There's absolutely no point in .... new computers if the ones we've got are perfectly adequate.
6 You'll have huge difficulties .... a job abroad if you don't learn the language.

> **Useful language**
> **Adverb–adjective collocations with the phrases followed by a verb + -ing**
>
> It's just/really/absolutely/probably/definitely no good / not worth / no use …
>
> There's really/absolutely no point in …
>
> There's little / not much point in …
>
> He had few / huge / great / serious / lots of problems/ difficulties …

Working in China and working in Europe

Listening

> **Mandarin Consultant**
> A leading China consultancy offering tailored services to help clients better understand and succeed in the Chinese market

1 Work in pairs. You are going to hear Rob Liu, who works for Mandarin Consultant, talking about working across cultures. Before you listen, discuss these questions.

1 How do you think working in Europe and working in China are different?
2 What are the benefits for people from Europe and China of working in each others' countries? What can they learn from the experience?

2 (2) 14 **Listen to Rob Liu. Choose the correct answer – A, B or C – for each question.**

1 What does Rob's job involve?
  A He recruits new employees.
  B He trains people for jobs in different countries.
  C He promotes his company's activities.

2 What attracted Rob to his present job?
  A It was connected with what he studied at university.
  B It was based in China.
  C It suited his particular abilities.

3 In comparison with Chinese jobseekers, Rob says Western jobseekers are more likely to
  A focus on how they can be useful to the company.
  B build up their skills and qualifications.
  C have the experience Western employers require.

4 Rob advises Westerners going to work in China to
  A work in places where there are many other foreigners.
  B adopt Chinese working methods and attitudes.
  C work as quickly and effectively as possible.

5 Rob suggests that European companies planning to do business in China should
  A employ local staff.
  B link up with a local company.
  C use a local development agency.

6 When Chinese job applicants go for job interviews in other countries, Rob advises them to
  A emphasise their qualifications.
  B reveal their real personality.
  C explain how hard they work.

3 **Work in small groups.**

What advice would you give foreign companies who are thinking of doing business in your country?

Speaking

Work in small groups. The company you work for is considering sending some of its younger staff to work in its offices abroad for six months. You have been asked to help select the staff.

Discuss the situation and decide:

- how younger members of staff can benefit from a foreign posting
- what problems they might have
- how to select the right people for these postings
- what preparation they will need.

Writing

1 A colleague has given you this memo with a job advertisement for checking. In some lines there is one wrong word. If there is a wrong word, write the correct word. If there is no mistake, put a tick (✓) .

2 You are a human resources assistant. Your company wants some of its employees to work in its overseas offices. Write a brief email to all staff.

- Announce the post(s).
- Explain the reasons.
- Say when and how to apply.

MEMO

To: all staff
From: Assistant HRO

We are currently recruiting internally ~~to~~ a   1 ...*for*...
younger member of staff to win experience of   2 ....
working in our London office and to know   3 ....
about British working culture. If you are   4 ....
interesting, please apply by 28th February at   5 ....
the last. Details of the posting can be found on   6 ....
the jobs page of the intranet.   7 ....

Grammar workshop 6

Units 21–24

Relative clauses

```
                    relative clause
              ┌───────────┴───────────┐
```

The factors which determine customer loyalty are easy to identify.

There are three types of relative clause:

1 **Defining relative clauses** tell you which person or thing the speaker is talking about:
   The meeting <u>which we went to in Guangzhou</u> was very useful, but the one <u>which we attended in Hong Kong</u> was not so useful. (The relative clauses tell us which meeting we are referring to.)

2 **Non-defining relative clauses** give extra information:
   Our principal suppliers, <u>whose factory is in Thailand</u>, have cashflow problems. (*whose factory is in Thailand* is extra information.)

3 **Co-ordinating relative clauses** come at the end of the sentence and add a comment about the previous part of the sentence:
   Hans arrived late for the meeting, <u>which was very inconvenient</u>. (The meeting was not inconvenient, but Hans's late arrival was inconvenient.)

There are differences in grammar:

Defining relative clauses
■ No commas
■ Use these relative pronouns: *who, which, whose, where, when, why*
■ *that* can be used instead of *who* or *which*
■ *who, which* or *that* can be omitted when they are the object of the clause, e.g. *The money (which/ that) you sent us has arrived. You* is the subject and *which/that* the object of the clause.

Non-defining relative clauses
■ Use commas
■ Use these relative pronouns: *who, which, whose, where, when, why*
■ Do not use *that*
■ The relative pronoun cannot be omitted.

Co-ordinating relative clauses follow a comma and
always use *which*:
Several customers are late paying us, which means we have a cashflow problem.

1 **Complete this email by writing a relative pronoun (*who, which, whose*, etc.) in each gap or writing ø if you think no relative pronoun is necessary. Add commas where necessary. In some cases, more than one answer is possible.**

Dear Farouk,

Thank you for your letter, **1** .which. arrived this morning, and in **2** .... you remind me of the need for a solution to the problem of pollution at our factory **3** .... we produce aluminium mouldings.

The most immediate problem **4** .... we have is an inspection by the environmental health officer **5** .... will take place next week. (You will remember her because she is the woman **6** .... report gave us so many problems two years ago.)

We have to present her with a solution **7** .... will convince her that we are serious about solving the problem. Our technical staff have also been working on it since last January **8** .... the new legislation came into force and they have come up with a number of ideas. We found the proposal **9** .... is most attractive is a purifying plant **10** .... will allow clean waste water into the River Klein **11** .... flows past the factory site.

Our bank manager **12** .... is very accommodating is ready to finance any project **13** .... viability we can prove. I enclose costings for the proposal **14** .... you might like to study before I send it to him.

15 .... would be most helpful would be an email with your thoughts as soon as possible, suggesting a date **16** .... work can begin.

Kind regards
Ingrid

---

2 ☉ **Business English students often make mistakes with relative clauses. Find and correct the mistakes in these sentences, which may include either a wrong relative pronoun or wrong punctuation, or both.**

1 Globelink has air freight available ~~that~~ means we can use it for urgent orders. *available, which means*

2 I am organising our staff training programme that starts on 21st June.

3 Regarding the meeting what was scheduled for next Friday, the date has changed.

4 The new discount, that we offer for cash payment, was one reason for this improvement.

5   The next method is online recruitment that is rather expensive.
6   The percentage of customers which are satisfied with our services is slightly above 50%.
7   They want us to introduce a bonus scheme what, in my opinion, would be very effective.
8   This will be a good service for our employees which have to drive a long way to our office.

Which pronoun: *it, this* or *that*?

> We use *it, this* and *that* (in the plural *they, these* and *those*) to refer to something we have already mentioned. Often more than one of them is correct in the context. However:
>
> ■ we use *it* when we are not making any emphasis:
> *We had a long, tense meeting with customers yesterday.* **It** *left us feeling very tired.*
>
> ■ *this* and *that* are more emphatic in drawing attention to the thing just mentioned:
> *We introduced a new production system in 2004, and* **this/that** *led to a huge increase in profitability.*
> Compare this with:
> *We introduced a new production system in 2004, and it led to a huge increase in profitability.*
> Here, the idea is expressed much less emphatically.
> We often use *this* when:
>
> ■ we still have something more to say about the thing we are referring to:
> *We've recommended opening an office in Belgrade.* **This** *will be discussed at the Board meeting next month.*
> *Many of our staff have been off sick this month.* **This** *has meant that we have fallen behind with our orders.*
>
> ■ we refer to the second of two things mentioned in the previous sentence. Compare:
> 1   *The bad weather has led to a delay in deliveries.* **This** *has caused a lot of inconvenience to our customers.* (This = the delay in deliveries)
> 2   *The bad weather has led to a delay in deliveries.* **It** *has also destroyed many crops.* (It = the bad weather)
> We often use *that* in conditional sentences:
> *We can meet at four o'clock if* **that** *suits you.*

Business English students often confuse *it, this* and *that*. Complete these sentences by writing the correct word in each gap. In some sentences, more than one answer is correct.

1   We've decided to make the theme of our seminar 'Achieving customer service'. .... is because our customers are very important to our company.

2   Unfortunately, due to a computer problem, we have been late in processing customers' orders. I am sorry for any inconvenience .... will cause you.
3   We only have five trainees for the course if .... is OK.
4   I want you to read this email. .... arrived this morning.
5   The language school offers courses in all the languages we need for our staff, and I think .... is the most important thing to take into consideration.
6   Freight costs have been falling recently. .... forms an essential part of our strategy for expanding into Africa and South America.
7   We would like to attend the seminar on 21 April if .... is possible.
8   The meeting is scheduled for Thursday. .... will start at 11 a.m.

Expressing results

> ■ *As a consequence of this / As a result / Consequently* + sentence
> *It snowed heavily last week.* **As a consequence of this / As a result / Consequently***, all our shipments were delayed.*
> ■ *mean / result in* + noun / *-ing* form
> *Your failure to deliver the goods on time* **meant / resulted in** *the loss of an important customer.*
> *Your failure to deliver the goods on time* **meant / resulted in** *us losing an important customer.*
> ■ *mean* + clause
> *Rising prices may* **mean** *that we will have to close the factory in Munich.*

Complete this memo with words or phrases from the box above.

> **To:**   Dispatch staff
> **From:**   Boris Vladev, Financial Director
> **Subject:** Cost savings
>
> ───────────────────────────────
>
> Rising oil prices have **1** .... greatly increased transport costs. This **2** .... that our profit margins are greatly reduced in those cases where we pay for delivery.
> **3** .... , we may have to raise prices, which could **4** .... our losing customers. Could I ask staff to:
> • make sure all lorries leaving the factory are completely full. This will **5** .... a 5% saving on present transport costs;
> • only use express delivery in really urgent cases. **6** .... , we will be able to save a further 6.5%.
> Many thanks.

Writing reference

Levels of formality

1 The table below shows some characteristics of formal and less formal English. Complete it by writing the words/phrases from the box in the gaps.

> agree with   asap   dashes   I look forward
> Meeting's Fri   pay back   satisfactory   show
> ~~We would appreciate~~   with reference to

more formal	less formal
■ no contractions: **1** We would appreciate ■ long words: *demonstrate, prepared* ■ less common words: **3** .... ■ one-word verbs: *collect, reimburse* ■ prepositional phrases: *I am writing* **5** .... *; We are broadly in agreement with ...* ■ **7** .... ■ no abbreviations: *September, as soon as possible* ■ complete sentences: *The meeting will be held in the Board Room on Friday.* ■ commas:, ■ brackets: ()	■ contractions: *We'd like ...* ■ short words: **2** ...., *ready* ■ common words: *good* ■ phrasal verbs: *pick up,* **4** .... ■ prepositions OR verbs: *I'm writing about; We generally* **6** .... ■ *I'm looking forward* ■ abbreviations: *Sept.,* **8** .... ■ incomplete sentences: **9** .... *– in Board Room.* ■ **10** ....: –

2 Read these two emails. Decide which is more formal and which is less formal, and why.

1

> Dear Montserrat,
>
> I am pleased to inform you that we have decided to award your firm the contract for website design. I will be in touch shortly with further details.
>
> Meanwhile, we would like to thank you for supplying such a competitive and professional quote.
>
> Kind regards,
> Ferenk

2

> Hi Sayed,
> Just to let you know that the link has been removed and the website is ready to go live again when you want.
> Sorry about the mix-up.
> Marta

3 Levels of formality in your writing depend on who will read what you write and your relationship with them. Decide what style (more formal or less formal) you would use when writing to/for each of these people.

1 someone you know well or have worked with a lot less formal
2 someone at the same level as you inside your organisation
3 someone in a more senior position than you
4 someone outside your organisation
5 someone you don't know, or don't know well
6 mixed groups of people, e.g. writing a report which might be circulated to different departments

4 Levels of formality also depend on the type and purpose of the document. Decide what style (more formal or less formal) you would use for each of these types of writing.

1 an email applying for a job more formal
2 an email congratulating a colleague on passing her professional exams
3 a letter apologising to a client for a mistake
4 an email to a colleague to change the time of a meeting
5 a report on customers' complaints
6 a proposal for a new business activity

5 Read these pieces of advice for when you are not sure what level of formality to adopt. Decide whether the advice is good (G) or bad (B).

1 Look at the level of formality in emails, letters or reports you have received from the person you are writing to and use the same.

2 Use an informal style with everyone – it makes business relationships friendlier.

3 It is safer to be slightly more formal if you are not certain.

Business correspondence: emails, memos and letters

Short emails

Many business people receive large numbers of emails each day. They want to be able to read them quickly, understand what they are saying without problems and answer them quickly. For this reason, many business emails are quite short.

The keys to good email writing are:

■ only say what is necessary
■ say it clearly and concisely.

1 Read the two emails below and answer these questions.

1 What is the purpose of each email?
2 What reason does each writer give?
3 What is Sanjay thanking Anita for?
4 Why does Malcolm start his email *Dear all*?
5 What action does Malcolm want in the second email?
6 Why does Malcolm apologise?

A

Hi Anita

Could you give me an idea of when you'll be able to get me the information I asked for? I have a conference call with our Chinese suppliers today and I need to give them a schedule.

Thanks in advance.
Sanjay

B

Dear all,

Unfortunately, one of my clients has rescheduled his visit for Thursday morning, so can we change our meeting to Friday afternoon?

Please confirm, and sorry for the inconvenience.

Best wishes
Malcolm

2 Complete the advice below about starting and finishing emails by writing a word/phrase from the box in each gap.

appropriate *Cheers* closely *Dear* first name
Hi *Kind regards* team

- Start emails with *Hi* or *Hello* or *Dear*. **1** _____ is least formal; **2** _____ is most formal.
- In English-speaking countries, if you use *Hi* or *Hello*, you will address the person using their **3** _____ .
- If it is not **4** _____ to use their first name, write *Dear* + the person's family name: *Dear Mr Fellini*.
- Use *Hi all* or *Hello everyone* when writing to several colleagues or members of your **5** _____ .
- Finish emails with *Cheers, All the best, Thanks, Many thanks, Thanks in advance, Best wishes, Regards, Kind regards*. **6** _____ is the least formal; **7** _____ is the most formal.
- When you work **8** _____ with someone, you needn't use any phrase to finish the email.

3 Match the emails below and on page 118 (A–F) with their subject lines (1–6). Ignore the options in italics for now.

1 Subject: appointment change
2 Subject: expanding our premises
3 Subject: re: customer enquiry
4 Subject: re: Fison's account
5 Subject: re: website project
6 Subject: Vilnius development conference

A

Hi Javier,
I'm afraid I won't be able to make it this morning **1** *as / so* we have an urgent job to finish for one of our clients. Let's check our diaries to find a more suitable and less rushed time **2** *and / to* meet and discuss our respective businesses.
Cheers,
Kevin

B

Hello Tanya
Thanks for the emails yesterday. When will you send me the link to the demo website? I can see a few simple changes to make to **3** *that / it*, but hopefully nothing that takes much time.
Regards
Piotr

C

Hi all,
Have we managed to backdate the accounts **4** *as / which* discussed in the emails below?
I'm meeting with the customer in two days and need to have an answer for them **5** *for now / by then*, as their end-of-year accounts are due.
Please advise ASAP.
Kindest regards,
Werner

D

Dear Simone,
I hope you are well.
As you know, we are currently renting three rooms.
6 *However / Although*, I would like to enquire about rates and availability of an additional one **7** *due to / because* we are hoping to take on more staff. I'm in the enquiry stage at the moment, **8** *however / but* I would certainly appreciate any information that you might have.
All the best,
Pierre

E

Dear Magda
I have been asked by the organisers if you could write your presentation for the event using PowerPoint. The reason for **9** *this / it* is that it will give them flexibility if they decide to adapt the presentation at a later date.
If you like, I would be happy to check **10** *it / this* for you when you are ready.
Best wishes
Grazyna

F

Hi Ron,
No problem. Leave it with me **11** *and / so* I'll give our client a quote this afternoon after I've done the figures. **12** *Then / So* if it's OK, I'll get the job done tomorrow if **13** *this is / that's* all right.
Thanks
Vince

4 It is important to link ideas together in emails using linking words/phrases and references. Choose the correct options in *italics* in the emails in Exercise 3.

5 Read emails A–F in Exercise 3 again. Decide if each is written in a more formal or less formal style.

6 Find examples of these functions in the emails in Exercise 3. (You may find more than one example for some.)

1 agreeing to a request/instruction
2 asking about someone's health
3 giving a reason
4 making a request or giving an instruction
5 making a suggestion
6 offering/promising to do something
7 referring to previous communications
8 requesting information

Memos

Memos are messages, information or instructions sent to one person or a number of people in the same organisation. They are usually in the form of emails and use similar language and styles.

1 Which of the emails A–F in Exercise 3 above do you think are memos written to people in the same organisation?

2 Read these two memos, ignoring the numbered gaps, and write the subject lines.

A

Subject: ....
Dear all,
A delegation from our Japanese suppliers will be visiting the office on Friday **1** .... get first-hand experience of our working methods, **2** .... I'd be grateful if you'd all dress more formally than usual for the occasion.
I'm sure you'll make **3** .... welcome.
Francesca

B

Subject: ....
Dear colleagues,
The Board of Directors has decided to rationalise our use of training resources in **4** .... to meet budget constraints in the present economic climate. It has **5** .... been decided that:
• all training requirements should in future be approved by the Human Resources Department
• requests for training should be submitted in writing and contain an explanation of how **6** .... will result in increased efficiency and profitability for the company.
For further details, please see the office bulletin of 15th August.
Thank you for your co-operation in **7** .... matter.
Nelson Bruger
Secretary

3 Complete the memos in Exercise 2 by writing one word in each numbered gap.

Letters and longer emails

Many letters these days have been replaced by email. However, when you write a letter, there are certain conventions you should follow, and many of these apply to longer, formal emails.

A letter of invitation

1 **Read this letter of invitation. What characteristics of a more formal style can you see?**

Dear Dr Kasic,

I am writing to invite you as our guest speaker at the International Shipping Confederation's Annual Conference, which will be taking place in Livorno on 18 June.

As you will see if you visit our website at www. isc/annualconference, the theme for this year's conference is 'Meeting global challenges for the years ahead', and the organisers feel that your unique academic qualifications, combined with your practical experience in the shipping business, make you the ideal choice for the opening session, for which you would be paid a fee of €2,500. ISC would in addition meet all expenses for you and a partner to attend this conference, including accommodation in a top-grade hotel.

I would be very grateful if you would let me know if you are available to do this.

I look forward to hearing from you

Yours sincerely

Angela Carrasco

Conference Organiser

2 **Match each of the paragraphs in the letter in Exercise 1 (1–4) with its purpose (a–d).**

paragraph	purpose
1	a the action you should take
2	b rounding off
3	c the reason for writing
4	d the reason for inviting you and your fees

3 **Match the sentence beginnings (1–9) with the sentence endings (a–i) to complete some letter-writing conventions.**

1 If you know the person's name,
2 If you don't know the person well,
3 If you know the person well enough,
4 If you don't know the name,
5 If you are writing to an organisation,
6 You can usually start your letter with a short paragraph
7 If you start your letter *Dear* + name,
8 If you start *Dear Sir/Madam* or *Dear Sirs,*
9 Put your name and your position or job title

a finish *Yours faithfully,*
b finish *Yours sincerely / Yours truly.*
c stating the reason for writing.
d under your signature.
e write *Dear* + first name: *Dear Paola.*
f write *Dear* + the name, even if you have never met them.
g write *Dear Mr/Mrs/Ms/Dr* + their family name.
h write *Dear Sir/Madam.*
i write *Dear Sirs.*

A letter applying for a job/grant, etc.

1 **Which of these details should you include in a letter of application?**

1 the reason for writing the letter
2 the name of the job you are applying for
3 how you found out about the vacancy
4 how much you want to earn
5 a reference to your CV and its contents
6 a brief summary of the things which will make you most interesting to the employer
7 how you spend your free time
8 some of the attractions of the job
9 why you want to leave your present job
10 your availability

2 **Normally, business letters are written on company paper with the address and logo already printed and with spaces for other details. However, if you are sending a letter of application, not email, you need to put details in the right places on the letter. Place each of these details (a–f) in the correct box (1–5) on the letter in Exercise 3 on page 120.**

a the date
b the name and address of the company you are writing to
c the name and/or position (e.g. Human Resources Manager) of the person you are writing to
d your address
e your email address
f your printed name

3 **Read this letter. Which of the details (1–10) from Exercise 1 does it include, and which paragraph are they in?**

[1]

[2]

[3]

[4]

[5]

Dear Sir/Madam,

I am writing to apply for the post of Public Relations Trainee in your organisation. I heard about this position through my university careers office.

As you will see from my curriculum vitae (attached), I am a final-year student in Marketing and Public Relations at the University of Novosibirsk, where I expect to graduate with a good degree at the end of this month. Apart from my studies in the field, last year I completed a six-month internship with Koestler-Farb GmbH, a German aerospace company based in Düsseldorf, and I have worked for three summers as a Public Relations Assistant at Novosibirsk Trade Centre. Consequently, I am able to work confidently in Russian, English and German.

I am interested in this position because, apart from the top-quality training it provides, it offers the sort of international opportunities for a long-term career that I am looking for. I welcome the chance for learning and growth that arise from working in a multicultural environment.

If you wish to pursue my application, I am available for interview at any time.

I look forward to hearing from you.

Yours faithfully,

Olga Murugova

[6]

A letter of enquiry

Read this letter of enquiry and answer these questions.

1 What is the purpose of each paragraph?
2 Why does Emilio use *we*, not *I*, in the first two paragraphs?
3 In the third paragraph, does he use direct or indirect questions? Why?
4 Why does he use the second conditional in the third paragraph?

Dear Mr Pfeiffer,

We are a large soft-drinks wholesaler based in Córdoba, Spain, delivering drinks to supermarkets, restaurants and bars throughout the country.

We have seen your advertisements recently for a GPS which will help our drivers to plan their routes efficiently, as well as allowing us to locate where they are in real time. We are interested in the possibility of installing a system like this in our fleet of delivery lorries, as it should produce significant savings in terms of efficiency.

I would be grateful therefore if you could let me know what the cost per unit of these systems is, whether they require installation by an expert technician and what discount you would be offering if we purchased approximately 240 of these devices. Also, if we placed an order, could you tell me how soon you would be able to deliver and install them, and whether staff would require any training in their use?

I look forward to an early reply.

Yours sincerely,

Emilio Tamarit
Operations Manager

Business documents: Reports and proposals

A report on a survey

1 **Complete the report on page 121 by writing the title and section headings (a–e) in the correct gaps (1–5). Ignore the options in italics.**

a Conclusions and recommendations
b Findings
c Introduction
d *Our website: the figures*
e Report on user feedback on our website

1 ....

2 ....

The purpose of this report is to summarise feedback we have received about the company's website **A** *and / also* to make recommendations on **B** *what / how* it can be improved to more closely meet our clients' needs. The information comes from an online survey of our users.

3 ....

Our website receives between 3,000 and 5,000 visits per month from customers and people who are interested, **C** *these / which* result in direct online sales of €280,000 last year and 1,356 online enquiries about products. Last month, 148 users agreed to complete an online questionnaire **D** *which / it* appeared as a pop-up box the second time they visited the site.

4 ....

Over a third of our respondents said that they found the site easy to use, nearly half stated that it was quite easy to use, **E** *while / when* about one in five complained that it was hard to use. Amongst those who said it was quite easy or hard to use, the majority complained that it takes too long to confirm and approve credit-card details **F** *after / while* they have decided to buy.

Another general area of dissatisfaction was the small size and lack of detail in photographs of the products, **G** *who / which* a significant percentage (31%) complained about.

5 ....

In order to speed up transactions, we should investigate the possibility of one-click purchases for repeat customers **H** *whose / and their* payment details are already in the system. I would also recommend that we offer the option of higher-resolution photographs **I** *so that / because* customers can see our products in greater detail, **J** *even though / however* this means that they will load more slowly.

2   The report in Exercise 1 uses quite long sentences with a number of linking words. Choose the best options in italics (A–J).

3   Read the report again and answer these questions.

1   Is the report written in a more formal or a less formal style?

2   When does the writer use an impersonal style, and when does she use a personal style? Why?

3   What figures does the report quote, and why?

4   Which section …
   a   explains the aim of the report?
   b   says how many people use the website, and what this means in terms of money?
   c   says how the information was gathered?
   d   says what people like and dislike about the website?
   e   suggests ways in which the website could be improved?

A personal report

1   The writer of the personal report below uses words and phrases to link ideas (e.g. *moreover*), introduce general points (e.g. *on the whole*) and introduce his attitude (e.g. *unfortunately*). Complete the report by writing words and phrases from the box in the gaps. Some words can be used more than once, and in some cases, more than one answer may be possible.

> There was also a tendency   Although   For example
> However   Moreover   On the whole   Unfortunately

Report on our premises in Cuxhaven, Germany

Introduction
I carried out a surprise inspection of our store in Cuxhaven, Germany, on 19th April this year, and the following is a report of my findings while there.

Appearance
1 .... , I found the store to be tidy, clean and attractive.
2 .... , the staff, who did not know I was an inspector, were welcoming and helpful, and I felt that visiting the store was a pleasant and satisfying experience. **3** .... , I found certain articles such as belts and umbrellas hard to find, and different parts of the store were not clearly signposted.
4 .... to turn the music up too loud, and this interfered with customers' conversations.

Prices
5 .... price guidelines for merchandise are issued by Head Office in Vigo, stores have some flexibility in pricing to suit the local market. **6** .... , I found discounted prices tended to be hard to understand. **7** .... , when a price tag announced a 15% discount, it was not easy to determine what the final price in euros would be.

Conclusions
The store offers a generally excellent level of service.
8 .... , directions and other written information within the store should be made clearer, and steps should be taken to make the music less intrusive.

2   Read the report in Exercise 1 again to find:

1   positive comments
2   points where action is required
3   verbs in the passive to avoid saying who did something / who should do something.

Proposals

1 Read the title of the proposal below. Is the objective to suggest a solution to a problem or a new business activity?

A proposal for reducing complaints about our customer helpline

Introduction
We have recently received a large number of complaints concerning our customer helpline. This proposal outlines possible solutions and suggests a plan for dealing with the issues.

Customer complaints
Our customers have expressed irritation at having to hold the line for up to ten minutes before an operative answers the phone. This means that many ring off before they are attended to and therefore they do not receive the information they require.
In most cases, these problems arise because there are not enough operatives working at the times customers call.

Possible solutions
We need to balance the cost of dealing with customer enquiries with the benefits of providing good customer care. There are two possible solutions to the problem. We can:
1 take on extra staff at peak times
2 outsource the customer helpdesk to a specialist firm.

Employing extra staff
We would need to employ up to five part-time workers, train them in our systems and make sure their timetables coincide with times of peak demand. Recruitment and training of suitable staff would be a significant cost.

Outsourcing customer care
While this solution is not cheap, the outsourcing firm would have trained staff available at the times required, thereby saving resources on recruitment and training. Our concern would be to monitor the quality of the service provided.

Conclusion
As the accompanying projection of costs shows, the second solution of outsourcing will almost certainly generate greater customer satisfaction in the medium to long term at a lower cost, and this is the solution that should be adopted.

2 Read the proposal in Exercise 1, ignoring the orange words, and answer these questions.

In which section(s) does the writer …
1 state the purpose of the proposal?
2 outline the problem and the cause of the problem?
3 offer a choice of solutions?
4 evaluate each solution?
5 say which solution she prefers?
6 refer to documents and/or charts which go with the proposal?

3 Which formal words/phrases printed in orange in the proposal in Exercise 1 mean the same as these less formal words/phrases?

1	a lot of *a large number of*	8	explains briefly
2	about	9	happen
3	anger	10	money
4	check on	11	need
5	chosen	12	problems
6	dealt with	13	produce
7	expensive	14	worry

A short proposal

When you write a short proposal, it should have a title, but it is not always necessary to divide it into sections.

1 Read this proposal and choose the best options in italics.

Proposal for leasing unused space to Fenollar S.A.

This is a proposal that we should lease unused property behind our premises to Fenollar S.A. as parking space for their lorries.

Fenollar S.A., which is on an adjoining factory site to our own, has a continuous stream of lorries arriving and waiting in the street in front. **1** *Due to / Because* the nature of their business, the lorries often wait for up to two hours **2** *until / before* loading or unloading, with the drivers inside.

My proposal is that we should offer to lease the unused ground to the left of our factory to Fenollar **3** *so that / therefore* they can leave their lorries there **4** *until / when* they are needed. Their drivers could then be redeployed and the street would be less cluttered. This would **5** *in addition / also* make access to our premises easier.

I have already spoken to their Transport Manager, **6** *he / who* has expressed interest, and I would suggest we ask for a rent of 800 euros pcm. **7** *This / It* would make unproductive land in our ownership profitable.

If **8** *this / that* is of interest, I suggest that we should contact their Transport Manager more formally.

2 Match the notes the writer made before he started writing (a–e) with the paragraphs (1–5).

paragraph 1	a *My suggestion – Fenollar could use our waste land*
paragraph 2	b *Our next step*
paragraph 3	c *Outline the business opportunity and its benefits*
paragraph 4	d *Outline the problem*
paragraph 5	e *The steps already taken*

3 Find where the writer uses *could* and *would* in the proposal in Exercise 1. Why does he use these verbs and not *can* and *will*?

Functions bank

Starting a letter / longer email

I'm / I am writing to apply for / complain about / apologise for / enquire about, etc.

Thank you for your letter of 18th June in which you invite me …

Further to our telephone conversation, I am writing …

We are a small software development company based in Krasnoyarsk, Russia, and I am writing to …

Rounding off a letter or email

I'm looking forward to hearing from you. (less formal)

I look forward to an early reply. (more formal)

Introducing information

Just to let you know that … (less formal)

This is to say that …

I am pleased/delighted to inform you that … (more formal)

Requesting information

Can you tell me/us … (less formal)

Can/Could you (please) let me know when/how …

I was wondering when/if …

I'd/We'd like to know …

I would like to enquire about …

We would appreciate it if you could supply us with the following information: (more formal)

Asking the price

How much will … cost? (less formal)

Could you tell me the price of …?

Could you please quote for …?

Could you please give us a (competitive) quote for …?

I'd like to enquire about the price/rates for … (more formal)

Asking indirect questions

I would like to know if/whether the brochure is available in German. (less formal)

Can/Could you tell me / let me know when you will be visiting St Petersburg?

I would like to have details about …

I wonder if you could tell me …

Could you please send me information about … (more formal)

Asking for comments

What do you think? (less formal)

Do you agree?

Could you let me have any feedback or comments by 15th January?

Please let us know what you think.

I would be grateful if you could get any feedback to me fairly soon. (more formal)

Referring to an email you have received

Thanks for this / your email. (less formal)

Thank you for this / your email. (more formal)

Referring to part of an email or to a topic

Regarding payment, we will make the transfer tomorrow. (less formal)

With reference/regard to payment … (more formal)

Referring to an attachment to an email

Please find/see the attachment / the attached document where we specify the terms of the contract.

Referring to a document enclosed with a letter

As you will see from the enclosed invoice/leaflet/ document, …

Referring to a conversation

Good to talk to you / meet you this morning. (less formal)

Further to our telephone conversation, … (more formal)

Giving instructions / Requesting

Can/Could you please …? (less formal)

I'd like you to please …

I wonder if you could please …?

Would you please …?

I'd be (very) grateful if you would …

I'd appreciate it if you would … (more formal)

Giving reasons

We want to / I am keen to …, so …

Therefore, …

The reason why we want to do this is …

The reason for this is that …

This/That is because …

This/That was due to the fact that …

Agreeing to requests

No problem – we'll start working on this next week. (less formal)

Yes, we'd be happy/glad to …

We'd be delighted to … (more formal)

Expressing purpose

The aim/purpose of this report/proposal is to …

The reason for this report/proposal is to …

This report is being written with the aim/purpose of …

Thanking

Thanks. (less formal)

Thank you for the instruction manuals, which we received this morning / which arrived this morning. (more formal)

I/We appreciate your contribution to this project. / Your contribution to this project is much appreciated.

Giving bad news / communicating unpleasant information

Sorry that … (less formal)
Unfortunately, …
I'm sorry to say that …
I/We regret (to inform you) that …
We regret that you have not been selected for interview on this occasion. (more formal)

Apologising

Apologies for the confusion. (less formal)
I'm sorry if this has caused you problems.
We would like to / We do apologise for …
Please accept our apologies for … (more formal)

Offering

If you like, I'll … (less formal)
Shall I …?
I'd be happy to …
It would give me great pleasure to … (more formal)

Asking for a reply

Please let me know asap. (less formal)
I look forward / I'm looking forward to hearing from you.
I look forward to an early reply. (more formal)

Expressing figures

nearly / about / over / more than a quarter / a third / a fifth, etc.
one in three/five BUT *two/three* etc. *out of ten.*
A large/small percentage of customers thought …
Only/Just 15% of customers said …
The vast majority …
A small/significant minority …

Making recommendations

We should/ought to …
I think we should/ought to …
I recommend that …
I would strongly recommend that …

Making suggestions

How about …? (less formal)
Why don't we …?
We can/could …
We should …
I suggest that we should …
I would suggest that we … (more formal)

Making generalisations

generally / on the whole / in general
They tend to be …
There is/was a tendency to …

Some abbreviations

pcm: per calendar month
pa: per annum
ASAP/asap: as soon as possible
FYI: for your information
BTW: by the way
BW: best wishes

Word lists

The numbers in brackets indicate the page on which the word first occurs. Some of these words appear in the transcripts at the back of the book. CD1 T1 means that the word appears in Track 1 on CD1.

n = noun, *n phr* = noun phrase, *pl n* = plural noun, *v* = verb, *v phr* = verb phrase, *phr v* = phrasal verb, *adj* = adjective, *adj phr* = adjectival phrase, *adv* = adverb, *adv phr* = adverbial phrase

UNIT 1

bonus *n* (8) an amount of money given to an employee in addition to their salary as a reward for working well

committed *adj* (11) loyal and willing to give your time and energy to something that you believe in

computer literate *adj phr* (10) able to use computers effectively

consistent *adj* (8) always behaving or happening in a similar, especially positive, way

core skill *n phr* (10) a particular ability that you develop through training and experience and that is necessary to do a particular job

corporate culture *n phr* (10) the beliefs and ideas that a company has and the way in which they affect how it does business and how its employees behave

dedicated *adj* (8) used only for one particular purpose or job

diverse *adj* (8) varied or different

do overtime *v phr* (11) to work after the usual time needed or expected in a job

earn an award *v phr* (8) to be given money or a prize following an official decision

goal setting *n phr* (8) the process of deciding what you want to achieve or what you want someone else to achieve over a particular period

hands-on training *n phr* (CD1 T1) a way of learning in which you do things instead of just reading or learning about them

headhunter *n* (10) a person who is hired by a company to find someone who has the qualifications for an important job and is willing to leave their present job

in-house *adj* (8) being done by employees within an organisation rather than by other companies or independent workers

intensive *adj* (8) involving a lot of effort or activity in a short period of time

learning goal *n phr* (CD1 T1) an aim or purpose that you intend to achieve by study

material incentive *n phr* (10) something, especially money, that encourages a person or organisation to do something

personal development *n phr* (8) the process of improving your skills and increasing the amount of experience that you have in your job

procedure *n* (CD1 T2) a set of actions which is the usual or official way of doing something

professionalism *n* (10) the combination of all the qualities that are connected with trained and skilled people

promote from within *v phr* (8) to raise someone who already belongs to an organisation to a higher or more important position or rank within that organisation

quotation *n* (CD1 T1) a statement of how much a job, service, or product will cost

recognition *n* (10) the act of praising or rewarding someone for something they have done

safety regulation *n phr* (9) an official rule that is meant to keep people protected from danger or harm

supervisor *n* (10) a person who is in charge of a group of people or an area of work and who makes sure that the work is done correctly and according to the rules

tailor-made *adj* (CD1 T1) specially made for a particular person, organisation, or purpose

take on *phr v* (CD1 T1) to employ someone

time management *n phr* (8) the practice of using your time effectively, and the study of this

training budget *n phr* (CD1 T1) the amount of money you have available to spend on teaching the skills that you will need to do a particular job or activity

UNIT 2

career coaching *n phr* (CD1 T4) the process of teaching the skills needed to succeed in a particular job

cashier *n* (CD1 T3) someone whose job is to take payments from customers or give out money in a store, bank, etc.

challenging *adj* (13) difficult, in a way that tests your ability or determination

discipline *n* (CD1 T3) the practice of making sure that people obey rules and do not cause problems

diversity *n* (CD1 T4) the fact of there being people of many different groups in society, within an organisation, etc.

effective promotional campaign *n phr* (12) a well-planned and successful group of activities which are intended to advertise something

efficient *adj* (12) using resources such as time, materials or energy well without wasting any

financial paperwork *n phr* (12) the part of a job which involves keeping records of how money is managed

fire *v* (CD1 T3) to make someone leave their job, especially because they have done something wrong

fulfilling *adj* (CD1 T4) making you feel happy and satisfied

issue *v* (12) to give someone something, especially officially

large-scale project *n phr* (CD1 T4) a large piece of planned work or building activity which is finished over a long period of time

performance *n* (12) how well someone does their job or their duties

personnel *n* (13) the department of a company or organisation that deals with employees when they join or leave, when they need training, when they have problems, etc.

personnel *n* (CD1 T3) the people who are employed by a company or organisation

pull the wool over someone's eyes *v phr* (CD1 T3) to deceive someone in order to prevent them from discovering something

role *n* (CD1 T3) the position or purpose that someone or something has in a situation, organisation, society or relationship

selling point *n* (CD1 T3) a characteristic of a product or service that will persuade people to buy it

thrive *v* (14) to grow, develop, and become successful

warehouse *n* (12) a large building for storing things before they are sold, used, or sent out to stores

workwise *adv* (CD1 T3) relating to work

UNIT 3

advertising campaign *n phr* (17) a planned series of advertisements that will be used in particular places at particular times in order to advertise a product or service and persuade people to buy it or use it

approval *n* (18) official permission or agreement for something

assign *v* (18) to give a particular job or piece of work to someone

be yourself *v phr* (CD1 T6) to behave in your usual manner, rather than behaving in a way you think other people might like

brand *n* (17) the name of a product produced or sold by a particular company, or what the characteristics, appearance, etc. a person, organisation, product, etc. is known for

colleague *n* (18) a person that you work with

compile documents *v phr* (18) to collect information from papers with written or printed information, especially of an official type, and arrange it in a book, report or list

embarrassment *n* (CD1 T5) when you feel nervous, worried or uncomfortable

emphasise *v* (CD1 T5) to show or state that something is very important or worth giving attention to

file *v* (CD1 T5) to store information or documents carefully so that they are easy to find, either in a place such as a folder or desk, or on a computer

follow up *phr v* (CD1 T5) to do something to finish a previous action or make it more successful

get a complete picture (of) *v phr* (CD1 T5) to understand someone or something better

go straight in the bin *v phr* (CD1 T5) to immediately put something into a container for waste, or refuse to consider something

image *n* (CD1 T6) the way that something or someone is thought of by other people

initiate *v* (18) to begin something

innovate *v* (16) to develop a new design, product, idea, etc.

inspire *v* (17) to make someone feel that they want to do something and can do it

intellectually stimulating *adj phr* (16) encouraging you to think and understand new and complicated ideas

interact *v* (17) to communicate with someone

internship *n* (18) a period of time during which a student works for a company or organisation in order to get experience of a particular type of work

intimidate *v* (16) to frighten or threaten someone, usually in order to persuade them to do something that you want them to do

logo *n* (17) a design or symbol displayed on a company's products, vehicles, signs, etc. that expresses the company's character and purpose and makes it easy for customers to recognize and remember the company

mobile technology *n phr* (16) the use of scientific knowledge or processes relating to phones or computers used while travelling from place to place, without being connected by wires

packaging *n* (17) the materials in which objects are wrapped before being sold

prospective employer *n phr* (CD1 T5) a person or organisation that might employ you in the future

referee *n* (17) a person who knows you and who is willing to describe your character and abilities in order to support you when you are trying to get a job, etc.

speak out freely *v phr* (17) to give your opinion about something without being controlled or limited, especially on a subject which you have strong feelings about

stay on one's toes *v phr* (16) to continue directing all your attention and energy to what you are doing

wisdom *n* (CD1 T5) the ability to use your knowledge and experience to make good decisions and judgments

workplace *n* (16) a building or room where people perform their jobs, or these places generally

UNIT 4

account for *v phr* (CD1 T7) to form the total of something

attitude *n* (CD1 T7) a feeling or opinion about something, especially when this shows in your behaviour

body language *n phr* (20) body movements that show someone's thoughts and feelings

carry out research *v phr* (23) to do or complete a detailed study of a subject, especially in order to discover (new) information

charge *v* (CD1 T8) to ask for a particular amount of money for something, especially a service or activity

check availability *v phr* (CD1 T8) to find out if something is able to be bought, used or reached

critical *adj* (23) extremely important to the progress or success of something

crucial *adj* (CD1 T7) extremely important or necessary

dress formally *v phr* (20) to wear a serious type of clothes

drive *v* (CD1 T7) to cause or influence something

finalise *v* (CD1 T9) to make a final and certain decision about a plan, date, etc.

form an impression (of sthg/sb) *v phr* (CD1 T7) to get an idea or opinion of what something is like

full-time *adj* (CD1 T9) for all the hours of the week that people normally work, not just for some of them

get sthg up on the screen *v phr* (CD1 T9) to make something able to be seen or read on a computer system

hold on *phr v* (21) to wait while someone else does something, especially when you are using the phone

incoming phone call *n phr* (23) when someone uses the phone to call you

instinctive *adj* (CD1 T7) Instinctive behaviour or reactions are not thought about, planned or developed by training.

intended recipient *n phr* (23) the person who is meant to receive something

part-time *adj* (CD1 T9) for only some of the hours of the week that people normally work, not all of them

progress report *n phr* (23) a description of an event or situation that explains how much progress is being made

rate *n* (CD1 T8) an amount of money that is charged or paid for a particular service

reinforce *v* (23) to make an idea or belief stronger

UNIT 5

affordable pricing *n phr* (29) when a company offers goods that are not expensive

app developer *n phr* (29) someone whose job is to create computer programs designed for particular purposes

appeal to *v phr* (27) to interest or attract someone

brand ambassador *n phr* (29) a manager who is responsible for creating and developing a brand and encouraging support for it, both inside and outside a company

capitalise on *v phr* (27) to use a situation to your own advantage

competitor *n* (29) a person, product, company, etc. that is trying to compete with others, for example, by trying to make bigger sales in a particular market

cross over *phr v* (29) the process or result of changing from one activity or style to another

customer loyalty *n phr* (CD1 T10) the fact of a customer buying products or services from the same company over a long period of time

emerging market *n phr* (29) a part of the world which is beginning to have economic power or success and where something might be sold

overheads *pl n* (CD1 T10) the regular and necessary costs, such as rent and heating, that are involved in operating a business

pay a premium *v phr* (CD1 T10) to give a larger amount of money than usual for something

premium price segment *n phr* (29) a part into which the economy or a company's business can be divided which involves charging or paying high prices for something

price ladder *n phr* (29) a way of referring to a series of several different prices to choose from, depending on the quality of the product

print ad *n phr* (27) an advertisement that appears in a newspaper or magazine, rather than on television, radio or the Internet

property consultant *n phr* (29) someone who is paid to give expert advice or training on buildings and land, considered as things to be bought and sold

publicity *n* (27) the activity of making certain that someone or something attracts a lot of interest or attention from many people, or the attention received as a result of this activity

supplier *n* (CD1 T10) a company that provides a product, or the materials to make a product

target *v* (29) to direct something, especially advertising or a product, at a particular group of people or a particular area

viral video *n phr* (29) an electronic recording of moving images which very quickly spreads or becomes popular through communication from one person to another, especially on the Internet

watchword *n* (29) (a word or phrase which represents) the main ideas or principles directing the way that someone behaves or the way that something is done

UNIT 6

a year in development *n phr* (CD1 T11) the period of 12 months during which something such as a new product or service is created

approach *v* (CD1 T11) to speak to, write to or visit another person or group in order to do something such as make a request or business agreement

big player *n phr* (CD1 T13) someone who has a lot of influence in an activity or organisation

break down *phr v* (CD1 T11) If a system, relationship or discussion breaks down, it fails because there is a problem or disagreement.

budget allocation *n phr* (32) a plan that shows the amount of money that an organisation is allowed to spend on particular things

generic *adj* (CD1 T11) shared by, typical of, or relating to a whole group of similar things, rather than to any particular thing

market research *n phr* (30) the collection and study of information about what people prefer to buy, how they react to advertising, and what other businesses in the same industry are doing

marketing spend *n phr* (CD1 T13) the amount of money that is spent on encouraging people to buy a product or service

pack *v* (31) to put something into a container

pitch *v* (CD1 T11) to try to persuade someone to buy your products/services or choose you to do some work for them

raise awareness *v phr* (CD1 T13) to make people realise that something exists

raise finance *v phr* (31) to manage to get money to invest in a business, project, property, etc.

range *n* (30) a number of similar things considered as a group

retail customer *n phr* (31) a person who buys goods, rather than a store or other business

set up a production facility *v phr* (31) to arrange a new building or area where goods will be made

strategy *n* (CD1 T13) the way in which a business, government, or other organisation carefully plans its actions over a period of time to improve its position and achieve what it wants

supply chain *n phr* (CD1 T11) the system of people and organisations that are involved in getting a product from the place where it is made to customers

transform the business *v phr* (31) to change completely the character of a particular company in order to improve it

turning point *n phr* (CD1 T11) a time when a situation starts to change in an important way

upmarket *adj* (CD1 T11) used to describe products and services that are of a high quality compared to others

UNIT 7

commercial edge *n phr* (36) an advantage over the people or businesses who are competing with you

control costs *n phr* (36) to limit the amount of money that has to be spent in order to buy, do or make something

custom-built *adj* (36) If something is custom-built, it is specially made for a particular buyer.

customised solution *n phr* (36) used to describe something that has been made to solve a customer's particular needs

enhance *v* (36) to improve the quality, amount or value of something

exhibit *v* (35) to show something publicly in a place such as a museum or trade show

fee *n* (CD1 T14) an amount of money paid for a particular piece of work or for a particular right or service

for hire *adj phr* (36) something that can be used temporarily in exchange for money

give you an edge over your competition *v phr* (36) to give you an advantage over the people or businesses who are competing with you in a particular market

guarantee *v* (CD1 T14) to promise that something will happen or is true

huge stock *n phr* (36) a large amount of goods that a store or business has for sale

install *v* (36) to put furniture, a machine, or a piece of equipment into position and make it ready to use

keen price *n phr* (36) If prices are keen, they are lower and offer more value than others.

legal requirement *n phr* (CD1 T14) a rule in law about something that it is necessary to have or to do

liaise *v* (36) to work with someone in order to exchange information with them

make an impact *v phr* (36) to have a powerful effect on someone or something

man the stand *v phr* (34) to work at a table or structure where someone can sell or advertise their products or services

marketing advantage *n phr* (36) an advantage over the people or businesses who are competing with you

marketing solution *n phr* (36) a way of finding out what customers want, using that information to design products and services, and selling them effectively

maximise visitor numbers *v phr* (36) to make the amount of people who visit as big as possible

monitor *v* (36) to watch a situation carefully for a period of time in order to discover something about it

mount *v* (36) to fix something on a wall, in a frame, etc. so that it can be viewed or used

on a first-come-first-served basis *adv phr* (CD1 T14) used to mean that people will receive something or be dealt with in the order in which they ask or arrive

project management *n phr* (36) the activity of organising and controlling a project

ready-made equipment *n phr* (36) the machinery, tools, etc. that you need to do a job in a finished form and available to use immediately

registration *n* (35) when a name or information is recorded on an official list

sales technique *n phr* (35) the ability to persuade people to buy a company's products or services

trade event *n phr* (36) a large event at which companies show and sell their products and try to increase their business

win new business *v phr* (36) to succeed in getting more people or companies to buy your goods or services

UNIT 8

acquire *v* (38) to get something

anchor *v* (40) to make something or someone stay in one position

blag *v* (CD1 T15) to manage to obtain something by using persuasion

financial gain *n phr* (39) with the purpose or aim of making money, rather than for any other reason

give a discount *v phr* (CD1 T17) to offer a reduction in the usual price of a product or service

give and take *n phr* (40) willingness to accept suggestions from another person and give up some of your own

give up on the first reversal *v phr* (CD1 T15) to stop doing something because of the first problem or failure in the process

identify needs *v phr* (40) to find and be able to describe something that you must have to achieve a particular thing

know their limits *v phr* (CD1 T15) If someone knows their limits, they are aware of the greatest amount of something that is possible for them to do.

make a profit *v phr* (CD1 T17) to earn money in trade or business, especially after paying the costs of producing and selling goods and services

novelty value *n phr* (CD1 T17) interesting because it has not been experienced before

opening proposal *n phr* (39) a formal suggestion, plan, or idea that comes near the beginning of something

persistent *adj* (38) Someone who is persistent continues doing something or tries to do something in a determined way.

place a repeat order *v phr* (CD1 T17) to order the same thing that you have ordered before

pushy *adj* (CD1 T15) behaving in an unpleasant way by trying too much to get something or to make someone do something

trustworthy *adj* (CD1 T15) able to be trusted

UNIT 9

achieve an ambition *v phr* (44) to successfully do something you wanted to do, especially after a lot of effort

buy into a franchise *v phr* (44) to pay money for the right for your business to sell the products and services of another company

cash infusion *n phr* (45) when money is added to a business to make it stronger or better

close down *phr v* (44) If a business or organisation closes down or someone closes it down, it stops operating.

cope with *phr v* (45) to deal successfully with a difficult situation

credit facilities *n phr* (47) arrangements for paying for goods or services at a later time, usually paying interest as well as the original amount

economic trend *n phr* (45) a general development relating to trade, industry, and money

entrepreneur *n* (CD1 T18) someone who makes money by starting their own business, especially when this involves seeing a new opportunity and taking risks

exploit a gap in the market *v phr* (44) to use the opportunity to sell a product or service because a need or demand for it exists but no one is supplying it

from strength to strength *adv phr* (CD1 T18) gradually becoming more successful

international presence *n phr* (45) when someone or something is known in more than one country

lay out guidelines *v phr* (45) to give information intended to advise people on how something should be done in a clear and detailed way

lose one's head *v phr* (45) to lose control and not act in a calm way

make redundant *v phr* (44) If you are made redundant, you lose your job because your employer no longer needs you.

new venture *n phr* (45) a new business activity

outlet *n* (44) a store that sells a particular company's products or products of a specific type

premises *pl n* (47) the buildings and land owned or used by someone, especially by a company or organisation

replicate the core concept *v phr* (45) to make or do the most important part of a business's idea again in exactly the same way

revenue stream *n phr* (45) the money coming into a company from a particular activity over a period of time, or the activity itself

roll out *phr v* (45) to make a new product, service, or system available for the first time

sign a contract *v phr* (45) to write your name on a legal document that states and explains a formal agreement between two different people or groups

social status *n phr* (44) the level or position of someone in relation to others in society

survey *n* (45) an examination of people's opinions, behaviour, etc. made, for example, by asking them questions

take charge of *v phr* (CD1 T18) to take control of something or of a group of people

take the plunge *v phr* (CD1 T18) to make a decision to do something, especially after thinking about it for a long time

tight lending market *n phr* (45) when the activity of lending money to people and organisations which they pay back with interest is controlled very carefully

time-consuming *adj* (45) taking a lot of time to do or complete

tone down *phr v* (45) to make something less forceful or offensive, usually a piece of writing or a speech

wealthy *adj* (45) rich

UNIT 10

build up a business *v phr* (CD1 T20) to increase the activity of buying and selling goods and services in quantity and make it stronger

business plan *n phr* (CD1 T19) a detailed document describing the future plans of a business

cold-call *v* (CD1 T19) to phone or visit a possible customer to try to sell them a product or service without being asked by the customer to do so

competitive rate *n phr* (CD1 T19) an amount or level of payment that is as good as or better than other amounts or levels of payment

consolidated shipments *n phr* (CD1 T20) combinations of large amounts of goods sent together to a place

create employment *v phr* (49) to make jobs exist

currency *n* (CD1 T20) the system of money that is used in a particular country at a particular time

debt *n* (49) the amount of money that is owed by a person, company, country, etc. and that they usually have to pay interest on

delivery on time *n phr* (CD1 T20) the act of taking goods, letters, parcels, etc. to a place, done when it should be and is not late

distributor *n* (CD1 T20) a person or company that buys products from a manufacturer and sells them for a profit to other businesses, stores or customers, often by transporting the goods to different places

encroach *v* (CD1 T20) to gradually cover more and more of an area

freight company *n phr* (CD1 T20) a business that transports goods by ship, aircraft, train or truck

go about *phr v* (CD1 T19) to begin to do something or deal with something

guarantee the loan *v phr* (49) If you guarantee someone's loan, you formally promise to accept the responsibility for paying the money back if the person fails to pay it.

invoice *n* (CD1 T20) a document that lists things provided or work done, gives their cost, and asks for payment

joint owners *n phr* (49) two or more people who own something

market sector *n phr* (CD1 T20) a part of an industry or a group of customers, products, etc. that are similar in some way

meet monthly repayments *v phr* (CD1 T19) to have enough money to pay amounts you owe every month

partnership *n* (48) an agreement between organisations, people, etc. to work together

principal payment *n phr* (49) a payment made to pay back all or part of a loan, rather than to pay interest on the loan

profit potential *n phr* (49) something that is able to develop into earning money in the future when the necessary conditions exist

prosper *v* (CD1 T20) to be or become successful, especially financially

recession *n* (CD1 T20) a period, usually at least six months, of low economic activity, when investments lose value, businesses fail, and unemployment rises

savings *pl n* (48) money that you keep, usually in a bank account, instead of spending it

ship in *phr v* (CD1 T20) to send something, usually a large object or a large quantity of objects or people, to a place far away

track back *phr v* (CD1 T20) to record the progress or development of something over a period of past time

UNIT 11

at current exchange rates *n phr* (CD1 T21) at the rate at which the money of one country can be changed for the money of another country at the present time

award a contract *v phr* (53) to have a formal agreement with a company for them to provide a service or do a job

commission *v* (55) to ask someone to do a particular piece of work for you

course of action *n phr* (52) the way something happens, or a way of doing something

cross-fertilisation of ideas *n phr* (54) the mixing of the ideas of different places or groups of people, to make it better for all

cutting edge technology *n phr* (53) the practical, especially industrial, use of all the latest scientific discoveries

divisional head *n* (52) a person who is in charge of one part of a large organisation

enjoy a reputation *v phr* (53) to have an advantage because people have a good opinion of someone or something

entity *n* (53) something which exists apart from other things, having its own independent existence

get down to *v phr* (CD1 T21) to start to direct your efforts and attention towards something

get onto *phr v* (CD1 T21) to speak or write to a person or organisation because you want them to help you in some way

ground-breaking *adj* (52) new and likely to have an effect on how things are done in the future

head up *phr v* (CD1 T21) to lead or manage a team, department, organisation, etc.

infrastructure *n* (53) the basic systems and services that are needed in order to support an economy, for example, transport and communication systems and electricity and water supplies

interested party *n phr* (53) any people or organisations who may be affected by a situation, or who are hoping to make money out of a situation

lease *n* (53) an agreement to pay money in order to use land, a building, a vehicle or a piece of equipment for a particular period of time

on a world scale *adv phr* (53) used to measure or compare the level of something around the world

purpose-built facility *n phr* (54) a building or area that is designed and built for a particular use

R&D facility *n phr* (52) a building or area for research and development (= the part of an organisation that works to improve its products and develop new ones, or the activity of doing this)

rank highest *v phr* (53) to have a position that is higher than others, or to be considered to have such a position

run a growing operation *v phr* (CD1 T21) to be in control of or manage a business organisation that is getting bigger

step across the threshold *v phr* (53) (formal) to go into a building or room

tax question *n phr* (53) a sentence or phrase used to find out information about money paid to the government

too many strings attached *n phr* (CD1 T21) If something such as an agreement has too many strings attached, it involves too large a number of special demands or limits.

viable alternative *n phr* (53) something that is different from something else, especially from what is usual, but is able to be done or likely to succeed

UNIT 12

advance their career *v phr* (58) to do things that help them to progress to better jobs and become successful

brainstorm *v* (58) to meet in a group to suggest a lot of new ideas very quickly, with the intention of considering them more carefully later

breakdown of costs *n phr* (CD1 T22) a division of how money needs to be spent, so that you can see all the details

credible *adj* (58) able to be believed or trusted

demand *n* (CD1 T22) a need for goods or services that customers want to buy/use

dry up *phr v* (58) to stop being able to talk in the normal way

feel free *v phr* (57) If someone tells you to feel free to do something, they mean that you can do it if you want to.

finding *n* (CD1 T22) information or a fact that is discovered by studying something

handout *n* (56) a document containing information that is given to people at a meeting or other event

mannerism *n* (58) something that a person does repeatedly with their face, hands or voice, and which they may not realise they are doing

outline a requirement *v phr* (CD1 T22) to give the main facts about something that you need

potential return *n phr* (CD1 T22) the amount of profit made by an investment or a business activity that is able to grow in the future

prompt *n* (58) words that help people to remember what they are going to say

reduce anxiety *v phr* (58) to make uncomfortable feelings of nervousness smaller in degree

rehearse *v* (58) to practise a play, a piece of music, etc. in order to prepare it for public performance

sound investment *n phr* (CD1 T22) when you put money, effort, time, etc. into something to make a profit in a way that shows good judgement

UNIT 13

avoid pitfalls *v phr* (CD1 T24) to prevent likely mistakes or problems in a situation from happening

build team spirit *v phr* (CD1 T23) to improve ways of thinking and acting that shows loyalty to your team and its members

cash in on *phr v* (64) to get money or another advantage from an event or situation, often in an unfair way

check in *phr v* (64) to show your ticket at an airport so that you can be told where you will be sitting and so that your bags can be put on the aircraft

flight status *n phr* (64) the situation at the present time about when an aircraft that is making a particular journey is likely to arrive or depart

get off to a dreadful start *v phr* (CD1 T24) to begin an activity very badly

loyalty programme *n phr* (64) a scheme rewarding customers for buying goods or services from a particular store or company

review *n* (64) a report that contains important information about a particular subject or activity

search engine *n phr* (64) a computer program that finds information on the Internet by looking for words that you have typed in a box on the screen

social network *n phr* (64) a website that allows users to post messages, information, images, etc. to other users

working hours *pl n* (63) the amount of time someone spends at work during a day

UNIT 14

behind the scenes *adv phr* (CD1 T28) If something happens behind the scenes, it happens without most people knowing about it, especially when something else is happening publicly.

boom *v* (CD1 T28) to experience an increase in economic activity, interest or growth

broaden the potential *v phr* (67) to increase the ability of something to develop, achieve or succeed

cater to *phr v* (CD1 T28) to try to satisfy a need

circumstantial *adj* (67) happening because of a particular situation

clear *v* (CD1 T27) to give official permission for something

collaboration *n* (67) the act of working together with other people or organisations to create or achieve something

counter-intuitive advice *n phr* (67) an opinion which someone offers you about what you should do in a particular situation which is not what you expect

cut off a conversation *v phr* (67) to stop a conversation suddenly

delegate *n* (66) a person who is chosen or elected by a group to speak or vote for it, especially at a meeting

estimate *n* (CD1 T25) a statement for a possible customer about how much a piece of work should cost

financial implication *n phr* (CD1 T27) the effect that an action or decision relating to money will have on something or someone

in due course *adv phr* (CD1 T25) at a suitable time in the future

industry peer *n phr* (67) a person who has a similar job to other people involved in one type of business

let an opportunity slip *v phr* (CD1 T27) to not use the possibility of doing something that you want to do or have to do)

old hand *n phr* (CD1 T26) someone who is very experienced and skilled in a particular area of activity

on request *adv phr* (CD1 T26) If something is available on request, you have to ask for it if you want it.

pen drive *n phr* (CD1 T26) a flash drive (= a small object for storing electronic data that can be connected to a computer and that can be carried about easily)

stroke of luck *n phr* (68) when something good happens suddenly by chance

up-and-coming *adj* (CD1 T28) likely to achieve success soon or in the near future

within close proximity to *adv phr* (CD1 T28) the state of being very near in space or time

UNIT 15

accountability *n* (71) a situation in which someone is responsible for things that happen and can give a satisfactory reason for them

agenda *n* (70) a list of things to be discussed during a meeting

bias *n* (71) the fact of allowing personal opinions to influence your judgement in an unfair way

chair *n* (70) a person who is in charge of a meeting

circulate *v* (70) to send something such as information, ideas or documents from one person to another

end in chaos *v phr* (CD1 T29) to finish in a state of total confusion with no order

face to face *adv phr, adj phr* (70) used to describe a situation in which you talk directly to another person, not by phone, email, online, etc.

know-how *n* (71) practical knowledge, experience and ability

meeting venue *n phr* (71) the place where a meeting happens

minutes *pl n* (70) the written record of what was said and decided at a meeting

morale *n* (71) the level of satisfaction felt by a person or group of people who work together

productive *adj* (CD1 T29) achieving good results

reach a conclusion *v phr* (CD1 T29) to make a decision about something

UNIT 16

correlation *n* (75) a connection between two or more things, especially when one of them causes or influences the other

front-office staff *n phr* (76) the people working in a company, bank, etc. who deal directly with customers

lucrative *adj* (75) earning or producing a lot of money

on the basis that *phr* (75) the reason why someone does something or why something happens

poor sales performance *n phr* (76) earning or producing only a small amount of money

rep *n* (74) abbreviation for 'sales representative': someone whose job is to sell a company's products or services, especially when this involves travelling to meet people or speaking to them on the phone

UNIT 17

align *v* (82) to change something so that it has a correct relationship to something else

at the last count *phr* (CD2 T3) when something was counted most recently

business function *n phr* (82) a particular area of responsibility of a company

counter-productive *adj* (CD2 T3) having an opposite effect to the one that was wanted, and therefore harmful

engage with *phr v* (82) to become involved with someone

hurt their budgets *v phr* (CD2 T3) reduce the amount of money you have available to spend

in an official capacity *n phr* (CD2 T3) as part of a particular position or job

insight *n* (82) a clear, deep and sometimes sudden understanding of a complicated problem or situation

intrinsically motivated *adj phr* (82) wanting to do something well as a basic characteristic of a person

next to nothing *n phr* (CD2 T3) almost nothing; very little

provoke a negative reaction *v phr* (CD2 T3) to do something that causes a bad feeling in people

special offer *n phr* (CD2 T3) goods that are sold at a lower price than usual

too good to miss *adj phr* (CD2 T3) If you say that something is too good to miss, you mean that it is a very good opportunity and that people should see it, do it, etc.

webinar *n* (82) an occasion when a group of people go online at the same time to study or discuss something

UNIT 18

anti-pollution law *n phr* (86) a rule, usually made by a government, that is opposed to or against damage caused to water, air, etc. by harmful substances or waste

boot up *phr v* (84) When a computer boots (up), it becomes ready for use by getting the necessary information into its memory, and when you boot (up) a computer, you cause it to do this.

breakdown in the system *n phr* (86) the failure of a way of doing things to work as it should

clean-air legislation *n phr* (86) a law or set of laws intended to prevent gases that harm the environment from being sent out into the air

climate change *n phr* (84) changes in the world's weather, particularly an increase in temperature, thought to be caused by things such as carbon dioxide in the atmosphere

emission *n phr* (CD2 T4) an amount of something, especially a gas that harms the environment, that is sent out into the air

environmentally friendly *adj phr* (84) designed or operating in a way that does not harm the environment

feature *n* (84) something that makes a product, machine or system different, and usually better, than others of a similar type

fraction *n* (85) a small part or amount of something

get staff involved *v phr* (85) to include people who work in a particular business in something, or to make them take part in or feel part of it

in nature *phr* (84) as the type or main characteristic of something

in practice *phr* (84) If something is true in practice, this is the real situation.

legal action *n phr* (86) the process of using lawyers, courts of law, etc. to solve disagreements, or an occasion when this happens

production process *n phr* (86) a method of producing goods

recycle *v* (85) to collect and treat rubbish in order to produce useful materials which can be used again

rent *n* (CD2 T4) the amount of money that you pay to rent something for a period of time

research lab *n* (CD2 T4) a room or building with scientific equipment where detailed study of a subject is done

resign *v* (86) to say that you have decided to leave your job

resource *n* (84) a useful or valuable possession or quality of a country, organisation or person

seek planning permission *v phr* (CD2 T4) to try to get an official agreement that something new can be built or an existing building can be changed

service charge *n* (CD2 T4) an amount of money paid to the owner of an apartment or office building for services such as cleaning and repairs

socially responsible *adj phr* (85) working or operating in ways that are not harmful to society or the environment

the paperless office *n phr* (84) a room or part of a building in which people work where information is kept on computers, not on paper

waste *n* (86) materials or substances with no use or value, for example, ones that are produced when other products are being made

waste power *v phr* (84) to use too much electricity or use it badly

work remotely *v phr* (CD2 T4) Employees who work remotely work mainly from home and communicate with the company by email and telephone.

UNIT 19

absenteeism *n* (88) the fact of staying away from work, especially without a good reason

at peak times *adv phr* (CD2 T5) at a time of day when a lot of people are using the same service, such as the Internet, phone, etc.

balance sheet *n* (CD2 T5) a financial statement that shows a company's assets and debts at a particular time

bandwidth *n* (CD2 T6) the amount of information that can be sent between computers, over a phone line, using radio signals, etc. in a particular amount of time

board meeting *n* (CD2 T5) an occasion when a group of people who are responsible for making rules and decisions on behalf of an organisation meet in order to discuss something

cashflow *n* (CD2 T5) the movement of money into and out of a company's accounts, used as a measure of how much money the company spends and receives and how much profit it makes over a particular period of time

channel ideas *v phr* (CD2 T8) to use suggestions or plans for doing something in a particular way

come in someone's remit *v phr* (CD2 T7) to be responsible for a particular area of work

cut down on *v phr* (CD2 T5) to reduce the amount or number of something

extra workload *n phr* (CD2 T5) a more-than-usual amount of work that a person or machine has to do within a particular period of time

implement change *v phr* (CD2 T8) to put the process of making something different into action

keep up with orders *v phr* (CD2 T6) to stay level with requests from customers for goods or services

on schedule *adv phr* (CD2 T5) not early or late

on the shop floor *adv phr* (CD2 T5) among the ordinary workers at a factory

output *n* (CD2 T5) the amount of goods and services, or waste products, that are produced by a particular economy, industry, company or worker

powers that be *n phr* (CD2 T6) important people who have authority over others

profit and loss *n phr* (CD2 T5) money that is earned or lost in trade or business

rush hour *n phr* (CD2 T5) one of the very busy times of the day on roads, trains, etc. in the morning when people are travelling to work and in the evening when people are going home

service provider *n* (CD2 T6) a company that provides internet connections and services

sick leave *n* (CD2 T5) a period of time that a worker is allowed to be away from work because they are ill

staff turnover *n phr* (88) the rate at which employees leave a company and are replaced by new employees

tie sthg in with *phr v* (CD2 T5) to plan something so that it happens as part of another activity

track orders in real time *v phr* (CD2 T6) to follow the movement or progress of requests from customers in the very short amount of time needed for computer systems to receive data and information and then communicate it or make it available

working conditions *pl n* (CD2 T6) the physical situation that someone works in or is affected by

UNIT 20

after-sales service *n phr* (94) the business activity that involves doing things for customers provided after they have paid for and received a product or service

base salary *n phr* (92) basic salary: the amount of money that someone earns every year in their job, not including any extra payments they may receive

benefits *pl n* (92) advantages such as medical insurance, life insurance and sick pay, that employees receive from their employer in addition to money

bookkeeping *n* (92) the activity of keeping records of all the money a company spends and receives

cashflow projection *n phr* (93) a calculation or guess about the future movement of money into and out of a company's accounts based on information that you have

cloud-based approach *n phr* (CD2 T9) the use of technology, services, software, etc. on the Internet rather than software and hardware that you buy and install on your computer

coding of systems *n phr* (CD2 T9) to represent information in a way that is not ordinary language, as with special signs or symbols, to make it easier to trade them between countries

competitive advantage *n phr* (CD2 T9) the conditions that make a business more successful than the businesses it is competing with, or a particular thing that makes it more successful

data centre *n phr* (CD2 T9) a place where a number of computers that contain large amounts of information can be kept safely

dissatisfied customer *n phr* (98) a person who buys a product or service and feels that that it is not as good as it should be

emergency hotline *n phr* (95) a special direct telephone line that people can use for dangerous or serious situations

file sharing *n phr* (93) the practice of distributing computer files, for example, images, films or music, among several computers

geeky *adj* (CD2 T9) used to describe someone who knows a lot about science or technology, especially computers

graphic design *n phr* (92) the skill or the work of arranging text and pictures, especially in the production of books, magazines, software, etc.

log on *phr v* (CD2 T9) to connect to a computer system by putting in a particular set of letters or numbers

monthly retainer *n phr* (92) an amount of money that you pay to someone in order to be sure that they can work for you when you need them to

net new clients *v phr* (92) to be successful in getting new customers to buy goods or services from your business

payroll tax *n phr* (92) any tax that is based on employees' pay, and is either paid by an employer or partly taken by an employer from what employees earn

people person *n phr* (CD2 T9) someone who is good at dealing with other people

perception *n* (CD2 T9) the way that someone thinks and feels about a company, product, service, etc.

realise cost savings *v phr* (93) to make money or a profit from spending less money than was planned

redundant site *n phr* (93) a place on the Internet which is no longer needed where a person, company or organisation can give information about their products or services

server *n* (93) a central computer that controls and provides information to other computers in a network

storage *n* (94) the act of keeping things somewhere so that they can be used later, especially goods or energy supplies

time zone *n phr* (93) one of the 24 parts into which the world is divided. The time in each zone is one hour earlier than in the zone east of it, and one hour later than in the zone west of it.

virus infection *n phr* (95) a harmful computer program intended to prevent computers from working normally

website hosting *n phr* (95) providing the computer equipment and software necessary for a website to be available on the Internet

UNIT 21

bring in *phr v* (CD2 T10) to introduce something new such as a product

car dealership *n phr* (98) a company that has permission to sell particular cars

deal with *phr v* (CD2 T10 to take action in order to achieve something or in order to solve a problem)

employee attitude *n phr* (98) the feelings that someone who is paid to work for someone else has, and the way this makes them behave

integrity *n* (99) the quality of being honest and having strong moral principles that you refuse to change

provider of choice *n phr* (98) the most popular company or organisation that sells a particular type of product or service

repeat customer *n phr* (98) someone who buys again from a company that they have used before

responsiveness *n* (99) used for talking about how quickly and well a person or organisation reacts to something

teamwork *n* (99) the activity of working together as a team, or the skills needed to do this

voucher *n* (CD2 T10) a printed piece of paper used to pay for particular goods or services, or to pay less than the usual price

UNIT 22

build long-term relationships *v phr* (CD2 T11) to create and develop ways of connecting with people over a long period of time

call-centre operative *n phr* (102) a person who works in a large office in which a company's employees provide information to its customers, or sell or advertise its goods or services by telephone

clear up *phr v* (CD2 T11) to give or find an explanation for something, or to deal with a problem or argument

exceed expectation *v phr* (103) to be even better than you were expecting

extend your customer base *v phr* (103) to increase the size or range of the group of people who buy or use a company's products or services

golden rule *n phr* (105) an important rule or principle, especially in a particular situation

handle an awkward customer *v phr* (103) to deal with a difficult person who is buying your product or service successfully

helpline *n* (103) a telephone service provided by an organisation or company to offer help and advice to people

lack of people skills *n phr* (103) not enough ability to deal with people in a friendly and effective way that achieves good results

point of purchase *n phr* (105) a place such as a store where a product is bought

project professionalism *v phr* (103) to have the combination of all the qualities that are connected with trained and skilled people, in a way that people notice

rapport *n* (103) a good understanding of someone and an ability to communicate well with them

retain a customer *v phr* (103) to keep or continue to have a person or an organisation that buys a product or service

reward *v* (105) to give someone money or other advantages in exchange for good behaviour or good work, etc.

valuable feedback *n phr* (105) useful information about something such as a new product or someone's work, that provides an idea of whether people like it or whether it is good

written brief *n* (CD2 T11) instructions on a piece of paper that explain what someone's work or task is

UNIT 23

have a lot on one's plate *v phr* (CD2 T12) to have a large amount of important work to deal with

line manager *n* (110) someone directly in charge of workers

work long hours *v phr* (110) to do a job for a large amount of time

UNIT 24

aptitude testing *n phr* (111) a test to find out whether someone has a natural ability for a particular type of work

autocratic *adj* (CD2 T13) controlled by one leader who has total power, and who does not allow anyone else to make decisions

best predictor *n phr* (111) the best way of saying what will happen in the future, based on knowledge or experience

career progression *n phr* (CD2 T14) the process of making progress to better jobs

corporate client *n phr* (CD2 T14) a large business that receives professional services from an organisation

culture-bound construct *n phr* (111) an idea based on the way of life or customs and beliefs of a particular group of people at a particular time

entry level *n phr* (CD2 T14) at or relating to the lowest level of an organisation, type of work, etc.

expat assignment *n phr* (111) the process of giving someone who does not live in their own country a particular job, task or responsibility

fill the position *v phr* (111) to employ someone to do a job

fit into their context *v phr* (CD2 T13) to do something that is accepted in the existing situation

intangible *adj* (111) used about a feeling or quality that does not exist in a physical way, or that is difficult to describe

integrate with local business culture *v phr* (CD2 T14) to become part of the ideas and ways of working of an organisation in a particular place

integrated marketing plan *n phr* (CD2 T14) the business activity that involves finding out what customers want, using that information to design products and services, and selling them effectively, in a combined form

international track record *n phr* (111) all the achievements or failures that someone or something has had in the past involving more than one country

middleman *n* (CD2 T14) a person or company that buys goods from the company that has produced them and makes a profit by selling them to a store or a user

pass this first hurdle *v phr* (111) to have to solve a problem at the start of something before you can make progress

post the position *v phr* (111) to advertise that a job is available

psychometric testing *n phr* (111) the activity of using tests that are designed to show someone's personality, mental ability, opinions, etc. in order to decide whether or not to employ them

risk-averse *adj* (111) not wanting to take risks

service line *n phr* (CD2 T14) a range of similar business activities that are sold by the same company, with different features and different prices

soft skill *n phr* (CD2 T14) a particular ability, idea or knowledge that helps a business to be successful

standard business norm *n phr* (111) a way of buying and selling goods and services or doing things that is generally accepted

steep learning curve *n phr* (111) the rate of someone's progress in learning a very difficult new skill

straightforward *adj* (CD2 T14) easy to understand or simple

take lightly *v phr* (111) to treat in a way that is not serious

take up employment *v phr* (CD2 T13) to start doing a new job

transferable skill *n phr* (CD2 T14) a particular ability used in one job or career that can also be used in another

withstand the rigours *v phr* (111) to deal with unpleasant or severe conditions successfully

Exam skills and Exam practice

Contents

Note that this section of the book focuses only on the sections of the BULATS Test that require most practice at this level.

About BULATS

BULATS stands for the Business Language Testing Service. It is a service for companies designed to help them find out the level of language skills among their staff, trainees or job applicants. It assesses language skills which are needed for the workplace, and for students and employees on language courses or on professional/business courses where foreign-language ability is an important element of the course.

BULATS provides tests for all learners of a foreign language. There is no 'pass mark'. Candidates are placed in one of six levels. These levels are expressed as ALTE (Association of Language Testers in Europe) levels, which are linked to the Council of Europe's Common European Framework of Reference for Languages (CEFR) levels. This is explained in the table below.

ALTE levels	Common European Framework of Reference for Languages (CEFR) Level	BULATS scores	Level description	Equivalent Main Suite Exam
Level 5	C2	90–100	Upper-Advanced	Cambridge English: Proficiency (CPE)
Level 4	C1	75–89	Advanced	Cambridge English: Advanced (CAE), Business Higher
Level 3	B2	60–74	Upper-Intermediate	Cambridge English: First (FCE), Business Vantage
Level 2	B1	40–59	Intermediate	Cambridge English: Preliminary (PET), Business Preliminary
Level 1	A2	20–39	Elementary	Cambridge English: Key (KET)
Level 0	A1	0–19	Beginner	–

At the moment, six different types of test are offered: the BULATS Computer-based Tests (Online Reading and Listening Test; Online Speaking Test; Online Writing Test) and the BULATS Paper-based Tests (the Paper-based Standard Test; the Paper-based Writing Test; the Paper-based Speaking Test).

BULATS Online Tests can be taken on any computer with a fast internet connection. No software needs to be downloaded or installed. A tutorial and demonstration test are available for candidates to familiarise themselves with the task types. On-screen help guides are available throughout the tests and information-for-candidates handbooks are also available.

Test lengths

The **Paper-based Standard Test** lasts 110 minutes and tests listening and reading skills and knowledge of grammar and vocabulary. The **Paper-based Writing Test** lasts 45 minutes and tests writing skills and knowledge of grammar and vocabulary. The **Paper-based Speaking Test** lasts a maximum of 12 minutes and tests your ability to speak in a foreign language in a business context. The **Online Reading and Listening Test** lasts about an hour; the **Online Speaking Test** lasts about 15 minutes and the **Online Writing Test** lasts 45 minutes.

The Standard Test

Skill	Part or section	Type of task	Number of questions
Listening	1	Understanding short conversations or monologues	10
	2	Taking down phone messages, orders, notes, etc.	12
	3	Listening for gist: identifying topic, context or function	10
	4	Listening to extended speech for detail and inference	18
Reading and language knowledge	1.1	Understanding notices, messages, timetables, adverts, graphs, etc.	7
	1.2	Gapped sentences	6
	1.3	Reading passage with multiple-choice questions	6
	1.4	Short reading passage; gap filling	5
	2.1	Four short reading passages; sentence matching	7
	2.2	Short reading passage; multiple-choice gap filling	5
	2.3	Short reading passage; gap filling	5
	2.4	Gapped sentences	6
	2.5	Long reading passage with multiple-choice questions	6
	2.6	Error correction	7

The Writing Test

	Part or section	Type of task	Time (approx.)
Writing	1	Short message/letter (50–60 words)	15 minutes
	2	Report or letter (180–200 words)	30 minutes

The Speaking Test

	Part or section	Type of task	Time (approx.)
Speaking	1	Interview	4 minutes
	2	Presentation	4 minutes
	3	Information exchange and discussion	4 minutes

Listening Test Part 4: Exam skills

Part 4 consists of:

- three interviews, discussions or conversations with two or more speakers or a presentation or report with just one speaker
- six multiple-choice questions for each section.

You must choose **A**, **B** or **C**.

You practised similar skills in Unit 6 (page 30) and in Unit 18 (page 87).

This part of the exam tests your ability to:

- follow longer listening tasks
- interpret what the speakers say in order to choose the correct option.

Multiple-choice questions in the Listening Test

Each question has three options. One is the correct answer, the others are 'distractors'. You have to distinguish the relevant information from the distractors. Be careful when you listen, because the speakers will usually mention something connected with the distractors. You must be alert in order to decide that they are the wrong answers.

Suggested exam technique

1 Use the pause between listening to the instructions and listening to the recording to:
   - read each question and underline the key words
   - study the options for the first few questions and predict how these might be expressed.
2 The speaker will probably say something about all three options. Listen carefully to discard the wrong options.
3 Remember: the speakers will probably not use the same words as are used in the questions – you have to listen for them to express the same meaning using different words.
4 Use the pause between listening the first time and listening the second time to check the questions which give you problems.
5 The Listening paper needs a lot of concentration. Make sure you keep concentrating hard until the end of the paper!

Exercises

1 a **You are going to hear an interview with Frances Greene whose company supplies cosmetics to hairdressers and beauty salons. Before you listen:**

   - underline the key words in these questions
   - check with a partner, and then discuss how Frances might express each option in the questions using other words.

   b ②15 **Listen and answer these questions.**

   1 How does Frances measure customer satisfaction in her business?
      A She employs a market research firm.
      B She carries out regular surveys.
      C She maintains informal contacts with all her customers.
   2 What is the most common problem she has with customers?
      A They are late paying for goods.
      B They demand higher quality than she can give.
      C They only buy at certain times of year.
   3 What is her most effective marketing tool?
      A word of mouth
      B her website
      C direct mail

   c **Check in the transcript to see how each option is discussed and which one is correct.**

To try a real exam task, go to page 137.

Listening Test Part 4: Exam practice

② 16 Section 1: Questions 33–38

- You will hear part of a lecture to business students about a transport group called Carter.
- For questions **33–38**, circle **one** letter, **A**, **B** or **C**, for the correct answer.
- You will hear the lecture twice.

33 What is the Carter Group's strategy?
  A to offer all its services in a number of countries
  B to sell off loss-making divisions
  C to focus on growth in its strongest geographical markets

34 One of Carter's strengths is its system of
  A constantly improving its management processes.
  B using customer surveys to improve service.
  C collaboration between its businesses.

35 Carter has won awards for reducing
  A the fuel consumption of buses.
  B the amount of waste that cannot be recycled.
  C business travel by its employees.

36 One reason why the new CEO was appointed was because of his experience
  A with a competitor.
  B in an international company.
  C within the Carter Group.

37 How did Carter perform financially last year?
  A better than many analysts had expected at the beginning of the year
  B quite well, considering the problems it faced
  C worse than in the previous year

38 According to the speaker, what is the main reason why Carter's future looks positive?
  A demand for train services
  B savings that the Group plans to make
  C growth in bus services

② 17 Section 2: Questions 39–44

- You will hear a discussion between a man called James and a woman called Trish, who both work in a conference centre's marketing team.
- For questions **39–44**, circle **one** letter, **A**, **B** or **C**, for the correct answer.
- You will hear the discussion twice.

39 What does James think is a problem with their current newspaper and magazine advertising?
  A It is likely to attract only local interest.
  B It doesn't show the unique features of the centre.
  C It gives too much information about the centre.

40 What image do they think the conference centre should have?
  A luxurious
  B relatively cheap
  C relaxed and comfortable

41 Which type of bookings does Trish want to try to increase?
  A repeat bookings
  B conferences and other large events
  C meetings and other small events

42 What market research do they decide to carry out first?
  A written surveys for local organisations
  B telephone surveys of past customers
  C online surveys for visitors to the website

43 How do they decide the first survey should be produced and administered?
  A They will draft it themselves, then involve a market-research agency.
  B They will ask a market-research agency to do it all.
  C They will do all the work themselves.

44 What do they say about the budget for the new marketing plan?
  A They need to find out how much has been allocated.
  B The amount hasn't yet been decided.
  C The CEO thinks the budget is too small.

② 18 Section 3: Questions 45–50

- You will hear a radio interview with Sally MacArthur, an executive coach, about conflict at work.
- For questions **45–50**, circle **one** letter, **A**, **B** or **C**, for the correct answer.
- You will hear the interview twice.

45 Sally MacArthur thinks there is more conflict at work now than in the past because
  A rules have not adapted to suit changes in the workforce.
  B there is a greater emphasis nowadays on establishing rules.
  C rules now give employees greater rights than in the past.

46 Sally MacArthur believes the people who are most to blame for conflicts at work are those who
  A behave aggressively.
  B avoid disagreement.
  C express their opinions freely.

47 Sally MacArthur says that if we raise problems with colleagues early,
  A it risks focusing attention on a problem that might otherwise resolve itself.
  B we will be able to distinguish between the person and the problem.
  C they have a better chance to find a way of improving the situation.

48 What does Sally MacArthur say about dealing with a problem face to face?
  A It makes people aware of each other's reactions.
  B People may lose their temper and be rude.
  C There is no time for people to think about their responses.

49 What advice does Sally MacArthur give about dealing with problems?
  A Don't offend other people.
  B Don't suggest that other people need to improve.
  C Don't be concerned only to win.

50 Sally MacArthur says that certain TV programmes
  A give an unbalanced view of the business world.
  B show that strength is admired in the business world.
  C fail to suggest ways of dealing with aggressive colleagues.

Reading Test Part 2 (Section 2): Exam skills

Part 2 Section 2 consists of:

- one text of about 100 words
- five multiple-choice gaps.

You must choose the best word, A, B, C or D.

You practised similar skills in Unit 1 (pages 8–9) and Unit 13 (page 64).

This part of the exam tests your knowledge of:
- vocabulary
- dependent prepositions (e.g. *depend on, succeed in*)
- grammatical structures which go with particular words (e.g. *make* + object + infinitive without *to*)
- expressions
- phrasal verbs
- linking words
- collocations.

Collocations

Collocations are words that are often found together, but which are not fixed expressions. Collocations may be:
- adjectives with nouns, e.g. *You will have to work to **tight deadlines**.*
- adverbs with verbs, e.g. *Prices have **risen sharply**.*
- verbs with nouns, e.g. *He was unable to **repay his debts**.*

Suggested exam technique

1 Before looking at the options, A, B, C and D, try to think which word will go in the gap – you may be surprised to find it's one of the options!
2 The options will have similar meanings: look for a dependent preposition or a grammatical structure which only goes with one of the options.
3 Look for possible collocations: do you *do, achieve, succeed* or *provide a service*? (Answer: *provide*)
4 When you have finished, read the text again with your answers. Check and change anything which doesn't sound natural to you.

Exercises

1 Choose the best word for each of these gaps. In each case, the correct word is the only one which will go with the dependent preposition. (Note that the preposition is not always just after the gap.)

> When you **1** .... for an interview, your interviewers will **2** .... not just on your skills and experience but also your personality to see whether you will **3** .... comfortably into their organisation and do a good job.

  1   A attend   B present   C give   (D) go
  2   A look   (B) focus   C examine   D investigate
  3   A match   (B) suit   C fit   D relate

2 Choose the best word for each of these gaps. In each case, the correct word will form a collocation.

> Although Bernard Lasky has a reputation for **1** .... a hard bargain after many years in sales, he **2** .... recommends negotiators to give clients a good deal. That, he insists, is the only way to ensure **3** .... long-term customers.

  1   A forcing   (B) making   C driving   D fixing
  2   (A) strongly   B strictly   C totally   D hardly
  3   A faithful   (B) loyal   C friendly   D dependable

3 Choose the best word for each of these gaps. In most cases, the correct word will depend on the grammatical structure of the sentence as well as the meaning.

> When launching a new product, you are **1** .... to carry out market research which will give you enough information to **2** .... you position your product correctly in the market. Moreover, it will help you **3** .... your promotional activities better.

  1   (A) suggested   B advised   C insisted   D warned
  2   A let   B allow   C permit   (D) facilitate
  3   A produce   (B) plan   C invent   D create

To try a real exam task, go to page 140.

Reading Test Part 2 (Section 2): Exam practice

Questions 1–5

- Read this article about training for managers.
- Choose the best word to fill each gap from the words below.
- For each question **1–5**, mark one letter, **A**, **B**, **C** or **D**, on your Answer Sheet.

Example:

He wants you to (**0**) .... him the reason.

0 A speak   **B** tell   **C** say   **D** talk

Answer:

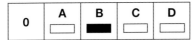

Consultancy training for managers

Consultancy is an important part of a manager's work, but we rarely (**1**) .... about it. Managers may spend a third of their time (**2**) .... what are really consulting activities, such as identifying ways in which to improve the company's processes and add value to its activities. (**3**) .... , in traditional management training, very little time is (**4**) ....

on helping potential managers to improve their consulting skills.

Our training sessions are (**5**) .... mainly for new managers. We show them that consultancy is an exciting professional activity that can immediately be applied in the workplace.

1	**A** consider	**B** imagine	**C** suppose	**D** think
2	**A** taking place	**B** carrying out	**C** taking part	**D** carrying off
3	**A** Therefore	**B** Unless	**C** However	**D** Despite
4	**A** spent	**B** passed	**C** made	**D** kept
5	**A** supposed	**B** intended	**C** aimed	**D** destined

Reading Test Part 2 (Section 3): Exam skills

Part 2 Section 3 consists of:

- one text of about 100 words
- five gaps which you must fill with one word.

You practised similar skills in Unit 7 (page 34) and Unit 21 (page 101).

This part of the exam tests your knowledge of grammar, especially:

- prepositions (*to, with, from, as,* etc.)
- articles (*a, an, the*)
- auxiliary verbs (*have, is, was,* etc.)
- pronouns (*this, he, one,* etc.)
- relative pronouns (*who, where, what,* etc.)
- grammar adverbs (*however, still, yet,* etc.).

What type of word?

The position of a word in the sentence will often tell you what type of word you need. For example:

- between the subject and the main verb, you need an auxiliary verb, a modal verb or an adverb: *Many businesses .... formed by serial entrepreneurs.* (auxiliary verb: *are*)
- before a noun, you need an adjective, an article or a preposition:
  He noted that .... businesses are formed by serial entrepreneurs. (adjective: *many*)
  Fewer than half of .... businesses formed by people under 25 are successful. (article: *the*)
  Banks are ready to lend money .... businesses which have solid assets. (preposition: *to*)

Suggested exam technique

1 Read the whole text first.
2 Look at each gap, sentence by sentence.
3 Consider what type of word you need – this will depend on the position of the word in the sentence.
4 When you know what type of word you need, think of options and try them in the gap.
5 Look carefully at the other words in the sentence, e.g. .... *interesting than* needs *more* to complete the comparative structure.
6 If you can't think of a word, leave it and come back to it later.
7 Don't leave any gaps blank – if you can't think of the correct word, make an intelligent guess: you may be right!
8 When you have finished, read the whole text again: does it read logically with the words you have chosen?

Exercises

1 Complete the table below with these words.

although   an   are   be   being   can   forward   have
it   much   so   than   the   they   to   what   who   with

Article	Pronoun	Relative pronoun	Auxiliary/ modal verb	Preposition	Other

2 a Read these sentences with a partner and decide what type of word would fit each gap.

1 During .... most recent recession, house prices fell by 23%.

2 The consultancy firm Brace and Nichols has put .... a plan for a complete restructuring of the company.

3 In his speech to the AGM, Mr Ishiguro stated that the price of shares .... risen by more than 20% last year.

4 Recently, the company has been performing badly, and .... of the main reasons for this is high oil prices.

5 The firm Bahrain International Imports has reached an agreement .... Isoltis to set up a joint venture in the Gulf region.

6 Despite the buoyancy of the electronics market, new electronic consumer products are .... more likely to fail than to sell profitably.

7 Sales targets for this year have been set at higher levels .... last year.

8 He argued that such long-standing clients should have .... given a much higher discount.

9 John Corfield, ... previously worked in sales for General Electric, has been appointed CEO.

10 .... customers don't want is to be faced with too many choices.

b Complete the sentences by writing one word in each gap.

3 Write one word for each gap below. If you are not sure, decide what type of word you need, then choose from the words in Exercise 1.

How rational are your investment and other personal finance decisions? In many cases, something may **1** .... seemed a good idea at the time, but when you review your investment portfolio, the haphazard pattern could **2** .... embarrassing. It may also reveal how often you bought into shares or funds at **3** .... top of the market. This is the most obvious example of illogical investor behaviour. About 70 per cent of the UK's private investors admit that their investments are a mess, according **4** .... a recent survey. It found that 135 of investors did not even know **5** .... they had invested in. All these examples of apparently bizarre activity **6** .... increasingly coming under a new microscope labelled behavioural finance. This is a branch of economic psychology that compares actual investor behaviour **7** .... the alleged purely rational approach dictated by classic economic theory.

4 Write one word for each gap.

In 2004, Benton Electronics announced that **1** .... were moving their head office from the centre of Burton to a new purpose-built office building on a green-field site on the outskirts. At first, **2** .... were a number of protests from staff **3** .... thought their journey times to and from work **4** .... be significantly increased. However, when the move was made, **5** .... soon became apparent that the new offices were a success, not just with customers but **6** .... with staff. **7** .... customers and staff found the company offices' proximity to the motorway extremely convenient. **8** .... addition to the easy access, free parking in the company car park **9** .... an added bonus. Another factor contributing **10** .... the success of the new site has been the comfort of the offices and the views of the countryside.

To try a real exam task, go to page 144.

Reading Test Part 2 (Section 3): Exam practice

Questions 6–10

- For questions **6–10**, read the text below and think of the word which best fits each space.
- Write only **one** word for each space on your Answer Sheet.

Example:

He is very interested (**0**) .... computers.

Answer:

0	*in*	▭ ▭

Remote working

Nowadays, more and more company employees are based (**6**) .... home. This means that the firm needs less office space, and workers have more flexibility with regard to when they work. However, some people adapt better (**7**) .... others to this way of working. The skills that are needed include self-motivation, an ability to deal

(**8**) .... various forms of technology, and an ability to organise their time. Perhaps (**9**) .... most important thing is not a skill but something practical: they also need a room, preferably a quiet one, (**10**) .... that they can work without being disturbed. This is particularly important if they have young children.

Reading Test Part 2 (Section 4): Exam skills

Part 2 Section 4 consists of:

- six sentences with gaps.

You must choose the word or phrase, A, B, C or D, which completes the gap.

You practised similar skills in your Personal Study Book: Unit 16 (page 36) and Unit 21 (page 46).

This part of the exam tests your knowledge of vocabulary and grammar, especially:

- meanings of individual words
- collocations (see page 139).

Suggested exam technique

1 Decide if the question is asking you about vocabulary or grammar.
2 If it is asking you about vocabulary:
   - choose the word which sounds natural in the context
   - look for clues in the sentence: prepositions, etc.
   If you don't know, discard the answers which you think are wrong and choose one of the others.
3 If it is asking you about grammar:
   - which word fits the grammar? For example, is there a verb + -ing (e.g. hoping) or an infinitive (e.g. to hope) after the gap? If there is a verb + -ing, perhaps the word you need is a preposition.
   If you don't know, discard the answers you think are wrong and choose from the others.

Exercises

1 **In this exercise, all the options have similar meanings, but only one is correct in the context. Work with a partner. Choose the option which is correct.**

   1 Unless production is kept on .... , we will fall behind with our orders.
      A timetable
      B schedule
      C agenda
      D programme
   2 Toyota are planning to launch a new .... of their Lexus range in June.
      A make B brand C model D trademark
   3 He's a skilled negotiator who is known to drive a hard ....
      A bargain B deal C agreement D contract

2 **Work with a partner. Choose the correct answers and say why the other options are wrong. Where possible, say which preposition they would need.**

   1 Comcam Ltd are looking for local suppliers in order to reduce their .... on imported components.
      A necessity
      B requirement
      C need
      D reliance
   2 One of the best decisions we ever made was to .... part of our profits in a new fleet of vans.
      A invest B spend C expend D pay
   3 If you're sending the goods by sea, it is essential to .... against any accidents which might happen during the journey.
      A guarantee B cover C insure D assure

3 **Work in pairs. Choose the correct answer and say how you would need to change the sentence to make one or two of the other options correct, e.g. *Despite their sales undergoing a record expansion, ...***

   1 Comcam's profits in the last year were disappointing, ... their sales underwent a record expansion.
      A despite
      B although
      C however
      D nevertheless
   2 Dieter Schmidt has just taken over as Managing Director after working as Head of Human Resources .... the last five years.
      A for B in C over D during
   3 We won't consider stocking their products .... them giving us a hefty discount.
      A providing B unless C without D except

To try a real exam task, go to page 146.

Reading Test Part 2 (Section 4): Exam practice

Questions 11–16

- Choose the word or phrase which best completes each sentence.
- For questions **11–16**, mark **one** letter, **A**, **B**, **C** or **D**, on your Answer Sheet.

11 .... all our efforts to find a new finance director, nobody suitable has been identified.
  - **A** Contrary to
  - **B** However
  - **C** In spite of
  - **D** Although

12 Financial services .... for a high proportion of the country's GDP.
  - **A** account
  - **B** comprise
  - **C** amount
  - **D** consist

13 The Marketing Manager has decided to turn .... a job offer from one of our competitors, and stay with us.
  - **A** up
  - **B** away
  - **C** down
  - **D** off

14 Before we go any further with development, we need to .... potential demand for our new product.
  - **A** count
  - **B** gauge
  - **C** reckon
  - **D** guess

15 The company needs some less able staff to leave, to .... people with fresh ideas.
  - **A** take up with
  - **B** stand up for
  - **C** go out with
  - **D** make way for

16 Struggling retailer KMO is going from one crisis to another – it's only a .... before it goes out of business.
  - **A** breathing space
  - **B** matter of time
  - **C** limited period
  - **D** well-earned rest

Reading Test Part 2 (Section 5): Exam skills

Part 2 Section 5 consists of:

- one text of 450–550 words
- six multiple-choice questions where you must choose the best answer, **A**, **B**, **C** or **D**.

You practised similar skills in Unit 5 (page 27) and Unit 21 (page 99).

This part of the exam tests your ability to:

- read in detail
- understand cohesive devices
- interpret opinions and ideas expressed in the text as well as facts.

Skimming

Skimming consists of reading very fast to get a general idea of the meaning and contents of the whole text (for example, you get a long email marked urgent just before you are going into an important meeting and you have to decide what action to take very quickly).

- When you see unfamiliar words or sentences you don't understand, do not spend time trying to understand them – continue reading.
- Only worry about difficult vocabulary or sentences if you find there is a question about them.

Suggested exam technique

1 Skim the text first to get a quick, general idea of what it says.
2 Read the stem of the first question (the part before the options A, B, C or D) and underline the key words.
3 Find where the question is dealt with in the text and read that part carefully.
4 Read the four options and choose the answer which matches what you understood when reading the text. Remember: the words of the text will not repeat the words of the question. You will have to find the same idea expressed in a different way.
5 Underline the words in the text which support your answer.
6 The answers to the questions come in the same order in the text, so when you have answered one question, move on to the next part of the text to answer the next question.
7 Be careful about time. If you take too long with this part, you won't have enough time for other parts.

Exercises

1 **Skim the text below in about two minutes. Then decide which of these is the best summary of the passage.**

1 How Tim achieved success
2 How the education system needs to change
3 Why graduates cannot get jobs

Degrees are not the only route to success

by Louisa Peacock

Tim Reynolds, 25, is feeling pleased with himself, and he has reason to be. It is just five years since he finished the apprenticeship which he did against the advice of his teachers, who had told him that unless he went to university, he would struggle to make something of himself. Tim had always known he wanted to do something 'hands-on' and potentially run his own business one day, rather than follow the route to university. He knew further classroom-based study was not for him, although he was more than capable, having achieved excellent exam grades, and he couldn't wait to leave school at 16.

Trying to convince his teachers that this was what he wanted to do was difficult, he recalls. 'My teachers were very one-track minded: university was the only way to become somebody and make something of yourself,' he says. 'There weren't a huge number of options – a degree was seen as the only way to go.'

Despite all that, he has already set up his own business and is looking to take on his first worker. His new firm, Younique, provides plumbing and heating services based on the skills he learned during his four-year apprenticeship at Aquacare, a local plumbing business. Upon finishing his training scheme, he was promoted to run the loss-making bathroom division of Aquacare, which he turned into a profit within six months. His newly gained finance and management skills, coupled with his craft skills, gave him the confidence to go it alone. When the firm was hit by the recession and had to make some redundancies, he saw it as the perfect time for him to become his own boss.

A growing number of employment experts want to see schools actively encourage entrepreneurialism, or vocational training, in the same way they highlight degrees. Professor Ewart Keep, of Cardiff University, says the most successful education systems in Europe combine apprenticeship and higher-education career paths, and these remove the stigma often associated with choosing on-the-job learning at 16 over a degree. 'A lot of kids don't want to stay in school or college, they want to get on into the world of work and earn a wage. Most other European countries make a significant effort to accredit people who go through that route. The UK Government is right to place the stress on apprenticeships, but quality needs to be improved,' he says.

A survey by Adecco, the recruitment giant, this week revealed one in three employers believe the university system fails to equip students with the skills required by business. Chris Moore, Managing Director, called for financial acumen and communication skills to form a core part of curricula from an early age.

Tim believes that expected increases in university tuition fees will make people think twice about university and pursue other options. 'I'm not anti-university, but young people need to go for the right reasons,' he says. He believes that had there been more awareness of the so-called 'real world' during school, learning the business-savvy skills needed to make it beyond getting a degree, he would have had the confidence to go it alone far sooner. And so might many of his classmates.

adapted from the *Daily Telegraph*

2 Underline the key idea in each question (1–5), but do *not* read the options (A–D).

1 Why did Tim <u>disregard the advice of his teachers</u>?
A He felt a university course would be too difficult for him.
B He wanted to do something more practical.
C He felt his teachers did not understand his ambitions.
D He wanted a career in international business.

2 What prompted Tim to start his own business?
A The knowledge he had acquired in a previous job
B The lack of alternative employment opportunities
C The encouragement he received from his bank
D The excellent economic situation

3 What does Professor Keep say about apprenticeships?
A They can cause anxiety for many trainees.
B They are a more effective way of learning than going to university.
C They are a good option for less-intelligent young people.
D They should be more closely integrated with other forms of study.

4 According to Adecco, young people should be taught the ability to
A make good decisions concerning money.
B express their needs clearly.
C handle mathematics and language well.
D manage office equipment and systems.

5 What point is Tim making in the final paragraph?
A For most young people, university is a wrong choice.
B With the right education, more young people would become entrepreneurs.
C It is hard to justify the cost of a university education.
D Young people need to have more belief in their own abilities.

3 Use the names and the key ideas you have underlined to find where the text deals with each question. For each question:

- read that part of the text carefully to find the answer
- when you are confident you have the answer, look at the options and choose the option which matches what you have understood
- underline the words in the text which gave you the answer.

To try a real exam task, go to page 149.

Reading Test Part 2 (Section 5): Exam practice

Questions 17–22

- Read the article below about recruiting new staff and answer questions **17–22** on the opposite page.
- For questions **17–22**, mark **one** letter, **A**, **B**, **C** or **D**, on your Answer Sheet.

Just as people like to think they're well above average as drivers, so it is in business when it comes to spotting and hiring top talent. Of course, this is rarely true, but it means that hiring great people too often remains a hit-or-miss affair, regardless of how much time and money are devoted to the process. The risks are magnified in the case of senior and board-level appointments, as the downside of getting such critical hires wrong is much greater. But it doesn't have to be that way. Here are a few pointers for those faced with employing new staff for their company.

Be methodical. Too often, recruiters compile long, even contradictory, lists of desirable qualities and lose any clear sense of priorities. Avoid the standard 'must haves' that every company seems to use, and instead take time to think through what the role *really* requires: a short, well-focused list is far more likely to pay off. Ask yourself what skills your company needs that it's currently short of. Don't just look for a junior copy of yourself, as so many do, on the basis that that person will fit into the company easily: keep your eyes open for strengths that will bring added value to the business.

When it comes to board-level appointments, strategic vision is an obvious requirement, but it isn't enough. The candidates who really impress are those who are able to connect the dots in a decision-making environment that isn't fully clear. They are able to see the impact of their decisions. They may or may not have IQs that put Nobel prizewinners to shame, but they have an ability to reason through the day-to-day challenges of a senior executive's job without getting lost in the details or misreading a situation.

For senior positions, it's worth involving external experts in the assessment: some major recruitment firms create short scenarios in which candidates must figure out the best course of action, with very little time to collect their thoughts. The pressure is enormous. Lose concentration for a moment and you're lost. Many scenarios involve long-lasting conflicts in corporate settings that demand clear resolution. The winning approach is seldom obvious: that's business. The candidates who can juggle these imaginary competing forces in their minds – and come up with a workable resolution – are the ones who are more likely to make the right calls in the everyday give-and-take of business.

Too often in top business circles, listening is regarded as a sign of weakness. All the glory belongs to the presenters, projecting their ideas and energy onto an enthusiastic audience. Start seeing the world that way, and new encounters become affected by an unhelpful desire to dominate the conversation. By contrast, good listeners gain authority by being extremely attentive to other people. These experts catch the gestures, pauses and inflections that hint at something beyond the words being said. The most important thing a person has to tell you is what they're not telling you. So when interviewing potential staff, at any level, make sure you find out whether they can listen as well as speak.

17 What is said about recruitment in the first paragraph?

    A   There is a shortage of talented people for senior positions.

    B   Companies often spend too much time and money on recruitment.

    C   Senior managers should play a greater role in recruiting staff.

    D   People responsible for recruiting often overestimate their skill.

18 One of the writer's recommendations about listing qualities is to

    A   aim to make the list as complete as possible.

    B   identify useful skills that your company currently lacks.

    C   compare them with those that other companies specify.

    D   focus on skills that will enable the candidate to fit in with colleagues.

19 What quality does the writer rate highest in board members?

    A   skill at making long-term plans

    B   the ability to understand a situation in detail

    C   a high level of intelligence

    D   the ability to see the broader picture

20 The writer recommends business simulations where candidates

    A   need to find solutions under pressure.

    B   are able to compare their solutions with each other.

    C   have time to consider alternative solutions.

    D   deal with situations suggested by the company for which they are being assessed.

21 According to the final paragraph, what does the writer consider a common fault?

    A   allowing oneself to be dominated in conversation by other people

    B   people believing they are better at listening than they really are

    C   considering the ability to persuade as superior to listening skills

    D   paying too much attention to gestures rather than the words that are used

22 What is the best title for this article?

    A   The best questions to ask when interviewing applicants

    B   How to ensure you appoint the best applicant

    C   Making your application stand out above the rest

    D   What makes the recruitment process harder than it seems

Reading Test Part 2 (Section 6): Exam skills

Part 2 Section 6 consists of:
- one text of 100–150 words; the text contains seven lines and in each line there may be one word which is not correct.

You must find the word which is not correct and write the correct word.

Some lines may be correct.

You practised similar skills in Unit 23 (page 108) of this book and Unit 24 (page 113).

This part of the exam tests your:
- ability to identify and correct errors in texts
- knowledge of grammar.

> **Wrong words**
>
> You should look for 'grammar words'. Here are some examples with the wrong word crossed out. The correct word is in brackets at the end of the sentence:
> - pronouns, e.g. *We put the product on the market last month and ~~he~~ is selling well.* (it)

> - relative pronouns, e.g. *I'm happy to stock your product, but ~~that~~ I don't want is for it not to sell.* (what)
> - conjunctions, e.g. *~~If~~ we can sell the product immediately, we will withdraw it from the market without hesitation.* (unless)
> - auxiliary or modal verbs, e.g. *Over the last five years, job cuts in the industry ~~are~~ lowered morale among workers.* (have)
> - prepositions, e.g. *We need to concentrate ~~in~~ quality.* (on)
> - short adverbs, e.g. *Running your own business is ~~so~~ a challenging job; it should not be undertaken unless you are prepared for hard work.* (such)

Suggested exam technique

1 Skim the text quickly to get a general idea of what it's about.
2 Although there will be an incorrect word in most lines, read the text by sentences, not by lines.
3 There will not be more than one wrong word per line.
4 Remember that some lines are correct, but read each sentence carefully to make sure.

Exercises

1 **Some of the lines in this letter have a wrong word. Cross out the wrong word and write the correct word in the gap on the right. If a line is correct, put a tick (✓) in the gap. All the wrong words are auxiliary verbs, modal verbs or verbs.**

Dear Mr Inskip,	
Thank you for the visit you paid us last Monday. It was most interesting	1 ....✓....
to see your latest range of swimwear, and I think it ~~would~~ do very well	2 ...will...
when the next season start.	3 ....
We would like to place an order for 2,500 items, which I list on the	4 ....
enclosed order form, as long as we may reach an agreement on payment	5 ....
terms. One of our managers have asked me if it is also possible to ask for	6 ....
different colours and patterns to being included in the range apart from	7 ....
the ones which are showing in the catalogue.	8 ....
I look forward to hearing from you shortly.	
Yours sincerely	
Fernando Delgado	

2   Some of the lines in this letter have a wrong word. Cross out the wrong word and write
    the correct word in the gap on the right. If a line is correct, put a tick (✓) in the gap. All
    the wrong words are prepositions.

Memo To: All staff From: CEO Subject: Staff meeting Management is considering changes ~~of~~ working practices, and we would welcome suggestions from staff. For this purpose, we will be holding a meeting at 4 pm on Wednesday 4 August by the staff canteen. You can either put your suggestions on an email to me, or you can make them at the meeting. Some ideas to think of include: • career breaks for staff from over ten years' service • flexitime, especially to parents with young children. Many thanks	1 *in/to* 2 ✓ 3 *in* 4 5 *or* 6 7 *for*

3   Some of the lines in this letter have a wrong word. Cross out the wrong word and write
    the correct word in the gap on the right. If a line is correct, put a tick (✓) in the gap. The
    wrong words are all the wrong type of word, e.g. an adjective instead of an adverb or a
    noun instead of a verb.

Dear Mrs Pereira You may ~~memory~~ that we met at the Footwear International Fair in Santiago last year. At present, we are extreme active in developing our business with South America and are particularly interesting in expansion our imports of clothing products from all over the continent. I shall be in São Paulo brief next month and I would welcome the opportunity to meet you and discussion the possibility of us distributing your products in Europe (which you mentioned at the fair). If you still find this possible of interest, please let me know, and we can arrange a meeting. My diary is already quite fill, so please let me know soon when you would find a meeting most convenient. Yours sincerely, Pierre Lauriac	1 remember 2 currently 3 interested 4 expand 5 appreciate 6 discuss 7 8 consider 9 agenda 10 arrange

To try a real exam task, go to page 153.

Reading Test Part 2 (Section 6): Exam practice

Questions 23–29

- The CEO of the company you work for has asked you to check this letter.
- In some lines there is one wrong word.
- If there is a wrong word, write the correct word on your Answer Sheet.
- If there is no mistake, put a tick (✓) on your Answer Sheet.

Example:
One of the items you ordered from our catalogue

0	✓

is <u>temporary</u> out of stock.

00	temporarily

Dear customer

23 I am writing to tell you about an exciting change affected MWH. Since my grandfather
24 set up the company in 1935, it has remained in family owners, and I succeeded my
25 father as CEO 27 years ago. The time has now come for me to retire, and hand up
26 the day-to-day running of the business to somebody else. Unfortunately, my daughter
27 has decided that her future lies in a field another than retail. I have therefore decided
28 to sell the company to one of our competitor, Thompson plc. MWH will continue to
29 trade under its own name, and I too much hope it can count on your continued patronage.

Writing Test Part 2: Exam skills

Part 2 consists of:
- either a letter or a report of 180–200 words.

You can choose to answer one of two questions.

You have approximately 30 minutes.

You practised similar skills in Unit 3 (page 18), Unit 16 (page 77), Unit 19 (page 91) and Unit 23 (pages 108 and 109).

This part of the exam tests your ability to:
- use the correct format and appropriate register for the type of task
- use grammar and vocabulary accurately to express your ideas
- communicate clearly in writing.

Levels of formality

The level of formality you use will depend on:
- the subject you are writing about
- who you are writing to.

For example, if you are writing an email to an important customer, the style will be quite formal, but if you are writing to a close colleague, you may use quite an informal style (see Writing reference section for levels of formality (page 116).

Suggested exam technique

1 Read the instructions carefully, underlining key information in the instructions:
- Is it a letter or a report?
- Who will read it? (This will decide the level of formality.)
- What points must you include?
2 Write a quick plan. Make sure your plan covers all the points you have been asked to include.
3 Organise your plan in a logical way.
4 Write your answer from your plan using:
- the correct format
- an appropriate level of formality (see above).
5 Use linking words and phrases to connect your ideas (e.g. *however, although, also, as a consequence, as a result, this means*, etc.).
6 Check your answer for mistakes.

Exercises

1 Work in pairs.

a Read this task and underline the key points, i.e. the things you must include in your answer.

> A number of staff have recently told you that they are unhappy about the times when they start and finish work in your company. You have been asked to write a report for the managing director about this.
> Write your **report**. Write about:
> - why staff are unhappy with the times
> - why it is important to keep staff happy
> - what solutions your company should adopt for the problem
> - any other points you think are important.
> Write **180–200** words.

b Answer these questions about the task.

1 What things should you include in your answer?
2 What ideas or information will you have to invent?
3 What information can you include which will make your report sound more realistic?
4 Who is going to read the report? So what level of formality should you use?
5 What format should your report have?

c Complete these notes for the task with your own ideas.

> **Introduction**
>
> **Problems with existing times**
> Working times at the moment: ....
> Problems with these times: ....
>
> **The importance of keeping staff happy**
> 1 Cost of recruiting new staff
> 2 ....
>
> **Solutions and recommendations**
> 1 ....
> 2 ....

d Read this sample answer and answer the questions below.

Report on staff working times

Introduction

The purpose of this report is to analyse why our office staff are unhappy with the times when they start and finish work and to suggest solutions to the problem.

Problems with existing times

At present, office staff start work at 9 a.m. and finish at 5.30 p.m. A number of problems have arisen with this timetable:

- Staff have to travel during the rush hour, which means longer and more uncomfortable journeys. As a result, they arrive at work feeling stressed.
- Many of our staff find it difficult to leave their children at school (between 8 and 8.30) and arrive at the office on time to start work.

The importance of keeping staff happy

Staff turnover as a consequence of this problem has increased from 10% per year ten years ago to 20% last year. This in turn has caused an increase in recruitment costs for the company. Also, happy staff are more motivated, work harder and give better service to our customers.

Solutions and recommendations

I recommend that we offer staff a number of the solutions:

- They can have flexible starting and finishing times at work.
- Where possible, they can do some of their work from home.

---

1 Does the report contain the same ideas as you put in your notes (in part b)?
2 What do you notice about the layout of the report?
3 Does the report have a title?
4 What are the purposes of the first and last sections?
5 Find phrases which express results. (For more work on expressing results, look at Unit 23 (page 109) and Grammar workshop 6 (page 115).)
6 Has the writer completed the task? Is there anything which has been forgotten?

To try a real exam task, go to page 156.

Writing Test Part 2: Exam practice

Task A

The CEO of your company has invited a firm of business consultants to suggest ways of making your company more efficient. You have been asked to write a letter to the firm of business consultants.

Write the **letter**, informing the business consultants about the problems they should try to solve.

Write about:
- poor customer service
- delays in production
- high levels of absence among staff

and any other points which you think are important.

Write about **180–200** words.

OR

Task B

Your company wants to improve its website. You have been asked to write a report on your company's website and your major competitor's website, and to suggest any changes that need to be made.

Write a **report** comparing your company's website with your major competitor's website.

Write about:
- the information that is included in the websites
- how easy they are to use
- what changes you would like to see

and any other points which you think are important.

Write about **180–200** words.

Speaking Test

The Speaking Test lasts about 12 minutes. You are assessed by the examiner, and a recording is made, which is assessed by another examiner later.

In the test, you are given marks for:
- accurate grammar and vocabulary
- range of language (how much vocabulary and grammar you know)
- discourse management (how well you speak when giving longer answers; how fluent you are; and how well you organise what you say)
- pronunciation
- interactive communication (your ability to share and participate in a conversation with the examiner).

Speaking Test Part 1: Exam skills

Part 1 consists of:
- general questions which the examiner asks you about
  - where you are from / where you live
  - your interests
  - your job or your studies
  - your hopes for the future.

This part of the test lasts about four minutes.

You practised similar skills in Unit 1 (page 9) and Unit 2 (page 15).

This part of the exam tests your ability to:
- talk about yourself
- perform functions such as agreeing and disagreeing.

Suggested exam technique

1 Make sure, before you go to the Speaking Test, that you can:
- describe what your job or your studies consist of
- talk about your ambitions/hopes for the future
- say what you like/dislike about your job/studies.
2 When you go into the interview, speak clearly so you can be heard.
3 Don't answer the questions with one or two words – answer with one or two sentences.
4 When you answer a question, give a reason for your answer or an example.

Some extra advice
- Try to speak naturally and confidently.
- Smile and look directly at the person you are speaking to.
- If you don't understand a question, ask the interviewer to repeat it.
- If you notice you've made a mistake, correct yourself.

Exercises

1 **Complete these sentences about yourself. Then compare your answers with a partner.**

1 My job/studies consist(s) of ....
2 The thing I enjoy most about my job/studies is .... because ....
3 There are some things I don't like, for example ....
4 I chose to do this job / this course because ....
5 I like this area for living/working because ....
6 I use / expect to use English in my work in order to ....
7 In the future, I hope to be working .... because ....

2 a **Work alone. Study the questions below and think how you could best answer them.**

- Can you give an example?
- Can you add a reason for your answer?

b **Note down two or three words you would like to use when you are answering each question.**

1 Where do you come from?
2 What do you like about the area where you live?
3 Is this a good area to work in?
4 What does your job consist of? / What do you study?
5 What do you most enjoy about your work/ studies?
6 Is there anything you don't enjoy?
7 Why have you been studying Business English?
8 How important is English in your job? / How important do you think English will be for you in the future?
9 What would you like to be doing in, say, ten years' time?
10 What do you enjoy doing in your free time?

3 a **Work in pairs. Take turns to interview each other using the questions from Exercise 2.**

b **When you have finished, discuss how you could improve your answers.**

Speaking Test Part 2: Exam skills

In Part 2:

- You are given a page with three topics printed on it. Each topic begins *Talk about …* or *Describe …* (for example: *Talk about how your company markets its products or services*) and ends *Why/Why not?* or *Give reasons for your answer.*
- There are some questions printed below each topic to help you.
- You are asked to choose one of the three topics.
- You have one minute to prepare your answer and make notes.
- You must speak for one minute about the topic.
- When you have finished, the examiner will ask one or two questions about your talk.

This part of the exam tests your ability to:

- speak for a longer period of time, as you might have to do when giving a presentation or speaking at a business meeting
- communicate a series of ideas clearly
- structure your speech and connect your ideas.

This part of the test lasts about four minutes.

You practised similar skills in Unit 12 (page 57) and Unit 18 (page 85).

Interview nerves

It is natural to feel a little nervous about this part of the interview. Overcome them by telling yourself:

- you have something interesting and important to say
- the examiner wants to hear your ideas
- he/she would be equally nervous if he/she had to give a talk in your language!

Above all, keep speaking. If you dry up, take a breath and start again. Don't worry if you repeat something you have already said.

Suggested exam technique

A You have **one minute** to prepare. Use it to:
1 choose the topic you think is easiest
2 think how you give longer answers to the questions by:
- giving reasons
- giving examples
3 make brief notes while you are thinking
4 note down key business vocabulary you want to use.

B If you can, use **your own experience** to answer the question.

C When speaking:
1 refer to your notes, but **look at the examiner**
2 introduce your talk by saying what topic you have chosen
3 sequence your talk by saying *firstly, secondly, finally,* etc.
4 signpost your talk with phrases like *this is because, for example* and *as a result of this*
5 watch the time and try to finish your talk with a brief concluding sentence at the end of the minute.

Exercises

1 a **Work in pairs. Study Topic 1 below and discuss how you could answer it. Take two or three minutes to do this and take notes.**

b **Change partners and give your talk. Your partner should listen and, at the end, ask you one or two questions about your talk.**

c **When each of you has given your talk, give feedback on what your partner did well and what they could improve.**

d **Do the same for Topics 2 and 3.**

---

1 Talk about the meetings you have to attend in your company.
   You should say:
   - how often you go to meetings
   - what sort of meetings you have to attend
   - how effective the meetings are
   How could the time spent at meetings be improved in your company? Give reasons for your answer.

---

2 Describe how your company promotes its products or services.
   You should say:
   - what promotional activities your company uses
   - who decides which activities to use
   - how effective you think these activities are.
   What changes would you like to see in the way your company promotes its products or services? Give reasons for your answer.

---

3 Talk about a job you have applied for. You should say:
   - what the job was
   - why you applied for the job
   - what happened during the application process.
   Was your application successful? Why? / Why not? Give reasons for your answer.

---

2 a Complete this talk by writing one of the words
   or phrases from the box in each space.

A further point	Another important thing is	
But, to conclude	Firstly	For example
I mean	So	This way

Well, I'm going to talk about what is important when
setting up a new business. **1** .... , it depends on the
type of business you are starting, but if it has just one or
two employees, management experience is not essential.
What is more important is knowledge of the product.
2 .... , if you're going to open a clothes shop, you
should know a lot about clothes. **3** .... a knowledge
of the market. You have to find out who your competitors
are, and your target customers. **4** .... you must be
sure that people are going to buy your product. **5** ....
, you don't want to invest your life savings in a business
which doesn't interest anyone! **6** .... is that you must
have a reasonable working knowledge of finance, so that
you can produce a sales forecast, estimate your costs
and make a cashflow prediction.
7 .... , you'll be able to persuade a bank to give you a
loan or overdraft. **8** .... , the most important thing is
interest in the product and your customers.

b ②₁₉ Check your answer by listening to
   Martin, a small business advisor, giving a talk
   to business students at an adult education
   college.

3 In his talk, Martin does the following things. Read
   what he said in Exercise 2 again and find where he
   did them.

   1 He introduces his talk.
   2 He makes three main points.
   3 He gives an example.
   4 He explains what he means using other words.
   5 He concludes his talk.
   6 He uses business vocabulary.

To try a real exam task, go to page 160.

Speaking Test Part 2: Exam practice

INSTRUCTIONS

Please read all THREE topics below carefully.

Choose **ONE** which you feel you will be able to talk about for one minute.

You have one minute to read and prepare your talk.

You may make notes.

Topic A

Describe an interesting business meeting you have taken part in.

You should say:
- who attended the meeting
- where it was held
- the purpose of the meeting.

Was the meeting a success? Why/Why not?

Topic B

Describe how your company recruits new staff.

You should say:
- who organises recruitment
- how job vacancies are advertised
- how the successful applicant is chosen.

Does your company have problems recruiting new staff? Why/Why not?

Topic C

Describe someone you don't like working with.

You should say:
- what work this person does
- what contact you have with this person
- why you don't like working with this person.

What would you change about this person? Give reasons for your answer.

Speaking Test Part 3: Exam skills

In Part 3:

- you are given a card with a role-play situation
- you ask the examiner questions to get the required information
- you must then give your opinion about the information the examiner has told you
- you then discuss a related topic with the examiner.

This part of the exam tests your ability to:

- ask questions
- express opinions
- agree and disagree.

This part of the test lasts about four minutes.

You practised similar skills in Unit 6 (page 33) and Unit 8 (pages 38–39).

Asking questions

You can ask questions directly by saying things like *How much does it cost?* or *When will you be able to deliver it?*

You can also ask questions more indirectly by saying *Can you tell me how much it costs?* or *I'd like to know when you will be able to deliver it.*

It's a good idea to practise asking both types of question before you go to the speaking test.

Suggested exam technique

1 Read the card carefully before you start speaking.
2 Greet the examiner and introduce the questions before you ask them, e.g. *Good morning, I'd like to ask you a few questions about …* The examiner will answer with something like: *OK, what would you like to know?* You can then sequence the questions, e.g. using *Firstly, Secondly* and *Finally*.
3 Make sure to ask the questions correctly.
4 Listen carefully to the examiner's answers and, at the end, give your opinion about what he/she says.
5 Be ready to agree or disagree with the opinions or ideas the examiner expresses. (For language of agreeing and disagreeing, see Useful language on pages 8 and 9 and Listening Exercise 1 on page 72.)

Exercises

1 **Read the task sheet and complete the questions below it with one word for each gap.**

TASK SHEET

Car suppliers
Your company has decided to buy a new fleet of cars for its executives. The examiner is a representative of a firm which supplies cars for companies. She/ He is visiting you to discuss the matter. Find out this information:
1 types of car available
2 prices
3 terms of payment.

Question 1
- What types of car ....
- .... you tell me what types of car .... ?

Question 2
- How much .... the cars .... ?
- I'd like to know how much ....

Question 3
- What .... terms of payment?
- What terms of payment .... offer?

2 a **Study these ways of sequencing questions and introducing indirect questions.**

Ways of sequencing questions	Ways of introducing indirect questions
First *First of all,* *Another thing* *Also* *One last thing*	*I'd like to ask …* *I'd like to know …* *Can you tell me … ?* *I was wondering …* *Could you tell me … ?*

b **Combine phrases from the table above to ask questions for this task sheet.**

TASK SHEET

A business hotel for a conference
Your company is looking for a business hotel for a conference they are going to hold in your city. You are visiting a hotel in the area. The examiner is the manager of the hotel. Find out this information:
1 facilities available at hotel
2 prices of rooms
3 discount for group booking.
You will then be asked to give your opinion about this information.

---

3 a Combine a comment from each column to form ways of expressing an opinion.

I like the price, but …	I don't think you are offering me a big enough discount.
The price is a bit high, but …	the facilities sound excellent.
I think the price is fine, and …	I'd prefer a hotel with more facilities for business people.

b Read this information, which would be given by the examiner. What opinion(s) could you express about it?

- Facilities at hotel: bar, restaurant, spa and business centre. No internet connection in rooms.
- Price: $150 per night (single room), $200 double room
- Discount for group booking: 10% on groups of ten or more

4 Work in pairs. Student A should take the role of candidate and Student B should take the role of examiner.

Student A (candidate)

Read this task sheet. Find out the information and give your opinion when the examiner asks for it.

TASK SHEET

Advertising in a newspaper
Your company is interested in advertising its products in a regional newspaper. Your examiner sells advertising space in the newspaper. He/She is visiting you to discuss the matter. Find out this information:
1 types of space available
2 price of full page
3 number of readers of newspaper.
You will then be asked to give your opinion on this information.

Student B (examiner)

Look at Student A's task sheet and answer with the information below. When Student A has finished asking, find out his/her opinion about the information. You can ask *So what do you think of the information I have given you?*

1 Types of space available: full page, half page and smaller sizes.
2 Price of full page: $6,000 per day
3 Readers: 50,000 a day

5 Work in the same pairs and change roles.

Student A (examiner)

Look at Student B's task sheet and answer with the information below. When Student B has finished asking, find out his/her opinion about the information. You can ask *So what do you think of the information I have given you?*

1 Spaces available: 50
2 Rates: 20% discount on normal price for one-year contract
3 Security: People park cars in car park at their own risk. Car park has no insurance.

Student B (candidate)

Read this task sheet. Find out the information and give your opinion when the examiner asks for it.

TASK SHEET

Car-parking facilities
Your company is considering renting car-parking facilities in a public car park near the office for office workers. The examiner is the manager of the car park. He/She is visiting you to discuss the matter. Find out this information:
1 Number of spaces available
2 Special rates
3 Security in car park
You will then be asked for your opinion on this information.

To try a real exam task, go to page 163.

Speaking Test Part 3: Exam practice

New office building

You have one minute to read through this task.

Information exchange

Your company wants to rent an office building for one department of your company. The examiner is the owner of an office building and is visiting you to discuss the building.

Find out this information:

1 the number of rooms in the building
2 the cost of renting the building
3 the date when the building will be available.

You will then be asked to give your opinion on this information.

Discussion

Now discuss this topic with the examiner.

What makes an office building suitable for the people working there?

Answer key

UNIT 1

Recruitment brochure

Reading

2 1 Advanced Sales, Goal Setting, Time Management
2 It gives staff the skills they need to succeed, they promote from within the company, they want to train their future leaders.

3 2 A 3 C 4 B 5 D 6 C 7 A 8 D 9 B 10 A

Vocabulary 1

2 qualifications 3 degree 4 course; certificate; knowledge; experience 5 development

Grammar workshop

2 U 3 C 4 C 5 U 6 U

Vocabulary 2

1 work 2 job 3 work 4 job 5 training course 6 training
7 training course

Training course

Listening

1 1 a name or type of company 2 *staff/employees*?
3 a length of time 4 something a Director of Studies can give

2 1 Forrest Insurance 2 graduate trainees 3 one/1 month
4 quotation

3 2 f 3 d 4 a 5 b 6 c

Training at Deloitte in China

Reading

1 *Suggested answers*
paragraph 1: Deloitte's dedication to training
paragraph 2: support for employees from managers
paragraph 3: managers' interest in staff development
paragraph 4: managers' attention to staff
paragraph 5: counsellors

2 1 *Suggested answer*: The connection between *clear upward path* and *ascend to the top*.
2 2 C 3 A 4 B 5 F 6 D

Vocabulary

1 b 2 c 3 a 4 d 5 f 6 e

Training scheme for new staff

Role-play

2 a 1, 3, 4, 6 b 2 c 5

UNIT 2

Getting started

2 *Suggested answers*
a 2, 6 b 1, 5, 6 c 1, 2, 4, 5, 6 d 1, 3, 4, 5, 6 e 1, 2, 3, 4, 6

Job responsibilities

Vocabulary

2 1 c 2 d 3 b 4 a 5 e

3 2 recruit 3 evaluating 4 promoting 5 investment 6 funds
7 performance 8 deadlines

6 1 of; are 2 have; been; have; been 3 did 4 are; for

A human resources manager

Listening

1 *Suggested underlining*
2 makes managing people easy
3 How / become
4 doing in ten years' time
5 advice / for job candidates
6 know / good at the job

2 1 A 2 B 3 C 4 C 5 B 6 B

Human resources

Vocabulary

1 1 c 2 b 3 a

2 2 ~~staffs~~ staff/employees 3 ~~staff~~ member of staff / employee
4 ~~staffs~~ members of staff / employees

What I like about my job

Listening

2 1 d 2 b 3 f 4 e 5 h

3 1 work; client 2 freedom; choices 3 fulfilling 4 inspiring
5 what; one 6 exciting

Staff training report

Writing

1 2 took 3 needed 4 fell 5 recruited 6 has signed 7 has set

2 employees – staff; budget – spend; agreement – contract; working methods – the way we work

3 The main reason for; because; because of this; For that reason

5 *Sample answer*
Two years ago, the Bank of Veronezh spent 3,500,000 roubles on language training for staff. The reason for this was that they needed to learn English in order to work with our Polish partners in the Bank of Gdansk. Last year, in contrast, our spending on training rose to 5,250,000 because we needed to teach them how to use the new IT systems which had been installed. Recently, we have introduced new accounting methods which have affected some members of staff, and as a result, this year's staff training budget has been set at 2,300,000 roubles.

UNIT 3

Job satisfaction at Sony Mobile Communications

Reading

1 *Suggested answers*
You can work with people from different countries and cultures, so there is a variety of behaviours and ideas and learning opportunities; opportunities for travel and work abroad; opportunities for promotion based on merit; opportunities may arise to work in other international organisations.

2 *Suggested underlining*
2 producing things / people / enjoy 3 improve our ways of working 4 affects the whole company 5 Recent recruits / encouraged / contribute ideas 6 wants / employees / variety of attitudes and opinions 7 To survive / continually / producing new products 8 aware / customers' different ways of thinking
Suggested paraphrases
2 making products people have fun with
3 make our working methods better
4 influences everyone in the organisation
5 new employees are given opportunities to say what they think
6 encourages diversity of points of view
7 To stay in business, you have to always innovate.
8 know about our clients' attitudes

3 1 B (*Developing my team and seeing them grow is what makes me happy – seeing them change over time.*)

   2 C (*I take real pride in creating applications that are fun and satisfying for our customers to use.*)

   3 B (*We work hard, but also we want to do it more intelligently, more efficiently and effectively.*)

   4 D (*… our team's thinking and plans shaping and changing all parts of the company from internal culture through to packaging, product design and advertising.*)

   5 C (*There's a great culture here where you can really discuss things with all your colleagues, even if you're a newcomer.*)

   6 A (*… different views and mindsets are accepted and encouraged.*)

   7 A (*There's also fierce competition that's always changing, forcing us to stay on our toes and innovate.*)

   8 D (*… it's about understanding the cultural sensitivities of different markets.*)

Vocabulary

1 mastered   2 crops up   3 to stay on our toes
4 an analytical mindset   5 to challenge the status quo

Advice on job applications

Listening

2 1 d 2 b 3 g 4 e 5 f

A short email and an email of a job application

Writing 1

2 1 for 2 on 3 it 4 give 5 with 6 If

3 *Suggested answer*
Dear Fatma, I saw this job for a technician advertised on my company's intranet and thought it might be right for you because you've studied electronic engineering. I'd be happy to help you with your application if you need it.
Sasha

4 *Suggested answer*: You should include all points except 4 and 10 (10 can be put in your CV).

6 *Christa's plan*
paragraph 1: the reason for writing the email, how she heard about the job
paragraph 2: her CV, what she studied, a summary of relevant work experience
paragraph 3: what she studied, relevant work experience in more detail
paragraph 4: why she is interested
paragraph 5: saying she is ready to be interviewed, references from her employers

7 3 now 4 time 5 *correct* 6 have 7 the 8 and 9 *correct*
10 more 11 However 12 *correct* 13 my 14 an 15 too

Vocabulary

2 ~~interested~~ interesting 3 ~~interest~~ interested 4 ~~opened~~ open
5 ~~convenience~~ convenient 6 ~~absence~~ absent

Speaking

2

	Adam	Harriet	reason(s)
1	✓		The organisation needs someone like you, you made it to the interview.
2	✓		
3	✓		
4	✓	✓	Gives impression that candidate is interested, they've done their homework, you'll be able to portray yourself better.
5		✓	They know what you're like.
6		✓	You get to know people there, and they know you.

UNIT 4

Getting started

1/2 1 much more important than 2 a lot less 3 easier
    4 a little more 5 not quite as important as

Grammar workshop

2 L 3 S 4 S 5 L 6 L 7 L 8 S

A phone call to a hotel

Listening

1 1 a person's surname, possibly spelled out
    2 the name of a company
    3 a type of room in a hotel
    4 the reason for needing the room
    5 a date
    6 something else that a person hiring a room might need

2 1 Kutsov 2 Top Flight 3 meeting 4 job interviews
    5 13th May 6 coffee

A telephone quiz

Reading

Suggested answers

1 B and C are normal if the call has been routed through a switchboard; D would be appropriate if you are a receptionist, for example; A is just unhelpful because the caller doesn't know if he or she has reached the right person or company.

2 B

3 C

4 A and C are both correct, but B is not.

5 A is quite formal, B is informal and C is neither correct nor polite.

6 C is formal, A is informal and B sounds rude.

7 A and B are both correct, although you would only use A with someone you know well.

8 B and C are both correct, depending on what information you are looking for.

9 B

Enquiring about a job

Listening

1 Speaking, My name's …

2 1 office administrator 2 mornings (only) 3 bookkeeping
    4 beginning 5 (by) email

Phone-answering tips

Reading

2 *Suggested answers*
paragraph 2: how you should answer the phone; paragraph 3: putting callers on hold; paragraph 4: taking messages correctly; paragraph 5: call back soon; paragraph 6: train other staff

3 B For example C it D these callers E However … this
    F Then … it G This

4 2 B 3 D 4 F 5 C 6 A

GRAMMAR WORKSHOP 1

Countable and uncountable nouns

1 U: advice, equipment, feedback, freight, information, knowledge, parking, recruitment, research, software, spending, teamwork, training, transport, travel
C: budget, car, computer, programme, report, team, training course

2 1 an advertisement 2 equipment 3 research; work 4 amount of information 5 advice 6 little travel; many training courses

Present perfect and past simple

1 1 have worked 2 went; have not gone/been 3 was; left; haven't seen; went 4 have changed; started; finished 5 posted; has been; has got; (has) started 6 wrote; haven't received 7 has grown; have taken on; opened

2 1 expected 2 have done 3 has decided 4 have arranged 5 increased 6 has become 7 decided 8 made

Talking about large and small differences

1 *Suggested answers*
1 far more / six times more / six times as many
2 nearly as many (letters) as ten years ago / far fewer (letters) than ten years ago
3 quite as many (meetings) as now
4 considerably / far / many / a lot more (phone calls) than now / twice as many (phone calls) as now
5 slightly fewer (text messages now) than ten years ago / not quite as many (text messages now) as ten years ago

UNIT 5

Getting started

1 1 b 2 d 3 f 4 e 5 c 6 g 7 a

2 *Suggested answers*
2 Free samples or gifts may be expensive to produce and distribute and may require extra staff for this. On the other hand, potential customers have a chance to actually experience the product.
3 Leaflets and brochures need to be well designed, which is also expensive. There are also distribution costs. However, they can explain the product/service in detail and make it sound attractive.
4 Point-of-sale displays are expensive because they need to be placed in a large number of shops which will charge for this. However, customers may make the decision to buy on the spot.
5 Sponsorship can be very expensive, but it links the company's image with a successful and attractive person, team or event.
6 Television and radio advertising is also expensive, but reaches a mass audience and may still be the most cost-effective.
7 The website may be the cheapest of the options listed and can also reach a mass audience if people can be encouraged to visit it.

Promoting AXE

Reading

2 Promotional activities: a slogan, online game, free samples, point-of-sale displays, media advertising, PR, a house party, direct mailing, online publicity, leaflets, advertisements in magazines, website, television show, free CD

3 1 B (… *young men's natural interest in pretty girls … appeal to American male youth culture.*)
2 D (… *young men to log on to the Internet to play a video game on the AXE website … If the player reached a certain level, he entered a lottery to win a trip to the party.*)
3 C (*AXE focused on the intrigue and discovery of the party.*)
4 A ('*It was all about getting into the mind of the 20-something guy,*' …)
5 B ('*To our knowledge, nobody has ever taken a consumer promotion and turned it into a television show,*' …)
6 C (… *a 22% increase in general brand awareness among males aged 11 to 24* …)

Vocabulary

2 d 3 c 4 e 5 b 6 a

Grammar workshop

1 to make 2 to bring 3 playing 4 doing 5 to dance 6 using 7 not to let 8 Building 9 to launch

Supermarkets' own brands

Listening

1 *Suggested answer*
Supermarkets can package, price and market the brand to suit their particular customers, their own marketing plan and make use of the supermarket's brand image. Own brands can be sold more cheaply because less advertising is required and production can be more easily adjusted to match demand.

2 1 C 2 A 3 B

Going viral in India and China

Reading

2 2 A (… *the video stacked up to 700,000 views on YouTube, even though it was criticised widely in the media.*)
3 C (*The launch of Denizen in China last month was the first time that Levi's has moved outside the United States for the global launch of a brand.*)
4 D (*With work environments becoming more casual, for the younger generation, denim is the clothing of choice.*)
5 C (… *is now keen on expanding the price ladder lower to prevent consumers from crossing over to competitors.*)
6 A (… *campaign to encourage consumers to take risks and move beyond the smart and sensible life* …)
7 B (*They blog about the brand and how the brand makes them feel.*)
8 A (*Most, if not all, have gone digital, and Levi's now seems to be doing the same.*)

UNIT 6

Developing and launching Drink Me Chai

Listening

2 1 A 2 A 3 B 4 B 5 C
3 She did market research to identify competing products; she tried importing it; she developed the product and tested it with customers at her station bar; she approached supermarkets with samples; she met a supermarket buyer and made a pitch; she branded and packaged the product for the supermarket.

Reading

1 1 When her customers said they would like to drink the product at home
2 At that stage, the product had no packaging or branding.

2 B *However* and *the journey*: The journey may refer to the journey to London.
C *it*: It may refer to *chai*.
D *But the major problem*: There may have been other problems mentioned earlier.
E *It*: Something which happened
F *Since then*: Refers to an earlier time mentioned in the text.
G *As a result*: This is the result of something mentioned in the text.

3 2 B 3 C 4 A 5 F 6 E

Launching and promoting a new product

Listening

2 Amanda mentions doing market research and testing the product on the market.

5	method	reason
	write-ups in magazines/ newspapers	raises awareness and increases sales
	sampling at shows/fairs/ festivals	people can try unique taste; she doesn't have a big budget, cannot advertise
	website	like a shop window; connects with customers and receives orders

A marketing report
Writing

1 2 by; from; to 3 ... spending on stands at trade fairs by A$75,000 from A$100,000 to A$25,000. 4 ... has risen by A$200,000 from A$450,000 to A$650,000.

4 2 the 3 *correct* 4 due 5 only 6 too 7 *correct* 8 down 9 being 10 *correct* 11 up 12 off 13 *correct*

5 *Suggested answers*
1 Spending on point-of-sale displays has fallen from £30,000 to £15,000; spending on magazine advertisements has risen from £12,000 to £46,000; spending on leaflets has been raised from £6,000 to £35,000.
2 Point-of-sale displays were not particularly effective because there was strong competition for customers' attention from other brands, but we managed to sell large numbers of chocolates through our magazine advertising because we advertised in slimming magazines. It is clear that our leaflets are reaching our target customers, who are generally people who are concerned about their health and like to keep fit.
3 The total budget rose from £48,000 last year to £98,000 this year. However, it will be reduced to £65,000 next year.
4 We should continue to spend the same amount on leaflets. However, we should stop promoting with point-of-sale displays, reduce our magazine advertising and consider using viral advertising on YouTube.

6 *Sample answer*
Introduction
The object of this report is to summarise how we have spent our promotional budget on Slimchocs over the last two years, its effectiveness and to make recommendations for next year's budget.
Our promotional activities
We reduced our outlay on point-of-sale displays from £30,000 to £15,000, as these failed to attract customers' attention due to strong competition from other brands. However, we raised our budget for advertising in slimming magazines by £34,000, as this proved an effective way of reaching target customers. We also increased our budget for leaflets by £29,000 because with these, we also managed to reach our target customers, who are primarily people interested in staying healthy and keeping fit.
Recommendations
Our promotional budget will be reduced next year to £65,000. As a result, I recommend that we should continue to spend the same amount on leaflets. However, it would be a good idea to stop promoting with point-of-sale displays, reduce our magazine advertising and consider using viral advertising on YouTube.

UNIT 7
Getting started

1 These are trade fairs, where companies hire space and set up stands. Company representatives and salespeople are talking to potential customers who visit their stands. People visit trade fairs to identify possible products and potential suppliers.

2 *Suggested answers*
Potential customers can see and handle the products on display. They can talk to sales staff.
Companies can invite potential customers to visit them at their stand.
A good stand can give a company prestige.

It gives the company an opportunity to promote its products to its competitor's customers.

The London Contemporary Design Show
Reading

1 1 A memo is an internal note circulated to people in an office (nowadays usually by email) containing information or instructions, possibly about a new policy or activity.
2 Directly, with the subject of the memo. If you wish, you can finish it with *Many thanks* (or something similar) and your initials or your signature.
3 Start with the name of the addressee and finish with *Thanks, Best wishes* or nothing and the name of the writer.
4 Contact the organisers of a trade fair to find out information about setting up a stand.

2 2 at 3 in 4 for 5 for 6 for 7 in/with 8 with 9 out

3 *Sample answer*
Dear Sir/Madam
We are a Swiss furniture design company. We are interested in exhibiting at the London Contemporary Design Show this year. Can you please tell us:
• how much it would cost to exhibit at the show?
• when we would need to make a booking?
Many thanks.

Grammar workshop

1 2 e 3 a 4 c 5 d
2 1 1b (It has the form of a question, starting with *Can.*)
2 2, 3, 4 and 5
3 we
4 details of, information about

Vocabulary

1 1 d 2 a 3 c 4 b
2 1 learn 2 find out 3 teach 4 found out 5 know; teach 6 learn 7 know 8 find out

Listening

1 *Suggested answers*
1 something with an area 2 something which costs £115
3 a date 4 something which can be sent by email
5 something which might happen to the space

2 1 Floor space 2 Insurance 3 13th June 4 bank details
5 guaranteed

3 *Sample answer*
Subject: London Contemporary Design Show
Hello Ulrike,
The organisers have given me the following information:
• Floor space costs between £295 and £340 per square metre plus VAT. We also have to pay £115 insurance and a £300 registration fee. The balance must be paid by 22nd August.
• The deadline for reservations is 13th June.
Best wishes
Marcel

Preparing an exhibition stand
Writing 1

2 *Sample answer*
Dear Sirs
We are a Swiss furniture company. We are planning to have a stand at the London Contemporary Design Show next September. We would be grateful if you could send us some sample designs and an estimate of costs. Can you also tell us roughly how long it will take to build?
Many thanks
Marcel Schaub

Reading

1 *Suggested underlining*
   2 international experience   3 on time   4 promotional activity
   5 can afford   6 needn't buy   7 as many people / as possible
2 1   A   (*Our prices are keen and competitive due to our huge stocks of ready-made equipment.*)
   2   B   (*We have delivered customised exhibition solutions worldwide and designed stands for almost every market you can name.*)
   3   B   (*Our project-management skills ensure deadlines are met …*)
   4   C   (*We can provide a complete marketing solution for your project, including pre-event promotions, stand design and show activity.*)
   5   B   (*… a solution that meets your brief and matches your budget.*)
   6   A   (*… by supplying custom-built exhibition stands – for hire or for sale.*)
   7   C   (*… we'll also work with you to maximise your visitor numbers.*)
3 1 D   2 B   3 A   4 A   5 B   6 C   7 C   8 D   9 B   10 A   11 A
   12 D   13 B   14 B   15 D

Writing 2

2 *Sample answer*
   Dear Mr Steel
   Thank you for your designs. In answer to your questions:
   1   We have booked 40 m² of floor space.
   2   Our stand is on a corner, and we would prefer it to be open.
   3   We would like to be able to accommodate up to 15 people at any one time.
   From the designs you sent us, the one we like the most is number 3. We look forward to receiving your design and quotation.
   Best wishes
   Marcel Schaub
3 *Sample answer*
   To: Sales staff
   From: Ulrike Schütz
   Subject: Stand at London Contemporary Design Show
   I'm pleased to inform you that the stand is being designed at the moment. Could you please let me know what equipment you will need for the stand? Also, I suggest you start preparing the graphics you want to put on the stand.
   Many thanks
   Ulrike

UNIT 8

Getting started

2

	K	A	R	D
1				✓
2	✓			
3				✓
4			✓	
5		✓		
6		✓	✓	
7	✓			
8		✓		

Breaking the ice

Speaking

2 2   Did you have a good trip?
   3   Lovely city, isn't it?
   4   Where are you staying?
   5   Now, can we show you a few of our products?
   6   Busy, isn't it?

7 Would either of you like a cup of coffee or a cup of tea before we get started?
3 Nice to meet you; That's great; Very smart; thanks for inviting us; we like people to see our stand; Very good; the airport's so convenient; Lovely city, isn't it; Yes, lovely; it's the best hotel in town; Oh, good; Busy, isn't it; Incredibly; This fair is getting more popular every year.

The art of agreeing

Reading

1 *Suggested answers*
   2 gain confidence / exchanging information (*They can build trust by telling each other things.*)
   3 in control of their feelings (*They should never get angry or upset.*)
   4 acquire / information / in advance (*They should find out as much as possible before they start.*)
   5 work out ways / other party / flexible (*They should try to think of ways for the other side to change their position.*)
   6 not always financial gain (*Their aim is not always to make money.*)
   7 non-verbal behaviour / influence (*Their body language will affect the outcome.*)
   8 opening proposal / advantage (*The person who starts the negotiation will be in a better position.*)
3 1   C   (*You can negotiate well only if you have the ability to walk away from an unfavourable agreement …*)
   2   B   (*While you are continuing to receive factual data, with both parties following the give-and-take principle, you are building trust gradually.*)
   3   D   (*Also remember never to lose your cool or emotions.*)
   4   A   (*The better prepared you are with factual data before heading into a negotiation, the more effective you will be.*)
   5   C   (*You should also factor in the fall-back options for the other side.*)
   6   A   (*… identify the real needs and goals. Though the most obviously stated need is money, it can be a proxy for other physical or more refined needs (shelter, reputation, self-esteem).*)
   7   B   (*… your body language will have an impact on people and on the outcome of your negotiation.*)
   8   D   (*Try and be the first to make an offer. It will help anchor the client to your view, and the final agreement is more likely to end closer to your proposal.*)

Vocabulary

1 proxy   2 vendor   3 impact   4 outcome   5 factor in
6 fall-back/back-up (options)   7 lose your cool

Listening

Names of actual speakers are given.
1 could (Jack)   2 took (Helga)   3 'll accept (could be either, but in fact it's Jack)   4 wouldn't make (Susie)   5 buy (Helga)   6 gave (Jack)

Writing

1 2 for   3 with   4 on   5 at   6 for   7 In   8 on   9 with   10 for
   11 in   12 for
3 Dear Helga
   Thanks for this – the pleasure was all mine.
   There are just a few details we need to clear up. First, the quantity we were talking about was 2,000 units, not 3,000 on the terms agreed. I hope this isn't a problem for you. Also, after discussions with my colleagues, would it be possible for us to return any units we haven't sold after six months instead of 12 months? We think this would be beneficial for both of us, as things tend to go out of fashion so quickly these days.
   Finally, we would be happy to pay in cash on condition that you deliver the goods at your expense.

I hope you can agree to all these points and that we can proceed with the order.
Kind regards
Jack

GRAMMAR WORKSHOP 2

Infinitives and verb + -ing

1 1 training 2 dealing 3 to get 4 Advertising; to invest
5 developing; to be 6 leaving; to start 7 (to) develop; lending
8 Studying; to be
2 1 choosing 2 to hear 3 closing 4 checking 5 to look
6 hearing

Prepositions in phrases describing trends

1 1 at 2 by; to 3 from; to 4 by
2 *Suggested answers*
Three years ago, the number of exhibitors stood at 450.
Two years ago, the number fell by 80 to 370.
Last year, the number of exhibitors rose from 370 to 515.
This year, the number has fallen by 125.
3 1 to 2 at 3 by 4 at 5 from; to 6 by

Formal requests

1 2 ~~give~~ could/would give 3 ~~you let~~ you could/would let
4 ~~can~~ could/would 5 ~~are~~ would be

First and second conditionals

1 1 are 2 decide 3 require 4 advertised 5 contained
6 book 7 were
2 *Suggested answers*
1 … our accountant approves.
2 … the project was more interesting.
3 … I'd spend far less time travelling.
4 … you pay the full price in advance.
5 … there are no interruptions.
6 … it's really urgent.
7 … it was a promotion.
8 I'll be happy to do business with him …

UNIT 9

Why start your own business?

Listening

2 1 f 2 b 3 g
3 *Suggested answers*
2 Advantages: franchisers supply you with an established business model and brand; they do market research for you prior to opening and perhaps provide finance for the start-up; they will take care of advertising and marketing; they may supply you with the products you sell; they will give advice and help in making the business a success.
Disadvantages: you are not completely free to implement your business ideas (you have to keep to the rules/guidelines established by the franchiser); it can be expensive to buy into a franchise; you have to share part of your profits with the franchiser.

Grammar workshop

1 in 2 on 3 for; until 4 at 5 for; by

An international franchise

Reading

2 1 They receive cash immediately, a percentage of revenue, an international presence, they can expand when the economy is weak at home, outlets in places with strong demand, new ideas.
2 It requires resources (especially time and other costs), the brand needs protecting from copying, maintaining control of the brand, distraction from home market.
3 1 B (*… an immediate cash infusion … an immediate international presence.*)
2 C (*As western businesses cope with tight lending markets and a weak economy, many emerging economies have strong consumer demand as well as investors with plenty of capital.*)
3 D (*… look at where it makes sense to go …*)
4 A (*Otherwise, a potential investor could soon turn into a troublesome copycat.*)
5 B (*Adler worries that the fresh, youthful atmosphere of Dlush's southern California locations can't really be duplicated in the Middle East, where the culture is more conservative.*)
6 D (*But Adler's main concern is that the Middle Eastern outlets have taken a lot of his time—and shifted his focus away from building the Dlush brand at home.*)

Vocabulary

1 capital 2 trademark 3 investors 4 outlets 5 concept
6 lucrative 7 retail 8 supply chain 9 gross revenue 10 resources

Financial terms

Vocabulary

1 1 b 2 h 3 d 4 a 5 c 6 g 7 f 8 e
2 1 turnover 2 costs 3 profit 4 credit 5 interest rate
6 asset(s) 7 tax 8 liability

A letter to a franchiser

Reading

2 1 working 2 was 3 ✓ 4 the 5 ✓ 6 is 7 for 8 more
9 ✓ 10 my 11 to 12 ✓

UNIT 10

Getting started

Suggested answers
1 a bank loan; personal savings
2 personal savings or a loan from family or friends
3 This is very variable, depending on the entrepreneur's individual circumstances, location and type of business.
4 cheapest: personal savings, a loan from family or friends, going into partnership, private equity, a government grant
most expensive: a bank loan, a mortgage
5 more control: a bank loan, a mortgage, a government grant, personal savings
less control: venture capital, private equity, going into partnership

Setting up a food consultancy

Listening

2 1 exhibitions 2 start(-)up 3 business plan 4 clients
5 (more) enthusiastic 6 part-time 7 pay back

Raising finance

Vocabulary 1

1 raise finance / money / a loan
borrow money
carry out market research / a business plan
launch a company
cover overheads
write a business plan
repay a loan / money

2 1 launch a company   2 carry out market research
3 raise finance / money / a loan / borrow money
4 write a business plan   5 repay your/the loan
6 cover (your) overheads

Reading

1 a 2, 3
b 1, 4, 5, 6, 7, 8
2 1 A (*Banks don't care whether or not your business has great
profit potential. They are only interested in the business's
ability to cover the principal and interest payments.*)
2 B (*You should prepare a written agreement …*)
3 B (*Don't be embarrassed to show financial statements, tax
returns or whatever else they want to see.*)
4 D (*… to facilitate … the generation of jobs …*)
5 C (*Venture capital is intended for higher risks …*)
6 D (*… terms of interest … are less than the market rate.*)
7 C (*… the investing institution acquires a share in the
business.*)
8 A (*Banks like to use assets such as premises, motor vehicles or
equipment as collateral (or security) against loans.*)

Vocabulary 2

1 assets   2 collateral/security   3 tax returns   4 ordinary shares
5 preference shares   6 equity finance   7 soft loans   8 market rate

Carter Bearings

Listening

1 *Suggested underlining*
2 succeed against competitors   3 way of finding clients
4 give / discount when   5 written communication / works best
6 advantage of buying from a distributor   7 sort of companies /
suppliers   8 key to survival
2 1 B   2 C   3 C   4 B   5 C   6 A   7 B   8 C

UNIT 11

Getting started

1 1 *Suggested answers*
- how much BioBok is willing to invest
- number of staff
- where the staff will come from

A new location in Europe

Listening

1 *Suggested answers*
1 another type of investment   2 number of staff   3 places where
staff can be recruited from   4 something/someone that can be
recruited   5 something that they need
2 1 equipment   2 60 / sixty   3 divisions   4 manager
5 (government) grants

Reading

1 1 C   2 B   3 C   4 A   5 A   6 D   7 D   8 C   9 B   10 A   11 D
12 B   13 C   14 B   15 C
2 2 B   3 H   4 B   5 H   6 H   7 B   8 H   9 B

Vocabulary

1 1 e   2 d   3 a   4 f   5 c   6 b
2 1 place   2 room   3 space   4 options   5 opportunity
6 possibilities
3 1 room   2 space   3 place   4 opportunity   5 option   6 possibility

A proposal

Reading

1 2 as   3 which   4 own   5 around   6 their   7 both   8 some
9 most   10 This   11 there   12 for
2 *I recommend that we …*; *Our next step should be to …*;
and *I suggest that, at a later stage we …*
3 *Suggested answers*
1 I recommend that we find premises which are close to the
airport.
2 I suggest we commission an architect to design a building for us.
3 Our next step should be to contact Lausanne University.
4 I recommend that we advertise for staff in international science
magazines.
4 1 *although, however* and *on the other hand*   2 *moreover, also*
3 *on balance*

Writing

2 *Sample answer*
Introduction
The aim of this proposal is to evaluate Gdansk and Wroclaw as
possible sites for our office in Poland.
Workforce
Both technology parks are attached to large universities where it
may be possible to recruit graduate students and teachers as staff.
Other IT companies
Since both parks already host a number of IT companies,
customers will be used to coming to these locations. Wroclaw
Technology Park contains some of the largest global IT companies,
which makes the possibility of co-operating with them easier. On
the other hand, the companies in Gdansk are very small, so they
are unlikely to be such useful partners.
Location
Although Gdansk is a pleasant city, Wroclaw undoubtedly offers
the advantage of being closer to international centres such as
Berlin or Prague, where many of our customers are based.
Other facilities
Gdansk offers subsidies or grants to new businesses setting up in
the area. This would be an excellent way of reducing the initial
investment in premises and equipment. On the other hand,
Wroclaw can provide us with business and legal counselling,
which will help us to comply with European regulations.
Recommendations
On balance, although Gdansk is a strong contender, I recommend
that we should choose Wroclaw because it is closer to our
principal markets and it will be easier to attract the right staff to
work there.

UNIT 12

Structuring a presentation

Speaking

1 c   2 e   3 d   4 f   5 b   6 g   7 a

Signalling the parts of a presentation

Listening

1 1 b, j   2 h   3 k   4 c, e   5 a, d, i   6 f   7 g
3 1 advertising   2 drivers   3 traffic conditions   4 main (road)
5 leasing   6 2,000   7 premium rates   8 500,000

Making the most of presentations

Reading

2 1 A   (*… some basic training …*)
2 D   (*Remember to speak slowly and clearly.*)
3 C   (*Recording and listening to yourself …*)

4   D   (... *make eye contact with members of the audience as often as possible.*)
5   B   (*The first step in making a really effective presentation is to prepare.*)
6   A   (*Rehearsing the presentation will greatly reduce anxiety.*)
7   B   (... *which things it is worth knowing about in case anybody asks you about it.*)
8   D   (... *put any lengthy detail into a handout ...*)

Grammar workshop

1 could   2 can   3 can   4 could   5 can   6 can

GRAMMAR WORKSHOP 3

Prepositions in time clauses

1   1 for   2 for   3 on/until   4 in   5 in/during; at   6 since   7 at   8 for; from; to/until   9 until   10 by   11 during/on   12 for
2   1 ~~until~~ by   2 ~~For~~ During/In   3 ~~at~~ on/–   4 ~~since~~ for   5 ~~since~~ from   6 ~~on~~ for

Linking ideas

1   1 although / even though   2 However; On the other hand; on balance   3 Although / Even though   4 However / On the other hand; On balance   5 However   6 However   7 Although / Even though
2   *Suggested answers*
    1   ... I have little time to study.
    2   ... I would like to find a more challenging job.
    3   ... always seem to have too much work on my desk.
    4   ... I wouldn't put it before my family and friends.

Can and *could*

1   1 could   2 could   3 can   4 can   5 could   6 could
2   1 could   2 could   3 could   4 could   5 can

UNIT 13

Getting started

Vocabulary

1   1 trip   2 journey   3 travel
2   1 travel   2 trip   3 trip   4 trip   5 trip/journey   6 trips/journeys

A company meeting

Speaking

2   1   Meeting clients: essential for building relationship, liking you, trust and persuasion
        Expanding your business: explore new markets – see them for yourself
        Meeting colleagues from different offices: get to know each other, builds team spirit, exchange ideas and communicate values
    2   a important   b vital   c essential
    3   All in all (other possible phrases: *to sum up, in summary, to conclude, in conclusion*)

Arranging to travel

Writing

1   1 at   2 who   3 in   4 at   5 while/when
2   1 I'm sorry to ...   2 I'd like you to ...   3 You could ...
3   *Sample answer*
    Hi Dimitri
    I'd be happy to go to the Congress. If you agree, I think it would be a good idea to take Paola with me, as she could make some useful contacts while we're there. We'll be at the Congress for the whole week.
    Best wishes
    Magda

4   *Sample answer*
    Pablo – I'm planning to go to the Mobile World Congress in Barcelona this month. Could you please book flights for myself and Paola and rooms at the Hotel Palace, arriving 24th and leaving 31st? Also, can you suggest places where we can entertain clients in Barcelona? Thanks, Magda

How business travel is changing

Reading

2   Hotels becoming more technological, having to do more than just advertise and offer discounts; business people less loyal to particular chains, looking for cheaper hotels, more loyalty programmes; travellers read reviews on websites and can choose rooms, booking while travelling, i.e. just before arriving.
3   1 A   2 C   3 B   4 D   5 B   6 A   7 D   8 B   9 A   10 D   11 C   12 D   13 C   14 A   15 C

Conference problems

Listening

2   1 E   2 D   3 F   4 H   5 B
3   1 should have sent   2 should have practised   3 should have hired

UNIT 14

Getting started

2   *Suggested answers*: networking, conference talks, presentations and seminars, entertainment events for conference-goers

Arranging conference facilities

Listening

1   *Suggested answers*
    1   numbers of people who are not delegates
    2   other people/things
    3   an event where there might be traditional dance
    4   something belonging to Air New Zealand
    5   a piece of equipment
    6   something speakers should bring
    7   something about the availability of sound equipment
    8   a place where exhibitors might have stands
    9   something always available
2   1 partners   2 guest speakers   3 Opening ceremony   4 logo   5 computer   6 pen drives   7 on request   8 reception area   9 (Free) refreshments
3   instructions: phone National Auditorium, tell them where to put projector
    reason: an urgent meeting
4   *Sample answer*
    Katya
    Unfortunately, I've had to take my wife urgently to the doctor, which means I haven't booked the teleconferencing facilities for Dr Lung. Remember, her talk is scheduled after the plenary in the main conference hall at 10 a.m., so could you please notify the organisers and book it for then?
    Thanks, Piotr

Making the most of business conferences

Reading

2   *Suggested answers*
    A   Put a star by the Action Steps.
    B   Think about what you learned from each session.
    C   Don't think you should go to every session.
    D   Make sure you meet people between sessions.

3 1 C (*Don't assume you should go to every event.*)
  2 C (*The greatest benefits of a conference are often
       circumstantial ... a chance conversation ... don't feel
       pressured by the structure.*)
  3 B (*... distill each presentation down to a central point.*)
  4 A (*... the Action Steps ... dealt with after the conference. I had
       recorded these Action Steps with a star ...*)
  5 D (*Reach out to your contacts in advance and suggest grabbing
       an early breakfast together, lunch, or dinner during the
       conference.*)
  6 B (*Perhaps there was a specific tip that you could adapt when
       you get back to your office ...*)
  7 D (*Encourage each person to invite one or two people that they
       deeply respect ...*)

Networking at a conference
Listening
1 1 g 2 a 3 b 4 c 5 e 6 d 7 h 8 f
2 1 f 2 d 3 e 4 b 5 a

A destination management company (DMC)
Listening
1 *Suggested answer*: A specialist company will know destinations,
  have contacts, and possibly be able to obtain discounts for
  facilities where events will be held. They will know event
  organisers. Also, by outsourcing this to a specialist company,
  your organisation does not need to devote time and resources to
  organising things themselves.
2 1 C 2 B 3 A 4 B 5 C 6 A

UNIT 15

Getting started
1 1 e 2 d 3 h 4 g 5 f 6 c 7 a 8 b

Talking about meetings
Listening
1 1 e 2 c 3 a 4 f 5 g 6 d 7 b
2 1 Martyna: 3   2 Sasha: 6   3 Mei Lin: 2   4 Paul: 1

A survey of meetings
Reading
1 *Suggested answers*
  You get facial expressions, hand gestures more easily; they
  develop transparency and trust; people feel more comfortable
  with each other; deadlines become more important; people make
  friends they respect on a personal level; they enable tailored
  solutions for business-to-business meetings; they facilitate
  opening the relationship, closing the decision, presenting critical
  information, moving forward on a project, getting a dialogue
  started.
2 the two (line 6): video conferencing and meetings held offsite
  none of them (lines 20–21): conference calls etc.
  them (line 27): team members
  its (line 34): a leading New York-based organization
  the majority (line 36): the majority of the organization's customers
  one (line 37): a hybrid meeting
  ones (line 40): meetings
  Both ... each other (lines 40–41): face-to-face meetings and virtual
  ones
  This emerging practice (line 42): hybrid meetings
  their (line 47): Sprint-Nextel's
  them (line 49): face-to-face meetings
  they (line 51): the company

the rest (line 52): the other members of the team
this (line 60): the mixture of face-to-face and virtual meetings
it (line 64): the dialogue with customers
3 1 C (*Instead of looking at video conferencing as an alternative to
       meetings held offsite, many companies are now combining
       the two, as well as using social networking tools as a
       powerful follow-up to face-to-face connections.*)
  2 A (*"It's harder to follow cues such as expressions on people's
       faces in two dimensions," ...*)
  3 D (*... her deadlines now take on greater importance for her,
       because the project is ... a friend and colleague who is now
       real to her ... people think twice before firing a colleague or
       friend that they respect on a personal level.*)
  4 B (*More and more, companies don't see a black-and-white
       divide between face-to-face meetings and virtual ones. Both
       are complementing each other.*)
  5 C (*As a result, Sprint trims meeting costs ...*)
  6 D (*"Social networking is important, because companies can
       keep the dialogue going with their customers" ... But getting
       it started depends on being face to face.*)

Vocabulary
1 e 2 d 3 b 4 c 5 a

Looking for solutions
Listening
1 a: 4, 7, 9
  b: 3, 10
  c: 1, 8
  d: 2, 5, 6
2 The phrases are heard in this order:
  What do you think?; Well, I think ...; Yes, and ...; I'm not sure;
  Personally, I feel that ...; ... don't you think?, Yes, but ...; Frankly,
  I think that ...; That's right; That's true;

Writing
Sample answer
Hello Barry,
I would be happy to visit China during the first two weeks of June. I
shall need to take about 100 leaflets, brochures and catalogues. I will
also need a case containing samples of all our main products.
Could you please let me know what expenses the company will pay
for my trip?
Many thanks,
Sandra

UNIT 16

Spanish sales
Listening
1 1 something which produces successful sales
  2 a number
  3 a place or time
  4 something related to customers and centres
  5 something reps know about
  6 something related to customers
  7/8 numbers
  9 something other than numbers that gives the team an ability to
  compete
2 1 planning 2 80/eighty 3 December 4 list 5 products
  6 relationship 7 5/five 8 6/six 9 quality
3 Existing customers – his team builds up a relationship with
  customers and visits them five or six times a year.

DF Software

Reading

1 *Suggested answers*
1 National sales have risen slightly; international sales have fallen a lot.
2 Total sales have fallen.
3 Their in-country budget has risen by 50%; their international budget has fallen by 50%.
4 There is a correlation between rising and falling sales and rising and falling budgets.
5 While visits to potential customers remain the same, visits to existing customers have fallen.

2 2 past/last 3 make 4 As 5 However 6 period 7 by
8 with 9 this 10 more 11 to 12 same 13 spent 14 them

4 1 a It is thought to be equally effective.
    b It was expected to be a more lucrative market.
    c They paid less attention to existing customers.
    d Customers prefer to meet sales staff face to face.
    e So that they don't lose them.
  2 a as b on the basis that c can be put down to the fact that
    d since e so that
  3 by using video conferencing
  4 by reducing the budget for the annual sales conference
  5 by means of, by

5 *Suggested answers*
1 I recommend using low-cost airlines for business travel when/ if/where/whenever possible.
2 I strongly suggest that we spend more time meeting customers instead of writing reports.
3 I strongly recommend that we incentivise sales staff by awarding prizes when they exceed their targets.
4 I would suggest that we offer our staff a training course to enhance their product knowledge.
5 I recommend that we should hire local staff in international markets, on the basis that this will save us money.

6 1 make 2 suggest 3 make 4 suggest 5 use

Grammar workshop

1 *Suggested answer*: Using the passive avoids saying who made the decisions; it is more formal.

2 *Suggested answers*
1 At a recent board meeting, it was decided to increase the number of sales staff / that the number of sales staff would/ should be increased.
2 Front-office staff are being encouraged to write emails to customers instead of phoning, as this is thought to save money / as it is thought that this will save money.
3 An incentive scheme has been implemented, as this is expected to encourage staff / as staff are expected to be encouraged by this / as it is expected that staff will be encouraged by this.

A report on the use of private company jets

Listening

3 1 G 2 B 3 D

Writing

1 1 Chart 1 shows the number of flights taken by top managers over the last two years and the number forecast for next year. Chart 2 shows what the flights were used for.

2 *Sample answer*
Report on the use of company aircraft by senior managers
Introduction
The reason for writing this report is to summarise and recommend changes in the use of the company aircraft by senior managers at Florentino International.

Number and purpose of flights
The number of flights per year has risen from 56 last year to 63 this year, with 80 expected next year.
Last year, the aircraft was mainly used to meet with clients (56%). Although this year the majority of flights have been for internal meetings, this is expected to change next year, when the plane will be used to meet customers on 60% of occasions.
Recommendations
We need to use the plane less, since the travel budget has been reduced. I therefore recommend that the plane should be used exclusively for meetings with key clients, as this boosts the company image. Furthermore, managers should switch to using scheduled airlines to go to internal meetings.

GRAMMAR WORKSHOP 4

Modal verbs: perfect forms

1 could/should have asked   2 could/should have stayed
3 could have rested   4 might/may/could have been
5 might/may/could have made   6 might/may/could have just dialled   7 could/should have told

Referencing

Suggested answers
1 … especially ones / those / the ones …
2 … to use it. That is why …
3 … and this will lead …
4 … and this has meant that they …
5 … ask them what training they need.
6 … with a client, we usually email each other to summarise …

Passives

1 1 … has been sent to head office.
  2 … will be opened by the Minister for Industry.
  3 … must be submitted by 19 March.
  4 … have been taken by the Board of Directors this morning.
  5 … are being interviewed for the job at the moment. / … for the job are being interviewed at the moment.
  6 … of finished articles are rejected as substandard.
  7 … was opened by mistake.
  8 … must always be kept in a locked safe.

2 1 … to fall next year due to increased competition.
  2 … are expected to rise by 50% in the next six months.
  3 … been announced that profits have reached record levels.
  4 … reported to be losing money.
  5 … by most people to be an excellent human resources manager.
  6 … to meet its deadlines.
  7 … to be bringing out a new smartphone.
  8 … items in our product range should be replaced.

UNIT 17

Social media and customers

Listening

1 1 an adjective which describes how websites are to use
  2 people who can be reached by websites
  3 something which is communicated
  4 a link or relationship between companies and customers
  5 a type of employee
  6 a number
  7 something new

2 1 cheap 2 younger consumers 3 brand message
  4 conversation 5 (unemployed) actors 6 25 million
  7 special offer

Vocabulary

1 1 miss 2 make 3 make 4 make 5 conducted
2 1 run 2 hold 3 place 4 made 5 conducted 6 make
  7 making
3 2 d 3 b, c 4 b, d 5 b 6 d 7 c 8 c 9 a 10 a, d
  11 c, d 12 a
4 1 make 2 do / carry out / conduct 3 arrange/hold/schedule
  4 carry out / implement 5 set/meet 6 arrange/schedule/set
  7 attend
5 *Suggested answer*
  Dear Igor, Martyna and Tatania
  Petra has asked me to organise a meeting in her office to discuss
  Felicity Bannerman's research into how we can use social media.
  Can you please let me know a day and a time which would suit all
  of you?
  Thanks
  Sasha

Some ways of using social media

Reading

1 *Suggested answers*
  1 mistakes 2 employees/workers; aims/goals/objectives
  3 Internet 4 customers; ends/aims/objectives 5 teaching/
  development/education 6 external; business/organisation
  7 listen to 8 using
2 1 C (… *acknowledge your mistakes …*)
  2 B (… *how they use social media within their global
      organisation to align all their employees to their overall
      business objectives.*)
  3 D (*Research published by Proctor and Gamble stated that an
      influencer's story spreads up to one million times within
      their social network on the Internet within one year.*)
  4 A (*Your strategy can then be to marry your business objectives
      with your insights into your customers.*)
  5 C (… *you can help them by providing everything from hands-
      on classroom work to virtual instruction, from written guides
      to recorded video and webinar-style sessions.*)
  6 D (… *making use of external influencers in the
      marketplace. These people have three characteristics:
      they like to try new things because they are new, they are
      intrinsically motivated, and they share stories with friends.*)
  7 A (*Your social strategy should include an element of listening
      to what is already being said in the space.*)
  8 B (… *use of social tools across all business functions, from PR
      to marketing to customer service.*)
3 1 mistakes 2 people who work for you / employees;
  objectives 3 Internet 4 customers; objectives 5 instruction
  6 external; organisation 7 listen to 8 use

Grammar workshop

3 the 4 the 5 the 6 the 7 – 8 – 9 – 10 the

An email enquiry

Writing

1 1 *Suggested underlining*
    introduce our company, say why we want to use social media,
    find out if she can help, how much she charges
2 2 1 that 2 *correct* 3 open 4 to 5 with 6 the 7 make
    8 a 9 employing 10 *correct* 11 about 12 making
3 1 told me this firm was good / consultancy has been
      recommended to us
      help /assist
      how much she charges / what your fees would be
  2 Bill's email is informal; Katrin's is more formal.

UNIT 18

The green office

Reading

2 a F b F c T
3 *Suggested answer*
  Paragraph 2: saving electricity by switching off your computer
  Paragraph 3: using standby mode
  Paragraph 4: printers still with us
  Paragraph 5: ways of saving printing costs
  Paragraph 6: sharing computers
4 *Suggested underlining*
  B Once you have finished with the documents
  C to set this up
  D these measures
  E Clearly this is not the case
  F An obvious solution would be / power it down
  G In addition
5 2 F 3 C 4 E 5 B 6 A

Vocabulary

2 b 3 e 4 g 5 a 6 f 7 d 8 c

Grammar workshop

1 1 Due to 2 due to the fact that
2 1 b 2 a 3 a 4 b
3 1 Due to / Owing to / Because of
  2 due to / owing to / because of
  3 because / due to the fact that / owing to the fact that
  4 because / due to the fact that / owing to the fact that
  5 Due to / Owing to / Because of
4 1 The reason why; is 2 cause 3 result in 4 The reason why;
  was 5 was caused 6 result in

Reducing waste

Vocabulary

1 1 way 2 method
2 1 methods 2 way 3 way 4 method(s) 5 way 6 method
  7 way

Writing

1 1 Because of 2 amount 3 grateful 4 ways 5 give
4 *Sample answer*
  Dear colleagues
  Due to rising costs, we need to cut down on the amount we waste
  in this office. Can you tell us how to make the office more efficient?
  The prize for the best idea will be two cinema tickets.
  Looking forward to your suggestions!
  Rajiv
5 *Sample answer*
  Hi Rajiv
  I think staff generally need to keep their desks tidier. If they do
  this, they will find papers and other documents more quickly and
  it will make the working environment more pleasant for all staff.
  Hassan

An environmental consultant

Listening

2 1 planning new buildings and the impact of the new buildings on
      the environment
  2 a science degree and a Master's in environmental science
3 1 C 2 A 3 A 4 B 5 C 6 B

UNIT 19

Getting started

1 a optional part-time working   b career breaks
   c flexible working hours
2 *Suggested answers*
   Benefits of the changes
   For the company:
   • Staff may be less stressed by outside factors, and therefore more efficient/effective.
   • Possibly less sick leave and other absences.
   • May be easier to retain staff, who, due to external circumstances, might otherwise leave.
   • Easier to recruit staff.
   • Generally, lower costs
   For staff:
   • Less stress.
   • Better work–life balance.
   • Ability to combine working life with family commitments.

Staff reactions

Listening

2 1 F   2 H   3 B   4 C   5 E

Reading a report

Reading

1 1 A   2 C   3 B   4 D   5 A   6 C   7 C   8 D   9 B   10 B   11 D
   12 B   13 C   14 C   15 A
2 1 to summarise staff's reactions to changes
   2 No, these are summarised. Normally a report would be accompanied by tables with the figures.
   3 Yes
   4 The company should go ahead with the changes (under *Recommendations*).
   5 Yes, also in *Recommendations*.

Vocabulary

1 1 c   2 a   3 b
2 1 g   2 f   3 e   4 c   5 a   6 b   7 d

Grammar workshop

1 1 for   2 about   3 with   4 me   5 to
2 1 ~~complaint~~ complained   2 ~~ask you more~~ ask you for more
   3 ~~tell that~~ tell you that / say that   4 ~~staff for a meeting~~ staff to a meeting   5 ~~tell about~~ tell you about   6 ~~agree to my~~ agree with my   7 ~~agree with the~~ agree to the

Calls to HR

Listening

1 1 the name of the department
   2 a complaint about something which is too slow
   3 something he needs to do
   4 something to change
   5 a place for lunch
   6 reason for meeting
   7 a type of manager
   8 something to calculate
   9 something in the staff survey
   10 something to be a member of
   11 something or someone from each department
   12 a type of website
2 1 logistics   2 internet connection   3 track goods
   4 service provider   5 staff canteen   6 working conditions
   7 assistant sales   8 expenses   9 proposals   10 working party
   11 one/1 representative   12 social media

3 *Suggested answers*
   2 they have/had to (be able to) track orders in real time.
   3 changing our service provider.
   4 to lunch (in the staff canteen).
   5 the meeting being held was to discuss working conditions.
   6 changing the way expenses are calculated.
   7 with most of the proposals in the staff survey.
   8 to be/form part of the working party.
   9 each department sending/that each department send one representative

A survey report

Writing

1 *Suggested answer*
   Chart 1 shows where staff feel the offices should be located; Chart 2 shows staff opinion about office design or layout; Chart 3 shows staff opinion about artificial light.
4 *Sample answer*
   Report on staff survey
   Introduction
   The purpose of this report is to summarise the results of our staff survey into the company's offices and make recommendations.
   Staff preferences
   Just under half of staff (46%) said they preferred new offices in this district. Although more than half of employees asked for open-plan offices, managers told me they needed to have their own offices in order to have privacy and quietness. The vast majority of workers also stated that their productivity would increase if their desks were placed near windows.
   Recommendations
   On consideration, I would recommend first that we renovate our current premises. Despite the disruption, the costs will be considerably lower than the alternatives. We should also accommodate managers in their own offices, while making the office for the rest of the staff open plan. Unfortunately, the shape of the building will not permit everyone to work with natural light.

UNIT 20

Getting started

1 *Suggested answers*
   Advantages
   The company may:
   • reduce costs (e.g. labour, land, premises)
   • benefit from more flexible working practices
   • achieve higher productivity
   • be able to produce higher-quality products
   • have access to more advantageous labour laws
   • be closer to markets
   • pay less tax
   The receiving country
   • increased employment
   • higher tax revenue
   • generation of wealth
2 **Disadvantages**
   The company may:
   • be more vulnerable to political changes
   • find offshore operations more difficult to manage/control
   • attract negative criticism, e.g. employing people at lower rates of pay abroad
   • have higher transport costs due to its operations being more widespread
   • have difficulty guarding company secrets/security
   The receiving country
   • may be vulnerable to changes in company policies, external market factors

When should we outsource?

Reading

1 reduced costs, chance to focus on what you are good at

3 1 A (*… to let them focus on the functions they specialize in.*)

   2 D (*… bring the actual cost of a full-time employee to nearly double their base salary.*)

   3 D ("*… outsourcing your legal might mean a bi-weekly teleconference with an attorney you couldn't possibly afford to hire full-time.*")

   4 B (*… entrepreneurs often come to his firm when they find they can't answer banks' questions about issues such as cashflow projections.*)

   5 B ("*Your potential cost savings are totally tied to the type of industry you're in and the complexity of what you're trying to do,*" *…*)

   6 C (*… offshore contractors may require more time to manage thanks to differences in time zones, language, and culture.*)

Outsourcing IT

Listening

2 *Suggested answers*

   1 more need for good people, growing, becoming more complex, coding of systems has been offshored, cloud-based IT, no need for companies to have their own data centre and servers

   2 computer science, but not necessarily

   3 understanding of technology, business understanding and ability to communicate with people

4 1 B 2 A 3 C 4 C 5 A

A proposal for outsourcing

Writing

2 1 b (more formal, less colloquial and therefore more suited to a formal proposal)

   2 b (same reason as in 1)

3 1 past

   2 a

4 1 would have saved 2 had not been infected
3 had not broken down; would have completed
4 would have delivered; had been

5 *Suggested answers*
If a round-the-clock emergency hotline had been available last year, we would have had an instant solution to our problems.
If staff had received IT support and training last year, they would have worked more efficiently.
If we'd used IT Remote's website hosting service, it would still have been necessary to design the website itself.

6 *Sample answer*
Proposal for outsourcing IT
Introduction
The purpose of this proposal is to recommend an external IT service provider from the two we have investigated.
DataDo
Although DataDo's charges are comparatively high, they include all our requirements for running our website in their fee. If we chose them, this would produce cost savings, since we would not have to staff resources to this job. They also provide systems protection and emergency services, and if we had had these last year, they would have prevented the disastrous virus infection.
IT Remote
This outfit is a low-cost alternative. Among the services they offer is staff training. This would have been useful last year, but since our staff are now fully trained, this is no longer of interest. Although they provide web hosting, they do not do web design. If they did, their services would be more interesting.
Recommendations
I recommend we employ DataDo, as their services are more tailored to our requirements.

GRAMMAR WORKSHOP 5

Definite article

1 3 – 4 the 5 the 6 – 7 – 8 – 9 – 10 – 11 the 12 the 13 the 14 – 15 the 16 the 17 the 18 the 19 the 20 the

2 2 ~~to your letter~~ to the letter 3 ~~of a marketing~~ of the marketing 4 ~~all documents~~ all the documents 5 ~~that our new~~ that the new 6 ~~A fall~~ The fall 7 *correct* 8 ~~on a same~~ on the same

Tense changes in reported speech

1 1 he/she found travelling to work at peak times stressful and time-consuming.

   2 the new scheme was introduced, he/she hoped he/she would be able to take a career break.

   3 had always wanted to travel round the world.

   4 we/they could provide on-site nursery care for pre-school children.

   5 in his/her last job, they (had) used flexitime, and it was / had been very successful.

   6 I/we/they introduced the changes, he/she might decide to work part time.

2 1 arrives/arrived 2 would sell 3 wants 4 would install 5 wouldn't/couldn't go; finished / had finished 6 had sent / would send 7 would be

Third conditional

1 would have rearranged 2 had given 3 would have signed; had been 4 had raised; would have stayed 5 had offered; would have bought 6 would not have broken down; had followed

2 *Suggested answers*: 1 we wouldn't have had a cashflow problem.
2 we had installed a good anti-virus program.
3 we had had sufficient sales budget.
4 we wouldn't have fallen behind with production.

UNIT 21

Getting started

1 1 25 2 8 to 16 3 thousands 4 91% 5 about 85% 6 4 to 100 7 68%

From satisfaction to loyalty

Reading

2 ideas mentioned in the article which make customers loyal to a company:

- good relationships between your employees and your customers
- the value of the product they are buying
- ease of doing business
- your staff's responsiveness, integrity, trust and professionalism
- having staff who are highly motivated, highly engaged
- staff have necessary customer-service skills

3 1 C (*… when your customers have a strong bond with you …*)

   2 B (*… people are your key competitive advantage.*)

   3 B (*… the impact that customer loyalty can have on your bottom line …*)

   4 D (*The top factor is value: 'Is this company's product or service having a positive impact on my business? Do I have a strong return on investment?'*)

   5 A (*… it's hard to be different from your rivals because best practices spread across an industry very rapidly …*)

   6 D (*… empowerment, which means that organisations need to empower employees to make decisions and take risks …*)

Vocabulary

1 f 2 h 3 d 4 c 5 g 6 b 7 a 8 e

Grammar workshop

1 which/that/–   2 which/that/–   3 which/that; which   4 who
5 which/that/–   6 which/that   7 where   8 which/that; who/that

Encouraging customer loyalty

Listening

1   1 service desk   2 comment card   3 loyalty card
4 (local) schools   5 rural areas   6 computer equipment
7 sample shop   8 shopping experience

A staff meeting

Writing and speaking

1   1 out   2 the   3 which   4 which/that   5 where   6 who/that
2   *Sample answer*
Dear Simone,
I'm afraid I shall be unable make it on time for the meeting on
Friday as I have a meeting with a client on the other side of town at
one o'clock. However, I should be able to get there by 2.30.
My apologies.
Karl

UNIT 22

Training in customer communication skills

Reading

2   *Suggested answers*
1   Satisfying/requirements by understanding how they are
thinking
2   customers/tell other people
3   writing skills
4   more certain/professional abilities
5   how/body language affects clients
6   ways of dealing with difficult clients
7   better service
8   using/popular media
3   1   C   (*To address your customers' needs, you must be able to see
things from their point of view, …*)
2   C   (*Word of mouth is the cheapest and most effective way of
marketing your business and extending your customer base.*)
3   A   (*… how email can be used for effective communication with
your customers.*)
4   B   (*… practise customer-handling skills … enabling a confident
return to the workplace.*)
5   A   (*… how non-verbal communication is interpreted by
customers.*)
6   C   (*… learn how to handle awkward customers appropriately.*)
7   B   (*… understanding of customer expectations and the skills to
exceed that expectation*)
8   D   (*Call centres and internet sales are the fastest-growing
operational departments for many organisations.*)

Vocabulary

1   1 good   2 large   3 wide
2   The following do *not* form correct collocations:
2 most significant   3 big   4 important   5 big   6 high   7 big
8 important   9 big

Customer communication at Not Just Food

Listening

1   *Suggested underlining*
2 original purpose / website   3 demonstrates / commitment to
clients   4 take trouble / small clients   5 avoided / dissatisfied
customers
2   1 B   2 B   3 C   4 A   5 B

3   1   By giving a discount when it costs less to do the work than they
originally quoted, and by swallowing the additional cost when
it costs more.
2   By being fair (see answer to previous question) and by helping
small clients who initially made them little money, but who
then grew.

Turning complaints to your advantage

Reading

2   It gives an opportunity to build a stronger relationship with
customers, increasing loyalty and business, improving reputation,
improving services.
3   *(with reasons based on Grammar workshop 6 explanations)*
1   it (not emphatic and no distinction needed between two things
already mentioned)
2   This (referring to the last thing mentioned – the opportunity for
a stronger, more profitable relationship)
3   it (not emphatic)
4   This (to refer to something we're going to say)
5   that (emphatic)
6   this (to refer to something you are going to say)
7   This (to refer to the second of two things – in this case, how
they can be rewarded)
8   this (emphatic)

UNIT 23

Getting started

Vocabulary

1   most recent
2   1 latest   2 latest   3 last   4 latest   5 last   6 last
3   1 the latest   2 the last   3 the last   4 the latest   5 the last
6 the last

A letter about a new service

Reading

1   1 B   2 C   3 D   4 C   5 B   6 D   7 B   8 A   9 A   10 D
2   1   The letter has a heading after *Dear Mr Müller*. Note: in the US,
the heading normally comes before *Dear Mr Müller*; in Britain,
a comma (,) or no punctuation is used after the name, while in
the US a colon (:) is used; in the US, titles like *Mr.* and *Mrs.* are
written with a full stop.
2   valued
3   we shall be offering the same level of service
4   trouble-free
5   contact me personally

Writing

2   *Sample answer*
Dear Mr Rodriguez,
New Services from TopTen Leasing
As a valued long-standing client of TopTen, I am sure you will
be interested to know that we are extending our leasing services
to the whole of Europe. This means we guarantee to deliver the
equipment you require anywhere in Europe within 24 hours of you
placing the order. Also, for each seven-day lease, we will give you
one free day. I enclose a leaflet detailing our service.
As you already know, we make sure that all the equipment we
supply is in perfect condition, so you can be certain to start using
it as soon as it is delivered. Also, as a premium customer, you are
not required to pay a deposit on the equipment you hire.
If you would like to know more about this service, or if you would
like to take advantage of it, please do not hesitate to contact me
personally.
Yours sincerely,

An email from a dissatisfied customer

Reading
1 2 ~~of~~ with   3 ~~Past~~ Last   4 ~~who~~ which   5 ~~of~~ to   6 ~~an~~ the
7 ~~Although~~ However   8 ✓   9 ~~last~~ latest   10 ~~they~~ which
11 ~~it~~ this/that   12 ✓   13 ~~more~~ extra   14 ✓   15 ~~in~~ over
16 ~~another~~ other   17 ✓   18 ~~it~~ which
2 1 Yes: when, where and the exact nature of the problem
2 Yes: especially if it caused injury, cost money or lost customers
3 Yes: this is essential, otherwise there's no point in writing the letter.
4 No: not unless it is related to the problem which occurred
5 Perhaps: but you should be careful about not angering people by threatening too much, and you should not make absurd threats which you will never carry out.
6 Yes: if this is true.
7 No: not necessary.
3 1 (paragraph 2); 2 (paragraph 3); 5, 6 (paragraph 4)

Grammar workshop
Suggested answers
1 You delivered the wrong model. As a consequence (of this), we had to send it back.
2 Some of the goods were damaged. As a consequence (of this), we lost an important order.
3 You were late sending the information. This meant that we missed an important deadline.
4 There were several mistakes in the invoice. As a result, we had to spend a day sorting it out.
5 You sent the components to the wrong factory. This meant that we had to stop the production line for an hour.
6 Two of the pieces were broken. Consequently, we had to return the entire consignment.

Preparing a letter or email of complaint

Listening
1 Remind them   2 five/5 days   3 the results   4 problem-free

Writing
2 *Sample answer*
Dear Mr Sarawi,
Late delivery of documents
I am writing to you to express my dissatisfaction with your document-delivery service.
Last Monday, we asked you to deliver some important legal documents to our clients in Katowice in time for a meeting with our lawyers on Monday morning. The documents did not, in fact, reach them until four o'clock on Friday afternoon, with the result that we had to cancel the meeting and reschedule it for this week. This nearly resulted in us losing an important contract.
I would like to remind you that we are a long-standing client of yours and that we rely on you to provide us with a trouble-free service. I must emphasise that we will only continue to use your service if deliveries continue to be problem-free in the future.
Yours sincerely,

UNIT 24

Working in another culture

Reading
2 *Suggested answers*
Paragraph 2: How to find out if you're suited for international work
Paragraph 3: The difficulties of getting an international posting
Paragraph 4: International workers' difficulties
Paragraph 5: Advice for working in a new culture
Paragraph 6: Adapting to new conditions

3 *Suggested underlining*
1 assessments / conducting business
2 problems / Thus, the choice / not be taken lightly
3 to even pass this first hurdle
4 the rigors of a foreign assignment and foreign culture
5 inter-culturally sensitive way / What we may assume / constructs
6 will not be business as usual / Added to the complexity
4 *Suggested underlining*
A they
B Instead, most difficulties
C However / refuse to see things this way
D It will instead contain
E Only then will they be allowed
F This
G –
5 2 B   3 E   4 A   5 F   6 D

Speaking
2 1 1 need to be culturally sensitive   2 learn the language   3 fit into the new context
2 1 You'll irritate people, won't work effectively.   2 If not, you'll have problems, people will misunderstand, get impatient.   3 You need to understand things from local point of view.
3 Russia: managers more autocratic vs USA: consulting and discussing
3 1 I think there are three things which are essential when taking up employment abroad.
2 a Firstly, Secondly, Finally
b because, If you don't, You see
c To take a personal example
d If you bear those things in mind

Grammar workshop
1 1 good   2 use   3 worth   4 problems   5 point   6 difficulty
2 *Suggested answers*
1 asking / applying to / going to
2 applying / going / trying / interviewing
3 attending / going to / holding
4 giving / showing
5 buying / ordering / installing
6 finding / succeeding in / making a success of

Working in China and working in Europe

Listening
2 1 C   2 C   3 A   4 B   5 A   6 B

Writing
1 2 ~~win~~ get/gain   3 ~~know~~ learn   4 ✓   5 ~~interesting~~ interested   6 ~~last~~ latest   7 ✓
2 *Sample answer*
Dear colleagues
This is to say that we are looking for three members of staff to work in our Guangzhou office for six months to gain experience of Chinese working methods and to integrate our operations more closely. Those interested should apply to me by email by the end of this month.
Thanks

GRAMMAR WORKSHOP 6

Relative clauses
1 2 which   3 factory, where   4 which/that   5 which
6 whose   7 which/that   8 January, when … force, and
9 which/that   10 which/that   11 Klein, which
12 manager, who is very accommodating, is   13 whose
14 proposal, which   15 What   16 when/that

2 2 ~~programme that~~ programme, which   3 ~~what~~ which   4 ~~that~~ which   5 ~~recruitment that~~ recruitment, which   6 ~~which~~ who/ that   7 ~~scheme what~~ scheme, which   8 ~~employees which~~ employees, who / employees who

Which pronoun: *it*, *this* or *that*?

1 This/That (emphatic)   2 this (referring to the second thing mentioned in the previous sentence – being late, not the computer problem)   3 that (conditional)   4 It (not emphatic)   5 this/that (emphatic)   6 This (something more to say)   7 that (conditional) 8 It (not emphatic)

Expressing results

1 meant / resulted in   2 means   3 As a result / As a consequence of this / Consequently   4 mean / result in   5 mean / result in 6 As a result / As a consequence of this / Consequently

WRITING REFERENCE

Levels of formality

1 2 *show*   3 *satisfactory*   4 *pay back*   5 *with reference to* 6 *agree with*   7 *I look forward*   8 *asap*   9 *Meeting's Fri* 10 dashes
2 Email 1 is more formal: uses *Dear …*, no contractions, formal phrases such as *pleased to inform*, complete sentences.
Email 2 is less formal: uses *Hi …*, incomplete sentences, informal phrases (*mix-up*, not *confusion*).
3 2 less formal   3 more formal   4 more formal   5 more formal 6 more formal
4 2 less formal   3 more formal   4 less formal   5 more formal 6 more formal
5 1 good   2 bad   3 good

Short emails

1 1   A   to find out when he'll get the information he needs
      B   to change the time of a meeting
   2   A   He needs to give a schedule to their Chinese suppliers.
      B   A client's visit has been rescheduled.
   3   The information which she will send.
   4   Because he is writing to several colleagues or his team.
   5   He wants his colleagues to confirm that Friday afternoon is OK for the meeting.
   6   Because he is causing his colleagues inconvenience.
2 1 *Hi*   2 *Dear*   3 first name   4 appropriate   5 team   6 *Cheers* 7 *Kind regards*   8 closely
3 1 A   2 D   3 F   4 C   5 B   6 E
4 1 as   2 to   3 it   4 as   5 by then   6 However   7 because 8 but   9 this   10 it   11 and   12 Then   13 that's
5 A less formal   B less formal   C less formal   D more formal E more formal   F less formal
6 1   No problem (F)
   2   I hope you are well (D)
   3   as we have an urgent job to finish (A); I'm meeting with the customer in two days and need to have an answer for them by then (C); as their end-of-year accounts are due (C); because we are hoping to take on more staff (D); The reason for this is that it will give them flexibility (E)
   4   I have been asked by the organisers if you could (E)
   5   Let's check our diaries (A)
   6   If you like, I would be happy to (E); I'll give our client a quote this afternoon (F); I'll get the job done tomorrow if that's all right (F)
   7   Thanks for the emails yesterday (B); discussed in the emails below (C)
   8   When will you send me …? (B); Have we managed to backdate the accounts …? (C); Please advise ASAP (C); I would certainly appreciate any information that you might have (D)

Memos

1 C   (and possibly B, E and F)
2 *Suggested answers*
   A   Visit from Japanese delegation
   B   New training directives
3 1 to   2 so   3 them   4 order   5 therefore   6 this   7 this

A letter of invitation

1 addressing the addressee by title and surname; no contractions; long words (e.g. *academic qualifications, combined*); less common words (e.g. *unique*); no abbreviations; complete sentences; formal phrases (e.g. *I would be very grateful if …*)
2 1 c   2 d   3 a   4 b
3 1 f   2 g   3 e   4 h   5 i   6 c   7 b   8 a   9 d

A letter applying for a job/grant, etc.

1 *Suggested answers*: 1, 2, 3, 5, 6, 8 and 10
2 1 d   2 e   3 a   4 c   5 b   6 f
3 Paragraph 1: 1, 2, 3
   Paragraph 2: 5, 6
   Paragraph 3: 8
   Paragraph 4: 10

A letter of enquiry

1 *Suggested answers*
   1   Paragraph 1: to introduce the company, its activities and importance
      Paragraph 2: to explain why he is writing – the product he needs
      Paragraph 3: to enquire about prices, installation, discounts and training
   2   Because he is speaking for the company, not as an individual.
   3   Indirect questions – they're more formal and polite.
   4   Because he is talking about an imaginary or hypothetical situation in which they might place an order.

A report on a survey

1 1 e   2 c   3 d   4 b   5 a
2 A and   B how   C which   D which   E while   F after   G which H whose   I so that   J even though
3 1   more formal
   2   She uses an impersonal style until the last section when she says *I would also recommend*. An impersonal style is more formal and serious. The personal recommendation shows that she supports it.
   3   the number of visits, the sales, enquiries and number of respondents to the questionnaire
      The first figures show how important the website is, and the number of respondents gives a comparison with the number of visitors and shows how representative their answers might be; in the third section, the figures give an idea of how representative certain comments were.
   4   a Introduction   b Our website: the figures   c Our website: the figures   d Findings   e Conclusions and recommendations

A personal report

1 1 On the whole   2 Moreover   3 However/Unfortunately 4 There was also a tendency   5 Although   6 Unfortunately/ However   7 For example   8 However
2 1   I found the store to be tidy, clean and attractive; the staff … were welcoming and helpful; visiting the store was a pleasant and satisfying experience; The store offers a generally excellent level of service
   2   directions and other written information … should be made clearer, and steps should be taken to make the music less intrusive.
   3   are issued; should be made; should be taken

Proposals

1 a solution to a problem
2 1 Introduction   2 Customer complaints   3 Possible solutions
4 Employing extra staff; Outsourcing customer care
5 Conclusion   6 Conclusion
3 2 concerning   3 irritation   4 monitor   5 adopted
6 attended to   7 a significant cost   8 outlines   9 arise
10 resources   11 require   12 issues   13 generate   14 concern

A short proposal

1 1 Due to   2 before   3 so that   4 until   5 also   6 who   7 This
8 this
2 1 a   2 d   3 c   4 e   5 b
3 He is using *could* and *would* (the second conditional) for a
hypothetical solution to a problem.

EXAM SKILLS AND EXAM PRACTICE

Listening Test Part 4: Exam skills

1 b 1 B   2 C   3 A

Listening Test Part 4: Exam practice

33 A   34 C   35 A   36 B   37 B   38 A
39 C   40 A   41 C   42 B   43 A   44 B
45 A   46 B   47 B   48 A   49 C   50 A

Reading Test Part 2 (Section 2): Exam skills

1 1 D   2 B   3 C
2 1 C   2 A   3 B
3 1 B   2 A   3 B

Reading Test Part 2 (Section 2): Exam practice

1 D   2 B   3 C   4 A   5 B

Reading Test Part 2 (Section 3): Exam skills

1

Article	Pronoun	Relative pronoun	Auxiliary/ modal verb	Preposition	Other
an the	it they	what who	are be being can have	to with	although forward much so than

2 b 1 the   2 forward/together   3 had   4 one   5 with
6 much/far   7 than   8 been   9 who   10 What
3 1 have   2 be   3 the   4 to   5 what   6 are   7 with /to
4 1 they   2 there   3 who   4 would   5 it   6 also   7 Both   8 In
9 was   10 to

Reading Test Part 2 (Section 3): Exam practice

6 at   7 than   8 with   9 the   10 so

Reading Test Part 2 (Section 4): Exam skills

1 1 B   2 C   3 A
2 1 D (*necessity/requirement/need for*)
2 A (*spend on, expend, pay for*)
3 C (*none of the others take a preposition*)
3 1 B   2 A   3 C

Reading Test Part 2 (Section 4): Exam practice

11 C   12 A   13 C   14 B   15 D   16 B

Reading Test Part 2 (Section 5): Exam skills

1 2
2 2 prompted Tim / start / own business
3 Professor Keep say about apprenticeships
4 Adecco, young people / taught the ability
5 point / Tim / final paragraph
3 1 B (*Tim had always known he wanted to do something 'hands-on' ...*)
2 A (*His newly gained finance and management skills, coupled with his craft skills, gave him the confidence to go it alone.*)
3 D (*... the most successful education systems in Europe combine apprenticeship and higher-education career paths ...*)
4 A (*... called for financial acumen ... to form a core part of curricula from an early age.*)
5 B (*He believes that had there been more awareness of the so-called 'real world' during school, learning the business-savvy skills needed to make it beyond getting a degree, he would have had the confidence to go it alone far sooner. And so might many of his classmates.*)

Reading Test Part 2 (Section 5): Exam practice

17 D   18 B   19 D   20 A   21 C   22 B

Reading Test Part 2 (Section 6): Exam skills

1 3 ~~start~~ starts   4 ✓   5 ~~may~~ can   6 ~~have~~ has   7 ~~being~~ be
8 ~~showing~~ shown
2 3 ~~by~~ in   4 ~~on~~ in   5 ✓   6 ~~from~~ with   7 ~~to~~ for
3 2 ~~extreme~~ extremely   3 ~~interesting~~ interested
4 ~~expansion~~ expanding   5 ~~brief~~ briefly   6 ~~discussion~~ discuss
7 ✓   8 ~~possible~~ possibility   9 ~~fill~~ full   10 ✓

Reading Test Part 2 (Section 6): Exam practice

23 ~~affected~~ affecting   24 ~~owners~~ ownership   25 ~~up~~ over
26 ✓   27 ~~another~~ other   28 ~~competitor~~ competitors   29 ~~too~~ very

Writing Test Part 2: Exam skills

1 a A number of staff have recently told you that they are unhappy about the times when they start and finish work in your company. You have been asked to write a <u>report for the managing director about this</u>.
Write your report. Write about:
- <u>why staff are unhappy with the times</u>
- <u>why it is important to keep staff happy</u>
- <u>what solutions your company should adopt</u> for the problem
- any other points you think are important.
Write 180–200 words.
b 1 You must include the underlined points (see above).
2 Why staff are unhappy, why it's important to keep staff happy, solutions to the problem
3 statistics
4 the managing director, so a formal style.
5 a title and sections with section headings
d 2 It has a title, is divided into sections with section headings and it uses bullet points.
3 yes
4 The first section introduces the purpose of the report. The last section recommends solutions to the problem.
5 Phrases which express results: *means, as a result, as a consequence of*
6 Yes. Nothing has been forgotten.

Writing Test Part 2: Exam practice

Task A

Sample answer

Dear Mr Jaworski,

I am writing on behalf of my CEO, Mr Jaune, to give you a little background to problem areas within our company which we would like you to look at and, if possible, suggest improvements or solutions. Our greatest area of concern is that we are not giving a sufficiently high level of service to our clients. In particular, we are late in completing orders, and on a number of occasions in the past year, clients have been invoiced incorrectly, leading to irritation and loss of trust.

Another connected problem has been that, on occasion, our production line has become disorganised, leading to delays in output and hence our unpunctuality in completing some orders. We hope you will be able to suggest ways in which we can organise our workforce more efficiently.

Finally, there has recently been more absenteeism both on the factory floor and in the offices. This is usually justified as sick leave, but we suspect that staff morale is low, and we would be grateful if you could look into this and suggest ways in which we can work as a happier and more cohesive team.

We look forward to your visit and your recommendations.

Yours sincerely,

Task B

Sample answer

Report on our company website

Introduction

The purpose of this report is to compare our website with GK Transport's website and to suggest modifications to make ours more competitive.

Our website and GK Transport's website

Our website shows details of our fleet of lorries, the loads they can carry, our rates and our major routes and our contact details. While GK Transport's site also contains this information, it has an interactive page as well, which allows visitors to calculate how much a load would cost for a journey.

Their site also permits customers to track their loads in real time and see exactly where they are in the international transport system.

Our website has some advantages over GK Transport's because it offers straightforward, clear navigation and responds quickly with any bandwidth, making it much easier to use. It also has the option of a quick link to a 24-hour helpdesk.

Recommendations

I would suggest offering a similar tracking system and an automated system for calculating costs, but with a direct link to our very successful helpdesk feature, so that customers using the system are automatically contacted with news of discounts and other special offers.

Transcripts

UNIT 1

①₀₁ Listening, page 10

WJ = Wolfgang Meyer, CS = Carmen Segovia

WJ: Skills Development College. Wolfgang Meyer speaking.

CS: Hello, my name's Carmen Segovia. I'm calling from Forrest Insurance Company to make enquiries about the company training courses you run.

WJ: OK, let me take down some details. How do you spell Forrest?

CS: F-O-double R-E-S-T.

WJ: … double R-E-S-T. OK. Um, what sort of course are you looking for?

CS: Well, we'd like a course in advanced computer skills and we were wondering if you do that sort of thing. The course is for a number of graduate trainees we've recently taken on.

WJ: Well, we do standard courses, which are four hours a week for ten weeks, or we can offer you tailor-made courses adapted for your particular needs.

CS: Yes, that sounds more what we're looking for. We're really thinking of a more intensive course for just one month.

WJ: That's fine. We can design a programme which meets your requirements – you know, your learning goals and training budget.

CS: Right. All the training you give is practical, hands-on training, isn't it? I mean, it's not just theoretical, is it?

WJ: Yes, all very hands-on. All students work on their individual computers. Can I suggest we send around our director of studies so she can analyse what you require? Then we can design a course to suit you and give you an exact quotation of how much it'd cost.

CS: That'd be great. When can your director come?

①₀₂ Role-play, page 11

M = Man, W = Woman

M: OK, um, shall we imagine we work for a software company with a hundred employees?

W: Fine. So what should the course include? I suggest that on the first day, we should explain what the company does and how it's organised.

M: Yes, that's a good idea. Um, we could also spend some time introducing people in the company, so that they meet them and learn who they are and what they do.

W: Yes, and how about getting them to spend two days learning how our computer systems work?

M: Good idea. That way, when they go to their jobs, they won't always have to ask other people. And I think another useful thing is to explain what to do when they have a problem—

W: —for example when they want time off, or they're off sick or something.

M: Exactly, so that they know what the procedures are and how to deal with them.

W: Good idea. Do you think the course should be internal or given by an external organisation?

M: Well, why don't we ask an external organisation? That'll mean that staff don't have to give up time to work on the training course.

W: I'm not sure. I think that it should be given by people within the company who know how everything works. Outside people won't know.

M: Mm, maybe, but the problem is that internal staff will need a lot of time to prepare the course and give it, and that'll distract them from their normal work.

W: Yes, but it's still probably cheaper than getting someone from outside to give the course.

M: Yes, possibly. Um, I'm not sure I agree though. Do you think the trainees should do the course in working hours or in their free time?

W: I think it depends how many hours they do each day. If the course is going to be all day, it should be in working time. If it's just a couple of hours, they can do it in their free time after work.

M: I don't agree. I think they'll be very tired after work.

W: You may be right. OK, what about holding the course for two hours every day, from nine to 11 in the morning?

M: Ah, I think *that's* a good idea – and we can then get different members of the staff to do sessions with the new recruits here in one of the meeting rooms.

W: Fine, that's agreed then.

M: Yes.

UNIT 2

①₀₃ Listening, page 13

I = Interviewer; C = Christina Bunt

I: What do you most like about your job?

C: I suppose the most enjoyable for me is training because it's what I started out doing, so it's the, er, bit that I enjoy most … um, there's not many things that I dislike, to be honest. I suppose, um, the most challenging part of it is when you're talking in the area of discipline or, um, sometimes the firing part … Um … That's … one of our major considerations is getting the right people in the right job to start with. If you, if you employ the right people, you don't have a problem managing them once they're in the … the workplace. Um, our cashiers, obviously customer service is our … our major selling point when it comes to our company. Um, if you employ a cashier who is naturally friendly, naturally smiles, naturally polite, it's not a problem. If you try and teach them to be polite and to smile, it doesn't necessarily work …

I: And how did you get into this line of work?

C: Um, I originally worked, er, trained as a nurse, um, when my daughter was born, needed a part-time job and, um, took a part-time job with Tesco. I used to work nine hours a week on the checkouts, er, covering lunch reliefs. And then they offered me an evening checkout supervisor's job which I took, and then … I took a full-time job, went into training about 15 years ago. I've worked with them for 22 [years], so, yeah, about 15 years ago I went into … as … into a job as a training manager, which is a kind of natural progression into personnel. So I did the training job for about four or five years, and then took my first role about ten or 11 years ago.

I: And where do you think you might be workwise in ten years? Where would you like to be?

C: Where would I like to be? I actually would like to still be working in personnel. Um, the career progression within my firm does tend to try and take senior team through to store management, but it's actually something that I'm not particularly interested to do. Um, I prefer the people side of the business and I would like to either be still in a personnel role in store or in a regional role as personnel.

I: Now, if someone came to you and said, 'I've … I've got a job interview, what should I try and make sure I do?' Can you give three tips for good interview technique?

C: Um, I suppose the first thing is to keep in mind that the first impression sticks, um, and I'm not looking for people to turn up to interview with me with … in a three-piece suit looking as if they've just stepped out of a fashion plate, but … tidy but comfortable, um, and that first step towards the person who's going to interview makes a huge difference if you're quite prepared to smile and be open and shake a hand, and sometimes for young people that can be really difficult because they're not used to a formal greeting … And to be totally natural and not try to put yourself forward as something that you're not. Because it's too obvious in an interview situation when you're, when you're trying to pull the wool over someone's eyes. … Um, talk about the things that you like and talk about the things that you're good at, because you do that naturally, if there's something that you're really interested in, even if it's got nothing to do with the job role that you're actually going into, the enthusiasm will come across. Um, I'll always know that I'm talking to somebody that's going to be enthusiastic about whatever I put in front of them, because they're enthusiastic about things that they like in their normal life.

① 04 Listening, page 14

Speaker 1: Jane Milton

I love being able to work out what a client needs and … and do it. And I love, you know, having an idea for a new food product for them and then seeing it, you know, in a supermarket, or, um, writing something and then having loads of emails from people because they've used that recipe so much and they can't believe how easy it was, or a whole lot of different things.

Speaker 2: Amanda Hamilton

I absolutely thrive on the freedom, just being able to make, you know, my own choices. It is, as you said, a lifestyle choice, although you probably end up working slightly more hours than you did working for a corporation, but you sort of somehow don't mind those longer hours because it's fulfilling. It's your own project, your own baby and there's also a sense of pride, I think, when you can make your own decisions.

Speaker 3: Rob Liu

We do, um, recruitment and we also do career coaching, that's targeting the Chinese-speaking jobseekers in the UK. Um, it's a lot of challenge, but it's quite interesting because I, I quite like the sort of 'people element', um, of it. You see people, sort of, improve, really, within a short, quite a short time sometimes. That's very, um, inspiring, I think. Um, it's, it's good to get to see people, um, making positive changes in, in their life.

Speaker 4: Adam Evans

… so that is my long-term aim – to make every single individual in this 30 – you know, in this team of 30 – to be the best, whether it's people who work in marketing, or whether it's somebody who is doing the paperwork, or whether it is somebody who visits, or it's an area manager. And so while they're doing the day-to-day business, what I'm doing is I'm getting their future ready, so when they arrive, there's a job there for them, and that's what I enjoy – that's one of the main things.

Speaker 5: Harriet Barber

Um, I like the diversity of projects because we always work with different clients and on different projects. We also work on very large-scale projects, so we're working on things like Crossrail and the Olympics, and lots of urban generation in London. And so it's exciting to see, like, how these projects are progressing, and all of the effort that goes into them, and that sort of thing, so that's really nice to see.

UNIT 3

① 05 Listening, page 17

P = Presenter, J = Jürgen, M = Marta, A = Alex, L = Luli, I = Ivan

P: So, finally, let's have some advice from each of you about how to go about getting that first job, the one you've studied so hard to prepare for. Jürgen?

J: My advice is this: especially with the first job, prospective employers want to get a complete picture of you, not just what you've been studying and your holiday jobs. So, include a section in your CV for the things which you like doing in your free time. These say a lot about you, and may make you a lot more interesting than all those other kids who just spend their evenings going to the pub or listening to music.

P: OK. Marta?

M: I was reading somewhere that, in the US, more than 80% of applications nowadays are made electronically – human resources officers don't want the trouble of having to file lots of applications, so what comes by snail mail goes straight in the bin. What goes into the computer is there in front of you at the click of a mouse.

P: Thanks for that, Marta. Alex, what's your advice?

A: Well, I agree with everything I've heard so far, but one thing I'd like to emphasise is that you've got to make yourself as attractive as possible to a potential employer, so make your good qualities stand out. On the other hand, don't ever tell a lie, because it'll catch up with you in the end – you know, you'll be found out. And when that happens, the only thing you'll achieve is a feeling of embarrassment.

P: That's good advice. Luli, it's your turn to offer some words of wisdom.

L: Words of wisdom!? Mine's just plain common sense and comes from long experience of non-native speakers writing applications in English. Get someone to look it over before you send it, someone who speaks the language well, preferably a native, because it's such a pity to lose that all-important chance for a job interview because of some slight grammatical mistakes – and they do make a difference to the impression you're giving.

P: Good point, Luli, and I couldn't agree more. What about you, Ivan?

I: Frankly, I agree with everything that's been said in the last five minutes. You know, I get pages and pages of applications every week, and I find it hard to sort people who are genuinely interested in working for us from the ones who just send the same application to every company on the Internet. So, though they all have names and addresses, they don't all get replies. My advice is to follow up that application with a call to ask if your application has been received and to show that you really are interested. It makes all the difference, and chances are you'll get invited in for a chat.

①⑥ Speaking, page 19

Adam Evans

Understand and do the research, because, um, the impression … when somebody comes in and they talk about your organisation, even though they've never worked there, and they know that you've been, you know, you've been around for 500 years, and you know that you're the leader in Asia and you know this, it's quite 'wow, this person has done the homework!' And it gives the impression that the candidate is really interested in the job, and that is wonderful, I mean, we just adopted a baby panda in China, you know, from the Chinese government gave it to us, and somebody in an interview actually brought that out. That was really quite surprising. I didn't expect that at all, and so my … the impression of that candidate was suddenly 'this person's interested,' you know – it's not just another job. Another piece of advice is, and I know it's difficult, is to be themselves, first and foremost. And how can you be yourself in an interview? That's the other thing, because you're not, because you're nervous … but let them … look at the interview process as, um, if they were talking to me – who's the most nervous? Is it me or the candidate? Because I don't know the candidate, and I need somebody for a position, and I would like them to work with me, but I have to sell that image. Now, on the other hand, they're nervous because they have to sell themselves, as well. So I see it as a kind of 50/50, and if they can have that in mind – that it's a 50/50, the company needs them – it's not just, you know: 'Will I get the job or won't I get the job?' It's 'Is the company really good enough for me?' Because they're important people, and if they've got to the interview stage, then they're on the way, they're on the way. And so … and ask questions, if there's any doubt or anything they don't understand, ask questions. And smile. Important. Really smile. Be pleasant, but be themselves – definitely be themselves.

Harriet Barber

I think one of the most important things is making sure that you understand the company, and what they do, and what their values are, and if possible emailing and contacting them by some way. Sometimes, they often won't reply, but now and again, they will put you in contact with someone who will answer your questions; and the more you know, the more likely it is that, that you will understand them and you'll be able to portray yourself in a better light. I did, um, a month or so work experience there before I started, just because I emailed someone and they said, 'Yes, you can come in.' And then when I applied for my job, part of the forms said: 'Do you know anyone in the company?' So, I could put all that information down, and then when I was interviewed, I could talk about things I knew from the company, and they already knew who I was. And so it was like I'd had, like, a month-long interview, and they were much happier about taking someone that they were able to try, sort of, how they work first before. Otherwise, they've only met you for about two hours and they're, like 'Well, I'm not really sure.'

UNIT 4

①⑦ Getting started, page 20

I = Interviewer, C = Chandra

I: So, why are first impressions so important in business?

C: Well, you know, I think all our activities in business are driven by objectives, whether it's to get that first job or to achieve a sale, and I think psychologists generally agree that it takes only about seven seconds for someone to form their first impression of you before you've even had a chance to open your mouth!

I: And a first impression is very hard to change, isn't it?

C: Exactly – once it's been formed, you have to work much, much harder to change it. So, how you dress, the way your hair looks, even how clean your shoes are matters – and so does your body language. All these things tell people things about your attitude before you even get down to business. In fact, it accounts for 55 per cent of the impression we form.

I: Interesting. What other things influence our impressions?

C: The sound of your voice accounts for 38 per cent of the first impression, and surprisingly, because it's the thing we probably worry about most, the actual words we're going to use only account for seven per cent of the first impression.

I: In other words, it's not what we say, but how we say it.

C: Quite – but even more, how we look when we're saying it! It's all very subliminal and instinctive.

I: And how does that work when you can't see the person, say, you're on the phone?

C: Well, that's interesting. Even on the phone, the actual words you choose are not nearly as important as the tone of your voice – it works at about 70 per cent for tone and 30 per cent for choice of words – so those sort of subconscious things are really crucial.

I: Thank you.

① 08 Listening, page 20

R = Receptionist, A = Alexei

R: Princes Hotel. How can I help you?

A: Good afternoon. My name's Alexei Kutzov, and I'm calling from Moscow. I want to book a meeting room while I'm there in Geneva.

R: OK, sir. Let me get your details first. Could you give me your name again, please?

A: Yeah. It's Alexei Kutzov, that's K-U-T-Z-O-V.

R: Fine, Mr Kutzov. And can you tell me the name of your company, so I can put it on the invoice?

A: No problem. The name of my company is Top Flight International.

R: OK, and what size room would you like? Our smallest meeting rooms hold about ten people and our largest about 150.

A: The smallest is fine. We'll be using it for job interviews – we're looking for staff for the office we're opening in Switzerland. Um, there'll be three of us plus the interviewees.

R: And when would you like the room for?

A: I was hoping for May the 13th – that's in a month's time.

R: Right, sir. Um, I'm just checking availability. Um, yes, that's fine.

A: Good. Um, could you let me know the rates, please?

R: Sure. Um, they're taken by the hour, and we charge 40 Swiss francs an hour.

A: OK, well, I'd need it all day actually, from nine in the morning through to about eight in the evening, although I hope we'll finish earlier than that.

R: OK, that's fine, sir. And is there anything else you'd like while you're here, Mr Kutzov?

A: Well, um, we're going to be interviewing eight candidates for a job, so could you provide tea and coffee during the day for interviewers and interviewees? Several of them will be travelling down from outside Geneva.

R: No problem. We look forward to seeing you then, Mr Kutzov.

A: Thanks. Bye.

R: Goodbye.

① 09 Listening, page 22

J = Juanita, V = Vasily

J: Amposta Metals, Human Resources Department.

V: Hello. Could I speak to Juanita Camps, please?

J: Speaking.

V: Good morning. My name's Vasily Kasankov. A friend of mine suggested I phone you because she told me you might have a vacancy for an office administrator.

J: Yes, that's right. We haven't advertised it yet, but we'll be needing somebody.

V: I see. Do you mind if I ask you some questions about the job?

J: No, not at all. Can you just hang on a sec while I get the details of the job up on the screen … That's it. Now, what would you like to know?

V: Can you tell me if the job is full time or part time?

J: Well, we haven't finalised details yet, but I imagine it'll be mornings only. Would that suit you?

V: Yes, very much. I'm interested in finding a job for while my children are at school. And what would the job consist of?

J: Basic office administration, typing letters and reports, bookkeeping – that sort of thing. Do you have any experience of office work?

V: Yes. I worked in an office for ten years. When would the job start?

J: Let's see. At the beginning of September, I imagine.

V: OK, and how should I make my application?

J: Could you make it by email, please? It's so much easier to process that way.

V: Yes, of course. Could you give me your email address, then, please?

UNIT 5

① 10 Listening, page 28

CB = Christina Bunt

CB: Tesco were actually the first supermarket to introduce an own brand, and it was Tesco tea, um, when … and that was before the supermarkets … um, the main reason for it, I would imagine, er, started off as overheads … if you're not paying a premium to another supplier to produce that brand. You also have much better control over the brand, the product that's going into the packet, and you also get recognition, so if Tesco produce a particularly good biscuit or a particularly good kind of coffee, you're building up all the time customer loyalty, because they've got that Tesco brand in their cupboard, and it's good, and they'll go back to that store to get it … Some are cheaper, some are more expensive. Tesco Own Brand Finest, for instance, may be more expensive than a similar product, but it'll be much better quality, and Tesco will be able to control that quality. Um, our value brands are branded specifically to be at a better price, and we can do that because we're a large business that, you know, has an awful lot of product going through it.

UNIT 6

① ⑪ Listening, page 30

I = Interviewer, AH = Amanda Hamilton

I: Now, just explain exactly what *chai* is and how you came about it.

AH: *Chai*, um, is actually a generic word for 'tea', and in India, *chai* has been drunk for centuries in the same way that we would drink a normal cup of tea. It's a blend of spices … mixed with milk, sugar and black tea, and in India it's traditionally boiled on the side of, um, train stations in huge woks where they've freshly boiled the ingredients and offer *chai* to thirsty commuters coming into the train station. In America, as they do, they've westernised the *chai* recipe and created many *chai* latte flavours, ready-to-drink *chai* options, um, and you can get *chai* in most groceries, delis and cafés in the US. The reason I'm mentioning the US is because that's where I discovered *chai*, not in India, and I … I should probably go back a step in that I actually had created mobile tea bars, um, at train stations in the south-east … So the idea was to create upmarket tea bars where commuters could have coffee, but have a nice range of maybe fruit teas, herbal teas, and this *chai* was the perfect addition to our diverse menu. We researched the market a lot and found very, very few people selling it in this country, um, but the only people that were were importing it from America. Problem was, it cost a fortune to exp…, imp… import, and the supply chain kept breaking down and so customers would, you know, get … get very annoyed with us. So really, the … the … the decision to try and create my own *chai* was born out of just supplying my own tea bars, not really anything wider than that …

I should say it took a year in development … Some of the early recipes were horrible, you know, and the beauty of having the tea bars was that you had a mini market-testing tool and that I could take the recipes straight to the tea bars and let the customers decide because they're the most important people …

… we'd reached the point where the customers either couldn't tell the difference between mine and the … the US version, or they preferred it and that was good enough to me. We stopped the US supply, and I started solely supplying my own tea bars … if I was producing *chai* for my customers and they were enjoying it, why could that not be expanded on a glo… you know, wider scale,

um, possibly selling to other café bars or, you know, even retail in supermarkets, so I decided to, um, to just approach supermarkets and just see what they thought, sent in samples to, er, Tesco, really not expecting much back … and, um, got a call back to say that they absolutely loved the samples and would be interested in meeting me, and so last summer we went in, um, to have a meeting with the buyer and pitched, you know, my, my research in the US and how I thought it would be placed in the UK, and he offered, um, 230 stores nationwide straight away, at which point my mouth dropped rather like yours is now, and, um, that was a massive turning point obviously because at that point I had to get a brand and packaging like really quickly in about six weeks, and I didn't have a designer, and it was all just full on for that period of time.

① ⑫ Listening, page 31, Exercise 2

I = Interviewer, AH = Amanda Hamilton

I: What do you think was most important, or is most important when launching a new product?

AH: Checking, testing that there's a sufficient market for it. I mean, are … are enough people going to want your product? Because there's no point in launching something that you're not going to have customers for, so that's why the tea bars were a perfect market-testing tool for me because I could have launched a flavour or drink that I thought might, you know, have been nice, but had not tested it on any customer base, so although it was a small market-testing tool, it was effective.

① ⑬ Listening, page 31, Exercise 5

I = Interviewer, AH = Amanda Hamilton

I: What promotional activities have you done?

AH: Um, we've had write-ups in, um, *Slimming* magazine, *Delicious* … most of the women's magazines, which is great … in the *FT* this weekend there was a piece, um … about me, which was great. Um, I mean that's obviously a really high-profile newspaper, so, um, it's just all about, you know, raising awareness to try and, you know, increase sales … Er, in terms of, er, getting new customers, we have one strategy, and that is sampling. Um, the more people that can try the drink, er, the more, you know, customers we'll get because it is unique taste. So we do, um, a number of, um, sampling shows; we did the BBC Good Food show last … last year, er, and sampling out on the road … and pick, you know, festivals or … er, large areas where there's lots of people … I don't have big budgets for advertising, so, um …

I: I mean presumably you use your website a lot.

AH: Mm, yes, yeah, absolutely. It's like, um … it's like your shop window, um … to … to the world, because, you know, the Internet brings us all together, you can receive interest and possibly … hopefully orders. I looked at that … that … that sachet on magazine thing and you're looking at sort of over a hundred thousand for a … for a run and some of the big players, they just have so much marketing spend, and my product is sitting on the shelf next to these big players. How do you compete? It's a real challenge to … to compete with, you know, a moderate budget. I recently did a … a show at, um, the London Food Fair, where we did some sampling of 'ice chai', actually because, um, it's all very well launching a hot drink, but then, you know, what do you do come the warmer months?

UNIT 7

① 14 Listening, page 35

M = Marcel, T = Tasha

M: Lucerne Design. Marcel Schaub speaking. How can I help you?

T: Hello, Mr Schaub. It's Tasha Markova here from 100percentdesign.

M: Oh, 100percentdesign. Good to hear from you, go ahead.

T: You sent me an email the other day asking about prices. I thought I'd just ring you to give you the information.

M: Right. Fine. Let me just note it down then.

T: Here it is. Floor space at the exhibition, which runs from the 22nd to the 25th of September, costs between £295 and £340 a square metre excluding VAT. The difference in price depends on when you book and whether you want us to supply a basic stand.

M: OK. And can you tell me if there are any other costs?

T: Sure. On top of that, you'll have to pay £115 for insurance. That's a legal requirement. And you have to pay £300 in advance as a registration fee.

M: OK, and when's the last date for registration?

T: The 13th of June, but you'll be leaving it a bit late by then, as the best places will've been taken.

M: Mm. And how would you like us to pay?

T: By bank transfer. I'll send the bank details to you by email.

M: Right, thank you.

T: I'll also email you a floor plan so you can see the spaces which are still available. The sooner you choose and reserve one, the better.

M: But didn't you say by the middle of June?

T: Yes, but for actual locations, we work on a first-come-first-served basis.

M: Ah, I understand. And when do we have to pay the full amount?

T: The deadline for that is one month before the exhibition starts … in other words, the 22nd of August. After that, your reserved space can't be guaranteed.

M: OK. I've got all that. Thanks, Tasha. I'll discuss this information with my boss and get back to you. Can I have your phone number, please?

T: Yes, it's 01399 445378.

UNIT 8

① 15 Getting started, page 38

Karl

I think you just have to be, erm, there's a very, sort of thin line between being pushy and being persuasive, and I think you have to be very, very polite. When someone's obviously busy, you need to give them the time and, and call back another time; but, at the same time you shouldn't just give up on the first reversal, you do need to continue, and continue.

Adam

First of all, it's planning, so it's, you know, which clients you want to go to, with what product you want to take them, why you think they're interested in it, what information you're going to give them and when, what kind of follow-up, what kind of event you'll organise for them … It's a whole sequence and it's on the day-to-day – how you phone them up, make an appointment with them. But if you're … and it's also believing in what you're selling to them, as well. I think to be persuasive you have to know what you've got in your hands, and you have to understand the philosophy behind it, the needs of the client, that's what makes it persuasive, and the way that you present it, as well.

Rob

Right, um, I think, first of all, it's the ability of, er, being able to listen to your client, um, to be able to understand what is it that they are really looking for, and what are their needs, um, essentially. And also to be able to communicate with them, and, um, and during that conversation, to actually make them aware that, um, you know, what you can offer could be the, would be the best, um, solution to what they need.

Duncan

We'll go out for lunch with people, and coffee maybe, and just get face to face with them, build, build that relationship. So, first point then, do you like somebody? So you've got to be likeable. Um, do you trust this person who you're going to allow or not allow to persuade you? So, you've got to be trustworthy, I think, and you've got to, you've got to, um, therefore, um, be honest, I think; um, not everybody in business is, but when you speak to people who are senior, they tend to be honest guys who, um, who will tell it how it is really, in, in … And also, know their limits. So, if, if, if you don't know something, it's fine to say you don't know, and say you'll go away and learn it – that's absolutely fine. But if you try and blag it or pretend that you know, then you're not going to be trusted by the person you're talking to.

① 16 Speaking, page 38

J = Jack, H = Helga, S = Susie, M = Mark

J: Hello. Good morning. Helga Marcovitz? My name's Jack Zhou, and this is my colleague, Susie Chen.

H: Hello. Nice to meet you. So you managed to come. That's great.

S: Hello. Nice to meet you, too. So this is your stand. Very smart! Thanks for inviting us, by the way.

H: Well, we've been wanting to talk to you people for some time, and we like people to see our stand at a fair. Did you have a good trip?

J: Yes, thanks. Very good.

S: Yes, the airport's so convenient for this fair. Lovely city, isn't it?

H: Yes, lovely. Where are you staying?

S: We're staying at the Ritz, in the city centre.

H: Oh, good. They say it's the best hotel in town. When did you get in?

J: Just last night, but not too late.

H: Oh, good. Now, can we show you a few of our products? Take a seat if you like.

J: Thanks. Busy, isn't it?

H: Incredibly, and it's been like this all week. This fair's getting more popular every year. Now, would either of you like a cup of coffee or tea before we get started?

S: Yes, please. I could really do with a cup of coffee myself. What about you, Jack?

J: Er, tea for me, please.

H: Fine. I'll just send one of our people out for it. Mark! Can you bring two cups of tea and one cup of coffee, please?

M: Sure.

① ⑰ Listening, page 41

H = Helga, J = Jack, S = Susie

H: Hello. Back again!

J: Yes, we've been doing a bit of thinking, and we've decided some of your products could interest us if the terms were right.

H: Well, that's good news. Which items are you thinking about in particular?

J: Let's start with the CorkPops, shall we? I think we might be able to sell some of those, if only for novelty value.

H: Well, I'm sure you'll have no difficulty in selling quite a lot. How many are you thinking of?

J: Well, we thought we'd start with 200 or so to see how they go.

H: Just 200? I think 2,000 would be a better number.

J: Two thousand!

H: Sure, because I think you'll find they sell really well. Look, I'll tell you what: if you took 2,000, I'd take back whatever you couldn't sell after a year at the price you paid for them. How does that sound?

J: Two thousand on sale or return? Yes, we'll accept that if we can agree on the other details.

H: Great!

S: I'm a bit worried about the price you're asking, because if we bought the CorkPops at €12 each, we wouldn't make any profit. We'd have to spend quite a lot on promoting them, you know.

H: So, what do you suggest, Susie?

S: We'd like to pay €9 a unit.

H: Um … well, I can agree to €10 per unit if you buy other products from us as well.

J: OK. I think we could go to €9.50 if you gave us a discount of 5% on sales of over 2,000.

H: You mean, if you place a repeat order, you'll want a 5% discount on the price we've just agreed?

J: That's it.

H: Agreed – I've noted down those details and I'll send you an email to confirm things.

J: Fine.

H: Now, what else can I interest you in?

J: Well, let's talk about the Battery Peeler.

H: Great, I'm sure we'll be able to offer you something …

UNIT 9

① ⑱ Listening, page 44

P = Presenter, L = Lisa, N = Naiara, M = Matylda

P: Good evening. Tonight on *Building Your Future* we talk to three women who have made a go of starting their own businesses. We talk to them about the excitements and risks of running your own business and find out what it takes to be an entrepreneur in the 21st century. But first, we ask them why they started up their businesses in the first place. First you, Lisa. Why did you decide to take the plunge?

L: Well, you know, my mother's Italian, although I was born and brought up in Wales. Anyway, I noticed that, in my home town, most specialist food shops had closed down in the last few years, and there was nowhere you could buy handmade pasta. So, I thought, here's my opportunity – no competition and a really good product – so, on March the 1st last year, I opened my own outlet.

P: Great, and you're doing well.

L: Really well.

P: And you, Naiara? What inspired you to become an entrepreneur?

N: I'd worked for an airline for 20 years in marketing, that is, until the end of last year, when I was made redundant. Suddenly, in my forties, I found myself, you know, with nothing to do. I mean, I found that pretty traumatic and I thought 'I don't want this to happen to me again. Perhaps I'd better take charge of my own future.' So, at the beginning of February, I bought into this franchise with my redundancy money. It's actually a travel agent's, as a matter of fact, and since then, I've got to say, I've … I've never looked back.

P: Gone from strength to strength.

N: That's right. Best thing I ever did.

P: Can you explain, for those listeners who don't know, what a franchise is?

N: Sure. Basically, it's your own business, but you buy the right to sell the products of a large franchising organisation – you know, you pay fees and part of your profits and you use their logo and benefit from their marketing. McDonald's, the fast-food chain, is one example. Each restaurant is, in fact, a small business.

P: Thanks, Naiara. And you, Matylda, why did you decide to go it alone?

M: I'll tell you. I'm one of those people who's ready to work really hard, but quite honestly, I was tired of being a secretary. You know, my boss would say, 'Can you organise this meeting for ten o'clock?' or 'Can you type up this report by tomorrow?' and there I was, working really hard and not really being appreciated. I wanted to be doing something with a bit more excitement, where I was taking some risks, not just organising meetings and typing up the same old things all day.

P: So, Matylda, if I can continue with you, how did you go about setting up your business? Where did you get the idea?

UNIT 10

① 19 Listening, page 48

J = Jane Milton, I = Interviewer

J: My name is Jane Milton, and my business is called Not Just Food.

I: And what does your company do?

J: Gosh. We … we do a mix of food-related marketing things from recipe-writing to preparing food for photographs to organising exhibitions …

I: And what market research did you do before launching your company, and how did you go about it?

J: Gosh. I was quite lucky, actually. I, um, was told about an organisation called the Training and Enterprise Council at that time, um, who ran business start-up courses, and I went on one of those, primarily really because at the end of it, they would help you to get any funding you needed, and you stood a better chance of getting money from a bank if you'd done one of their courses. Um … and I had a great, the two men who tutored me through the eight weeks, I think, of one or two hours at a time, um, they were incredibly rigorous about the setting up of my business and how realistic my business plan was, and they made me phone … cold-call companies to ask if they would use my services if I did this kind of work. And I nearly made myself ill doing it, I really hated the idea of doing it. But I phoned people and said, 'I'm not trying to sell you anything, I'm trying to do some research. Can you give me five minutes to answer some questions?' And some people said, 'Phone back another time,' and at that time I phoned back and about 50% of those initial people that I interviewed became clients when the business started. So it was a great system.

I: So really there's nothing to beat doing your own … doing your own market research rather than employing someone else to do it?

J: I think that's probably right, I mean, I'm sure a market-research company could have done some, but even in the office when somebody else answers the phone and explains what we do, they're less successful at getting work than I am because I'm just much more enthusiastic about it, I think. And I think that … that helps.

I: And, um, what options were open to you for raising finance to start up?

J: Um, initially I got a small business start-up loan at a very competitive rate with one of the banks, um, through this scheme that I'd been on, but, um, I didn't need much to start. I borrowed a laptop computer from somebody, um, and I just, you know, made do and I set up office in my spare bedroom and so my overheads weren't that high initially, and I also took a part-time job at first, so that I had enough income just to pay my most basic bills while I got started.

I: What do you think is important when looking for finance for a start-up?

J: I think you have to be realistic about how much money you need, and also realistic about how much you can afford to pay back, 'cause obviously nobody lends you it without wanting it back, and so you have to be sure that whatever you borrow, you could meet the monthly repayments …

① 20 Listening, page 51

I = Interviewer, K = Karl

I: And can you tell me a bit about what your company is, and what it does?

K: Basically, we're a specialist bearing company; um, we act as master distributors for a number of American manufacturers, German manufacturers and also supply specialist bearings into the nuclear and research industries.

I: And, er, can you tell us the story of how you set up this company?

K: Um, it essentially started because my father – who previously used to work in the bearing industry – decided he would approach a company to become their agent, which was Carter. He did some of the work to get that, into, into, um, process, and basically, because of his age, he was coming towards 60, I think he sort of backed off of it, and I spoke to him about it, and it seemed like a very good idea I would approach the company myself and to start, um, to run with it. It took about a year's work unpaid, just trying to build up the business and then achieved an order that was big enough for me to start properly, basically.

I: What's important about starting up a new company, or when you're thinking of a new business venture?

K: I think it's clear to have a, a good business plan. You need to know, um, what the market is, how you fit into the market. You need to know what your overheads will be and all of your costs, um, you also need to know your profitability. So it would be pointless starting a business if you didn't have any profitability in it. Um, I think you need to have something that's an advantage over your competitors, because obviously there's typically other people in that market place already, and you need to offer something different.

I: Carter Bearings supplies bearings to companies in many different countries … how do you find new clients?

K: Well, there's numerous ways. I mean, we actively, um, look for clients who will use the very specialist products we have, and we know their market sectors, and we know how to target them, and quite often it can be just calling them up; quite often people will find us on Google. Um, typically the Internet, Google AdWords, having our website show up very highly – because our products are very specialised, it is very easy to get high Google search results – we can normally come in top.

I: What would you say is the key to working with clients whose cultures are different?

K: Understanding, um, what they culturally expect. So, for example, northern Europe would expect to have a delivery on time, they'd expect to have a discount if they pay their invoice within ten days. Um, they typically don't negotiate pricing – they expect to get the best price first of all. Whereas, if we were, if we were working with somebody, for example, in a, a location such as Turkey or India, they'd expect to have a price given to them which they'd expect to negotiate down by 50%, at least – so, essentially, all we do is we give them a 50% higher price, and then negotiate down to where we want to be.

I: And how do you deal with clients whose level of English is not very high? Do you have any problems?

K: I think it's definitely a matter of being very clear, particularly in written emails. People nowadays can put things through translation tools on the Internet, and so long as it's written very clearly, they can translate it quite clearly. It's ambiguity that's the problem. And I think that the thing is, one of the issues, what we find is that younger people, in particular, like to have this sort of Facebook, MSN, backwards-and-forwards kind of email conversations, and that can become very, very problematic. And also, if you're trying to track back how, how an error has occurred, you need to go through lots and lots of emails. It's better to have everything in one email which is very succinct.

I: What do you think the advantages are of, um, buying through a distributor, instead of buying direct from the manufacturer?

K: Local support, um, you can buy in the same currency as your own currency, if … a lot of the companies who I represent are in the USA. The, the fact that we ship in consolidated shipments means that we'll be more competitive. If you had to ship just one bearing over, it would be expensive.

I: And how do you find new suppliers?

K: Um, it's very much a case of we'll try and define somebody that we can find that was doing something very specialist, they're not being properly represented – or not represented at all – and approach them, giving them our previous, some of our previous history, and, er, what we think we can do for them, and if that develops further, it's a matter of negotiating a contract. And as I said, find a manufacturer who doesn't have any sales locations in your area or territory, and really negotiate with them. It's something that's … We're always trying to find a company that we trust, as well. It's, it's very much a matter of judgement.

I: What do you think the keys are to survival or prospering in hard economic times?

K: Well, we've defined very specialist market sectors, and we defined the areas where we think are not very well supported by other companies, or don't have good coverage on product, or have various other problems. Um, I think also involved in, in that controlling finance, there's no need to pay too much for all the services that you, you require. It's very important to keep negotiating; for example, we use lots of freight companies, we negotiate it regularly, um, telephone services. We've actually grown 40% each year during the recession … just by encroaching into different market sectors, specialist sectors, and even last year we increased our turnover by 67%.

UNIT 11

①₂₁ Listening, page 52

C = Charles, A = Alicia

C: Charles Langley.

A: Hi, Charles. It's Alicia here, Alicia Flores.

C: Oh, hello, Alicia. How are you doing?

A: Fine, thanks, Charles, how are you?

C: Very well. And what can I do for you?

A: Well, it's about your email. I have a few questions I thought I'd better just clear up quickly before I get down to investigating.

C: OK, fire away. What do you want to know?

A: Well, it would be useful to know what sort of investment you're thinking of making in Europe.

C: Well, this is all a bit hush-hush at this stage, but we're thinking in terms of two million euros in the first year – that's about 21 million rand at current exchange rates – for laboratories, equipment and office space.

A: Wow! A major move, then.

C: Sure, but for biotechnology, we've got to be where the action is, and with a central European location, we should be able to attract some of the best brains.

A: So there'll be quite a lot of people employed there, I take it.

C: We thought that we'd start with ten of our own staff drawn from different divisions around the world, and then, if things go well, we'll build up to about 60 people, so the place you find must have room for expansion.

A: OK, I'll look for somewhere with plenty of office space. Will all the staff be recruited from our other divisions?

C: A few, because we want a bit of cross-fertilisation of ideas – that's one of our objectives – but mainly recruited in the local area.

A: OK, that sounds interesting.

C: And we're looking for a manager from inside the company to head up the new venture, so can you suggest some people, so we have, say, two or three options to choose from? It'll be a great opportunity for someone ambitious – to run a growing operation, I mean.

A: You're certainly right there.

C: And one last thing, Alicia.

A: What's that, Charles?

C: I hear that in some regions in Europe, they offer government grants for companies thinking of moving there. Can you check the possibilities and see what's going? It could save us some money if there aren't too many strings attached.

A: Sure, I'll get onto all this right away and let you have a proposal in a few days' time.

C: Great stuff, Alicia. I'll look forward to that. Bye.

A: Bye.

UNIT 12

①22 Listening, page 57

PF = Peter Furlong

PF: Good morning, and welcome to the Adelphi Hotel. Thank you all very much for coming; some of you have travelled a long way to hear us today, and I hope you've all had good journeys. So let me introduce myself: my name's Peter Furlong, and this is my partner, Mark Davies. The purpose of this presentation, as you know, is to explain our business plans to you and hopefully to get you interested in investing in Clock Options Express. In my presentation, I aim to do three things. First, I'll give you a short summary of our main business idea. Then I'll tell you the findings of the market research that we've been conducting, and finally I'll outline our financial requirements and plans, which should show you what a sound and exciting investment Clock Options Express represents. If you have any questions you'd like to ask, I'll be happy to answer them at the end of the talk. So let's start with my first point – our main business idea: information and advertising display panels. This idea arose from the observation that in this city and in surrounding towns, there's a definite need for reliable and accurate information to drivers and other travellers concerning the time, traffic conditions, parking and the public-transport situation, and that this information could be shown on public display panels strategically situated on main road accesses to the city and at railway stations. They'd be paid for by leasing advertising space on the same public display panels. Now, to move on to my second point: market research. We started last year by conducting a survey of over 2,000 motorists who travelled in this area over a two-month period. Simultaneously, we commissioned a study of public-transport users. The findings of these two investigations can be seen on this chart, which clearly shows that not only would the display panels attract interest arising from travellers' need for reliable information, but that they'd also be a major focus for advertisers who'd be prepared to pay premium rates for leasing space …

… and as you can see, our products have considerable market potential. I think that just about covers the market research, so let's deal with the third part of my presentation, which is to explain our financial requirements and plans. In this chart, you can see a breakdown of our initial costs into five main areas: suppliers, premises, equipment, staff and marketing costs. Now, you'll notice that although we've tried to keep our requirements to a minimum, there are …

… and I hope you'll agree that our concept's very valid and represents an extremely interesting investment opportunity. Now, if I can just summarise the main points again, they're as follows: first, we've got an interesting and useful product which, in this area, is not on the market at the moment. Second, our market research with both travellers and potential advertisers shows a clear demand for our product and a readiness to buy into it. Finally, our initial financial requirements of just £500,000 in the first year are modest, and the potential return on investment makes this a very attractive opportunity for involvement in the start-up of a new business.

So, finally, I'd like to finish off by saying that it's been a pleasure talking to you all and thank you for your patience and interest in listening to me. Now, if you have any questions, please feel free to ask them.

UNIT 13

①23 Speaking, page 63

D = Dimitri

D: I think there are three things which are really important when deciding whether to travel on business or not. First, and by far the most important, is meeting your customers, existing ones and potential ones. There's no way you can build the right sort of relationship, get them to like working with you and trust you, persuade them to buy more of your products unless you meet them face to face and talk to them. You can't do this nearly so easily or effectively by, for example, talking on the phone or video conferencing. Secondly, and also vital, you have to explore new markets and see what possibilities exist in different places. The Internet's very good for some basic research, but if you're going to make your business grow, you've got to get out there and see the potential markets for yourself. Finally, and also absolutely essential in today's global workplace, where your teams may be spread over several different countries, staff have to meet together from time to time and get to know each other. This builds team spirit, helps people to exchange ideas and allows the company to communicate its values. All in all, if you want your company to grow, well-planned, tightly budgeted business travel's essential. And it's money well spent.

1 **24** Listening, page 65

M = Mark, C = Candice, I = Igor, P = Paula, H = Harry,
S = Susan

M: Right, I've called this quick meeting because I've got to organise the annual sales conference this year and I want to avoid a few of the pitfalls. I know you've all been to a good number of conferences of one kind or another over the years, so I'd be grateful for a bit of advice if you can. What can go wrong, do you think, Candice?

C: Well, I really look forward to conferences, meeting colleagues from other offices and old friends who've moved to other jobs and other organisations, and it gets me out of the office in my working time, so what I really look forward to is going somewhere exotic, somewhere I couldn't afford to go to if it was me who was paying. I can remember a really awful conference held in some ugly industrial town just because it was easy for most delegates to get to, when what we really wanted was, you know, somewhere a bit more unusual. They should've sent us to South America or the Far East or something. I mean, it didn't even work out cheaper in the end.

M: Good point. What about you, Igor?

I: I can remember a one-day conference which got off to a dreadful start because the woman who was going to give the first speech – very distinguished she was too – just couldn't handle the technology, you know. I think she had a PowerPoint presentation prepared, but she couldn't make it work. Mind you, it wasn't the computer or anything like that – it was her, and she got nervous and lost her place and started repeating herself and it spoilt the whole day, got everyone in a bad, unco-operative state of mind. She really should've practised a bit beforehand. It's not that difficult.

M: OK, thanks, Igor. And you, Paula?

P: I can tell you about a conference held in an old 19th-century hotel in Oslo. The place really wasn't suited to the sort of conference this was supposed to be. For instance the keynote speech was in the dance hall, with everyone sitting on plastic chairs and nowhere to take notes. They should've hired one of those purpose-built conference centres. The organisers, I mean – much better: decent air-conditioned lecture theatres, comfortable padded seating …

M: Yes, but more expensive, I guess.

P: Sure, but it gives a better impression.

H: You're right about that, but I can tell you what most upset me.

M: What's that, Harry?

H: It was the people.

P: The people? But you go to a conference to meet people, Harry, be reasonable!

H: No, the people hired to run the conference, you know, the stewards and receptionists. This was that sales conference, a number of years ago now. You might remember it, you were there. They were all so rude and offhand. I just don't think they'd been given any

training in customer service, so we were lost and fed up. It completely ruined the four days we were there, and you know, it was a lovely place. Should've been a great conference.

M: So, we have to make sure we get the right people. Finally, you, Susan.

S: It's hard to remember, actually.

M: What?

S: I mean it's hard to remember a good conference, in my case. I hate them all. But, you know, being in a wheelchair doesn't help. It's not the lifts or things like that. It's staying in hotels – somehow, they're never quite right for someone like me. I just find the rooms unsuitable, too hot or too noisy, things like that, and I find it difficult to sleep in a strange bed.

M: There are several things there which I'll have to bear in mind. Thanks, Susan. So what other advice can you all give me before I go off and start emailing people?

UNIT 14

1 **25** Listening, page 66

Conversation 1

M = Martin, S = Sally

M: South Pacific Tourism Organisation. How can I help you?

S: Good morning. Can I speak to Martin Forbes, please?

M: That's me.

S: Oh, hello, Mr Forbes. This is Sally McBride from Pacific Events.

M: Good morning. Call me Martin, by the way.

S: OK, and I'm Sally.

M: Right, Sally. What can I do for you?

S: I just wanted to clear up a few details of the conference events we're organising for you, and then we can send you an estimate.

M: Right. Tell me what you need to know, and I'll see if I can help you.

S: Yes, well, first I've got to have numbers – delegates, delegates' partners, husbands, wives and so on – for the transport as much as anything else.

M: So far, we've got 550 who've booked up. I don't think there'll be any more, because the closing date was last week.

S: Does that include partners?

M: No, I'll have to email you the number of partners because I haven't counted them yet.

S: Fine.

M: And there'll be eight guest speakers.

S: Eight?

M: Yes, who'll want picking up from the airport by car, not in your fleet of buses.

S: Right. You'll let me know when they're arriving in due course, won't you?

M: Just as soon as I know.

S: Now, special events: you wanted a traditional dance for the opening ceremony, didn't you?

M: Yes, that'd be great – everyone enjoys that.

S: Yes, and it gets everyone in a positive mood after their journeys. I'll book the dancers. At the gala dinner, there are going to be fireworks, I see in my notes.

M: Yes, but you'll have to liaise with Air New Zealand about those because they'll want the company logo on the programme if they're paying for them.

S: Sure. Well, I think that's all my queries for the time being.

M: Well, if you need anything else, just pick up the phone or drop me an email.

S: I will. Thanks. Bye.

M: Bye.

① 26 Conversation 2

H = Hannah, S = Sally

H: National Auditorium.

S: Hello. Can I speak to Sam Fingal, please?

H: He's not in the office at the moment. I'm Hannah, his assistant. Can I help you instead?

S: Sure. My name's Sally McBride from Pacific Events, and I'm calling to find out about equipment at the auditorium for the conference in October.

H: OK. What would you like to know?

S: Can you tell me what you've got in the main conference room?

H: Well, it's quite big, so there are no flipcharts or anything like that – delegates wouldn't see them. Basically, a screen and a projector.

S: OK … you say the place is big. Will people be able to hear the speakers easily?

H: There's a microphone, of course, for those who want it.

S: And what about a computer link into the projector?

H: Yes, we've got that, so just advise your speakers to bring a pen drive with their presentation on it.

S: OK – I'll note that down and make sure they do. They're all old hands on the conference circuit.

H: Good. Anything else?

S: Yes. Um, what about in the meeting rooms? What equipment have you got there?

H: All rooms have screens and data projectors, and we can supply good-quality sound equipment on request.

S: I'd better note that down for the information sheet – on request – just so people know.

H: That's right.

S: Just out of interest, several companies'll be wanting to put up exhibition stands. Is there somewhere they can do that?

H: We've got a large reception area which is normally used for that.

S: Good. And what's the weather like in October? Pretty hot, I suppose.

H: Quite warm if you're not used to it.

S: So, will people be able to get something to drink?

H: Oh yes. We always offer free refreshments round the clock to delegates at conferences. It's part of the service.

S: Wonderful.

H: Anything else you'd like to know?

S: No, I think that's just about everything on my list. Thanks. You've been very helpful.

H: It's my pleasure.

S: Look forward to meeting you at the conference, then. Goodbye.

H: Me too. Goodbye and have a good day!

S: Thanks. Bye.

① 27 Listening, page 68

Conversation 1

Man: You know it's a pretty intractable problem, the one we've got.

Woman: I know. We had something similar a few years ago, and actually we went to Ireland and Strong. You know, they're based in Boston and they're not cheap, but actually they sorted out the financial implications pretty quick, so I'd suggest trying them. If you're interested, I could give you their number, and I'll tell you who we found was really efficient, actually …

Conversation 2

Woman: What you're talking about's exactly the sort of thing we specialise in!

Man: That's what I thought, and actually, you were recommended to me by Jerry Linklater, so if you'd like to do the job, we'd be delighted to give it to you. We'd pay you more than the market rate, I guess, though I'd have to clear those details with my colleagues, of course.

Conversation 3

Man: No, I feel that after five years in this job, it's time I was moving on and doing something a bit more challenging.

Woman: Well, for the sort of work you're looking for, I'd have thought Lyle Parkers would be ideal. In fact, I know someone in human resources there, and if there's an opening in marketing, I'm sure he'd know. Would you like me to give him a ring? It'd be better than you cold-calling.

Conversation 4

Woman: Well, the service you're offering is great, of course, but it's the way you brought it to market that was really clever. It's such a neat idea – in fact, I wish we'd thought of it ourselves … not that we'd want to copy you!

Man: Thanks, Maria! Yes, we're pretty proud of that one.

Conversation 5

Man: Well, I think your ideas are really interesting! We should talk about this some more.

Woman: I'd be happy to. And I'm sure we could do some pretty profitable business together. How about fixing something up where we talk about this properly? It's too noisy here, and there are too many other people around. Are you going to be in Amsterdam soon? Otherwise I could fly over to London. It's not that far, and it'd be a pity to let an opportunity like this slip.

① 28 Listening, page 69

I = Interviewer, C = Charlotte

I: Can you describe, um, Pacific World to me … what exactly is it?

C: Pacific World is a destination management company, um, they have offices all across Asia, South-East Asia and China. Um … a destination management company is a company that basically, when you go on holiday or you organise an event in Asia, they are the people that handle all of the ground arrangements, so if you were on holiday and arranging, um, tours, transfers, hotel accommodation, they are the people behind the scenes that organise those.

I: And are they also for business travellers?

C: Uh, not so much business travellers, but for event management agencies … if you are an event management agency in the UK organising a conference or incentive over there, you will always use a DMC – destination management company – to do that because they have all the local relationships, they organise all the dinner venues, they organise all the creative ideas to make your event special.

I: What sort of company might use you?

C: Um, someone like, er, World Event Management or, um, various different companies … probably names that wouldn't be that well known because they're agencies, usually about … maximum 100 people, um, so it could be marketing agencies with an event-management side to them. But the people using those are people like pharmaceutical companies, IT companies, who would, um, use an event-management agency to organise their annual conference for their staff or incentive for their sales staff, um, that kind of thing.

I: What's the biggest, um, event or conference that you've organised?

C: We're just working at the moment on a conference to … it's a corporate company that have come to us to organise a conference for all of their worldwide staff in Shanghai … it's for 1,500 people. So for them, we then have to … because they don't know, um, China, they don't know Shanghai, and they know that we do, um, we've then sourced all of the accommodation and the meeting space, so you're talking about several hotels for that size group, all within close proximity to the convention centre, um … I think China, more than anywhere, is based very much on relationships, nothing … no business is done on a phone call or an email, you can't phone up and say: 'Have you got availability for this?', they will … you have to take them out for lunch and talk weeks in advance, um, for things. So, um, so I think in that sense, China is one of the places where you absolutely have to use a destination management company, you can't get in through another angle, um, but yes, so for them, apart from organising all the meeting facilities, all the, um … then you'd have to do

transfers from the … all the hotels, a social programme, which will involve different, um, evenings' entertainment with a big … I think they've got a big 'welcome' dinner on the first night and a big gala dinner on the last night, um, but because it's all different nationalities as well, we'll organise translators, English-speaking staff … any kind of documentation that you need while you're there, um …

I: Why have they chosen Shanghai?

C: Um, they were looking at Shanghai and Europe. Shanghai has got huge, um, facilities for large meetings because it is booming, um, and the hotels go up so quickly; everything is built so quickly that it can cater to that size. Also, Shanghai is such a modern, up-and-coming city, it is *the* place to go at the moment. It's expensive; the rates are very high because they can do … just like Hong Kong was not so many years ago, that's what Shanghai is now, um, so I think prestige, actually, more … it's an exciting, exotic place to go and it's a … and it's also very much … it's a huge financial centre that is booming and so, in that sense, to a finance company, which this is, it's incentivising to their staff in they see the sort of affluence of a destination and that gives you a big … buzz.

UNIT 15

① 29 Listening, page 70

C = Consulant, M = Martyna, S = Sasha, ML = Mei Lin, P = Paul

C: So, the purpose of this workshop today is to talk about some of the problems you people have with meetings and to see if we can find our way to solving some of them and making your working life just a little happier and perhaps a bit more productive. So let's just get a few ideas of the sorts of problem you have with meetings. Let's start with you. Your name is …?

M: Martyna.

C: OK, Martyna, tell us a problem.

M: Well, this one's a fairly typical one in this company. I was sent an agenda for the meeting a week before, I spent a lot of time preparing for it – you know, getting together a presentation for my part, doing a bit of research, finding statistics and so on. Then I got a phone call saying my boss had suddenly had to go off on an urgent business trip to Paris and could I ring everyone to say it wasn't happening. The meeting still hasn't happened, and that particular boss has left the company.

C: How frustrating!

M: Totally!

C: And you …?

S: Sasha. Well, to tell you the truth, I find some meetings so stressful that about two months ago, there was this meeting, and I decided I just couldn't take it and I didn't go. When they asked me afterwards why I wasn't there, the only thing that occurred to me to say was that I was terribly sorry, but I'd just forgotten.

C: What is it that makes meetings so stressful in this company?

ML: Oh, I can tell you that. My name's Mei Lin, by the way. What makes meetings so stressful is that we never seem to reach any decisions. I'm probably especially to blame for this because I run a lot of meetings myself, and it's really my job to get the participants to reach a conclusion. But, for example, the one I held yesterday ended in chaos with everyone talking at once.

C: Well, that's a problem we can certainly work on. Now, finally you?

P: Paul.

C: OK, Paul, what problem would you like to mention?

P: Well, I'm the assistant office manager, and one of my jobs is to get people to go to meetings, and find a time when everyone can make it. The trouble is, everyone's so busy that it's sometimes nearly impossible. Take a meeting I was arranging last week for senior managers: I spent nearly an entire morning calling them and emailing them until I finally found a time they could all meet.

C: Um, well, we've certainly got a good range of problems here. So let's continue by looking at some potential solutions.

① ③⓪ Listening, page 73

B = Barry, S = Sandra, P = Patrick, M = Mark

B: Well, hello everyone. Let's start, shall we? Now, you've all seen the agenda which I circulated to you last week, so you've had time to think about this. Just the one question: we want to be in the Chinese market: how do we get there? Sandra, what do you think?

S: Well, Barry, I think we should start by finding a distributor. Perhaps we should visit the country and meet a few possible distributors first. Get the feel of the place.

P: Yes, and do some market research while we're about it.

M: I'm not sure.

B: Mark?

M: Um, personally, I feel that market research is something best left to market researchers, not to export department managers like ourselves who don't even speak the language.

S: Yes, but the distributors will have a pretty good idea of the market, don't you think?

M: If you know them, and if you know that they aren't exaggerating things. Frankly, I think that first we need an independent market-research firm to tell us what we can sell, how much we can sell and how to sell it.

B: That's right. We've got the money for it, and it's what we'd do if we were going to develop and market a new product in this country.

P: That's true. So let's begin with market research.

M: Still, I think your idea, Sandra, of visiting the country and getting a feel for it is a good one. Would you like to volunteer for that?

S: Sure, and perhaps you'd like to come with me, so we can get a different point of view …

UNIT 16

② ⓪① Listening, page 74

I = Interviewer, AE = Adam Evans

I: What's important when meeting customers?

AE: Planning is most important. Planning the time and the way that you're going to deal and which centres are you going to visit. If, for example, I'm a sales rep in an area and I've got 20 competing sales reps – in fact, there are probably about more, 80 – um, they will visit far more centres than I'll be able to. I can't even attempt to visit the same amount, it's impossible, and also, er, well, I'll tell you how we organise it. In December, what we'll do is we'll say: 'OK, where do we want to go next year? What products have we got coming out? What sales do I have to achieve?' And then we'll make a list of the different areas … different centres where we think we can get those sales – and that includes the customers we have already, we have to look after those. And then when a sale came, our competitors, um, are also gonna go for these customers, but, um, I know my products far better than competitors do, so my, the potential for a much stronger relationship … for them to trust me, is higher than our competitors. I would visit these clients and potential clients with the same rhythm that the competitors will. I won't visit as many, but … um, you need to have visited clients throughout the year between five and six times … on average. If you visit them once, it doesn't serve any purpose whatsoever, and neither does it twice, but if you can visit them five or six times, your competitors can't develop that relationship. And it's funny, the other day I was in an interview, and the director of the whole project said to me: 'Adam, what I don't want is a sales rep to come in and visit me in the month of May, and he doesn't appear again till the following month of May.' And I said: 'Well, neither do we, OK? We want to look after you.' We've got a whole plan to involve our clients and potential clients that's very attractive. So, we can't compete on numbers – we're a much smaller team – but we can compete on, let's say, the quality of the visits that we do, and the number of visits that we do.

② ⓪② Listening, page 77

Speaker 1

GB: My name's Gustav Bremitz, and I'm Senior Production Engineer with Florentino International. The reason I favour the company jet is simply convenience. Normally, when I fly, I'm on my way to solve some production problem, and I never know before I arrive how long it's going to take, so by having the aircraft waiting, I don't have to depend on the departure times of commercial flights.

Speaker 2

PF: I'm Pascuala Fernández, Senior Account Manager. I should say that about 75% of the time I'm in the office is spent in meetings. If I can get some of those done while I'm flying, it leaves time for other work when I arrive. On commercial flights, they're just impossible.

Speaker 3

PK: My name's Patrykcja Krawiec and I'm Chief Sales Director for Florentino International. I take the private jet simply because it's quicker, and since in our business time's very definitely money, it probably saves money as well.

UNIT 17

2 03 Listening, page 80

I = Interviewer, FB = Felicity Bannerman

I: So, Felicity Bannerman, can you explain for us, please, how the social media are an opportunity for companies?

FB: Yes. Many companies are realising this is an opportunity which is too good to miss, especially because using social media is a change they can make which won't hurt their budgets – it's cheap in comparison with other types of public relations. Really, the only cost you have are the people you employ to run or monitor the media, and there are lots of people around with the right technical skills. Lots of people have social media accounts and know how to handle them, and so it's a really good way of getting in contact with younger consumers especially.

I: Hm. Interesting. But there must be some pitfalls for companies trying to use these media, aren't there?

FB: Yes, I'd say the most common mistake that companies make is to treat the social media as if it was somewhere to advertise. You know, they just put up their brand message and expect the public to accept it. This is wrong and provokes a very negative reaction. People who use them expect to be communicating with each other. When I'm consulted, one of the recommendations I make to companies is that they need to train their staff to listen to customers and potential customers. The process must become a conversation, otherwise the exercise becomes counter-productive.

I: Do you have any good stories of successful use of these media?

FB: Mm-hm. Several. For example, a few years ago, Coca-Cola discovered two unemployed actors who were running an unofficial page devoted to their company. They gave them a job and asked them to continue running the page in an official capacity. It's been hugely successful, and according to research which the company conducted, the page itself has a phenomenal number of followers – about 25 million at the last count.

I: Amazing. But what about small businesses?

FB: Well, I know of quite a few small businesses who use Twitter to talk to their customers. They've got some new product or something or they've decided to promote it with a special offer, so they send out a tweet, which people pick up on their phones or iPads, and 20 minutes later, they're popping into the shop. It's very effective and costs next to nothing.

I: Felicity Bannerman, thank you.

FB: Thank you.

UNIT 18

2 04 Listening, page 87

I = Interviewer, HB = Harriet Barber

I: Can you tell me about your job, and what do you do, and what it involves?

HB: I'm an environmental consultant, but more specifically environmental impact assessment. It's to do mostly with planning for construction of new buildings, that's where the majority of our work is, and it's if you build something, you can't just build whatever you like, in the way that you seek planning permission, part of it is environmental permission. And so we do the evaluation of the impact the development would have if it were built on the environment as it stands now, and we do it from ecological point of view, air quality …

I: So, when a new client comes to you, er, what, what is their objective?

HB: It depends. Um, some businesses are obliged to report their emissions and waste and all of that sort of thing; so they may ask for help with how they should do their report. And some people just want to for the sake of their reputation, and energy saving, money saving, all sorts of different reasons. Um, but generally it works well if it's not just that they're reporting it – if they're monitoring it, then once they have the data and the figures, it's, like, the best time for them to then start managing what they're doing. And so, if it's a combined system of reporting, monitoring and managing all together, they can, they have the most sort of efficient impact, and that's what we would usually try and encourage people to do.

I: And in general, what can any company do to become greener?

HB: Um, I think thinking about it is the first step, and identifying your, your main areas of environmental impact. So even if you're just a one-person office, it's probably going to be waste, because you're throwing out paper and that sort of thing. So if you, if you just as one person thought about that, you could probably halve it by just not printing everything, or reusing paper, that sort of thing. And so then it's just on a larger scale, with a larger company. So it's also telling your staff that you want to reduce your environmental impact so that you can get everyone involved with it, but if you're, if you have a policy and no one knows about it, then it's completely pointless.

I: And what attracted you to this career?

HB: Well, I did a science degree for my first degree, and then I didn't really want to work just in a research lab; although I enjoyed it, I didn't find, like, the diversity that interesting, and it was very focused on one project in one lab. And then I wanted to do something similar that used science skills, but not solely science, so I decided to do a Master's in environmental science.

I: What do you think about new technology? I mean, the business world's gone through a huge process of change. What changes do you see might, um, present themselves in the future?

HB: I think there's, um, quite a big move towards people working remotely from home – or whatever location they want – and having, not having so many fixed desks in an office, because that's where they're paying their overheads. And, the majority of people, if they're on the Internet, and all of the files are accessible to everyone, they don't need to be physically sitting in an office. And I think that's where a lot of companies in London expend a lot of money, because rents are so high, and service charges, and everything like that. If they can reduce the office space they need, and maybe focus on just meetings, as and when, with their project teams, I think that's probably what people would want to do.

I: And can you prepare yourself for that change?

HB: Yeah, I mean, I, I think you do lose something in not sitting next to the people you work with, and it also means that you can't ask a quick question. So I think when you're new, it's really valuable to have people around you, and perhaps it will just be that more senior people do that, or people who know that they've got enough work to cover them for the next couple of weeks will only come in when they need to see someone. But, yeah, I do think it's a shame that you lose the social element of the office, and that is something that's really nice about working in big teams, and that sort of thing.

UNIT 19

② 05 Listening, page 88

A = Assistant, L = Linda, K = Konstantin, O = Oliwia, C = Chung, M = Martin

A: What do you think of these proposals, Linda?

L: What do I think? Well, I'm all in favour if I can tie it in to my work. I mean, if I can get out to the customers with their orders when they want them, you know, it'd be great not to have to do any driving at peak times, and I'd find the job a lot more relaxing – you know what I mean? I get really uptight driving in rush hour.

A: Thanks, Linda. Now, Konstantin, your turn. What do you think?

K: Well, it's going to take a bit of organising and getting used to down on the shop floor – especially for me, as I have to do all the organising and keep our output on schedule – but it should make folks happier, and that'd be great, because

there are far too many people going off on sick leave just now, so it's worth giving it a try, just to cut down on that.

A: So you're in favour, despite the possible extra workload for you.

K: On balance, yes.

A: And what about you, Oliwia?

O: I think it'd be great because between my husband and me, we'd have more time for being with the kids. In my case, at the moment, I do nine to five every day, but my boss works very flexible hours – sometimes he doesn't come in till just before a board meeting, sometimes he works till ten at night, especially if he's video-conferencing with China or Brazil or somewhere, so I don't see why my timetable shouldn't be just as flexible, you know, as long as I get my work done.

A: OK, and what about you, Chung?

C: I have to be flexible anyway, so I don't reckon much to the proposals, personally – I mean, I have to come in and fix things when they break down, even if it's the middle of the night. But I reckon that if flexibility keeps the staff happy so they don't go off and find another job, that'd be a good thing. Lots of the breakdowns are caused by new staff handling the equipment without proper training.

A: That's a very good point, and, er, what do you think, Martin?

M: I think they're a great idea. I've got this idea that I'd like to take some time out. I've always wanted to travel and see a bit of the world, and have a break from spending all day with figures, balance sheets, profit and loss, cashflow – just for a year or two while I'm still young enough. These proposals might just give me that chance.

A: Thanks, Martin. Thanks for your input, everyone. I'll put together a report …

② 06 Listening, page 90

Conversation 1

K = Katrin, C = Chen

K: Katrin Reiner.

C: Oh, hello, Katrin, it's Lee Chen here, do you remember me? I'm one of the senior managers from Logistics.

K: Oh, hi, Chen, how are you doing? Long time, no see.

C: That's right, we're very busy right now. Can hardly keep up with the orders.

K: Well, that's good – better to have too much work than too little.

C: You're right there. Anyway, that's really what I'm calling about. Our problem is keeping up with orders, and part of the reason for that is that our internet connection just isn't fast enough. I mean, it's just not up to the load.

K: Well, that's not really my department. You need to—

C: I know, but I thought, since you're doing the staff survey to improve working conditions, I'd mention it to you as well.

K: OK, but I can only pass on your complaint, which you could really make direct just as effectively.

C: Sure. You see, where we run into difficulties is when we track orders in real time – it just doesn't work the way it should and we really have to be able to do that.

K: So what do you want me to do about it?

C: Well, I think it would benefit you as well. It's not that we need to get new equipment – that's fine – but we probably need a new service provider, you know, someone who can offer us better bandwidth.

K: Yes, I see what you mean. OK, I'll put in a request as well with the powers that be.

C: Great, thanks.

2 07 Conversation 2

S = Stepan, K = Katrin

K: Hello?

S: Hi, Katrin?

K: Speaking.

S: Stepan Vasiliev here.

K: Oh, hi, Stepan.

S: Yeah, just ringing to ask you to lunch with us one day.

K: Lunch? That would be nice. Where would you like to take me? Somewhere fancy, I hope!

S: Well, not exactly. I'm afraid it's going to be in the staff canteen – we don't really have time to go out in the middle of the day, plus we're hoping to talk about our working conditions.

K: Not to complain about the canteen food, then?

S: No – actually, I think it's pretty adequate myself, though we could sometimes do with a bit more variety.

K: Mm. Yes, maybe … so will it be just you and me?

S: No, I've invited along the assistant sales managers – not the senior ones, because I think their situation's all right.

K: OK, and what's on the agenda?

S: Well, it's not an agenda exactly, but we have a few ideas for making the way we work out our expenses better and fairer. I don't know if that comes within your remit or not.

K: Not exactly, but if you explain what you mean, then I could help you when you take your ideas along to the accounts department – that's if I agree, of course.

S: OK, so how about tomorrow, then, at 12.30?

K: Mm, that sounds fine. See you then.

S: Bye.

K: Bye.

2 08 Conversation 3

K = Katrin, M = Manuela

K: I'm out of the office at the moment. If you want to leave me a message, please speak after the beep.

M: Hello, Katrin, this is Manuela Ferrer here. I'm calling about the staff survey which you've been carrying out. Just really to say that I'm fine about almost all the proposals in it. I'm really interested in the flexible working suggestion – that's something I'd really like to take advantage of – but I'd be interested in seeing how it's all going to work in practice. So really I'm ringing to offer to be a part of the working party that's going to look at how to implement the changes. I've been thinking about

it quite a bit and have one or two suggestions. Basically, I think every department in the company should send one representative who can then sort of … well, you know, channel ideas from their colleagues. I also thought it might be a good opportunity to get other suggestions and recommendations from staff by making use of one of those social media websites, you know, so the thing becomes more of a dialogue. What do you think? Please ring me back when you have a moment. Bye.

UNIT 20

2 09 Listening, page 94

I = Interviewer, DM = Duncan Mackintosh

I: Is the IT industry changing a lot, or is it still basically the same as it was 20 years ago?

DM: Um, I think it's changing massively, quickly. We need good people more than ever needed good people before. That's because the industry is becoming more complex, um, so, my perception is that the way things have changed, maybe in the last 20 years is that we've gone from a lot of development, coding of, of systems and doing it as, as the need comes along, um, and doing it in the country to offshoring all of that more low-level work; so, the actual technical work, the coding, and sending that all off to India, or the Philippines, or, um, or where else they do it now and, and generally sending it in that kind of direction, and managing it from this country. And that's offshoring, both in terms of a company who produces software, um, will set up an office in India, in Mumbai, or something, and employ people into that office …

I: But why would a company outsource its IT systems?

DM: A company which isn't a technology company has systems, because they all do, but it's not, that's not where its competitive advantage is, so it pays another company to look after its systems, and that company might be an Indian company, it might be a British company, um, we see it a lot in the cloud-based approach that's happening now, which is where companies just don't want to have to worry about technology, so they pay, um, an outsourcer to just provide their whole infrastructure. So, all they have to do is log on and it works: they've got a network, and they've got a system, um, but they don't need a data centre, they don't need servers, it's all, it's all done for them.

I: What sort of people do you think are suited to work in IT?

DM: People that work in IT could be a very geeky individual who doesn't see daylight very often, um, right through on the scale to the really slick consultant salesman. Um, all of those people could work in IT, actually, there's a place for all of them.

I: So they wouldn't necessarily have to study it at university?

DM: Um, no, they don't, although a good-quality kind of computer-science degree or systems degree is useful, but anyone can get into IT. But, if the question was 'who's gonna be successful in IT', well, it's, I think it's about marrying, because as I mentioned a lot of the technical work's come about offshored – not all of it, but most of it – and so the people that are successful are the people that will marry understanding of technology, um, practical and conceptual, I think, with a business understanding and an ability to communicate with people, a people person basically. And if you've, if you've got both, um, and you're ambitious, and driven, and want to move forward in your career, then you'll, you'll be brilliant, you'll have an excellent career in IT. There's some fantastic opportunities, and you'll move for—, you'll fly, you'll fly in your career.

I: What should someone planning a career in IT do at university?

DM: If I was doing it, from what I know now, I would probably go and get a computer-science degree. But if I made the decision during university that I wanted a career, it wouldn't matter; I would just, um, during university read up on technology, or, or, I don't know, design a website, or just do something so I had it in my CV. And then I would go and join one of the consultancies. One of our main clients is an organisation called Accenture, which have a fantastic graduate, er, recruitment, um, scheme, and career progression there – right from, right from junior level, right the way to senior management level, and it's very structured, and the, um, you know, your, you won't have a boring day, you'll be really pushed and really driven. But, if I was coming into the market now, that's the company that I would join, probably, and that's the kind of career progression I would look for.

UNIT 21

② ⑩ Listening, page 101

CB = Christina Bunt

CB: We've got, well, we've got a huge customer-relations department at Head Office, who deal with customers … What we like to do is to try and ensure that our customer-service desk staff will sort out your comment for you, um, so if you've got, if you feel there's something wrong with the service that you've had, we like to think that our customer-service desk can … staff can deal with that and send you away happy. But sometimes it'll be something that they can't sort out, so we have a system where, we have a system of customer comment cards, so customers are invited to fill out a customer comment card, they get looked at first of all in store to see if it's something quite simple we can sort out.

We're one of the first companies to bring in the loyalty card, so the Tesco Clubcard points are quite well known,

and it … I mean it … it works. People like getting their Clubcard vouchers, um, but you've also, we … we also try to do quite a lot within the community wherever the store is, so the personnel manager and customer service manager will quite often have links with local schools, um, different local groups that, um, we … we go out and talk to people, um … We run community buses to get people in from rural areas into the store. And of course there's 'Computers for Schools', where, depending on how much you spend, you get given a computer voucher, and those computer vouchers, your children can take to school with them, and the school collect them and then trade them in for computer equipment.

We have, um, we do a number of things around the way that the store is perceived. We have a mystery-shopper system, where, um, we will get … somebody will come into the store once every, er, four weeks and do a sample shop, and we then get a report back from Head Office to say what they've seen, so they will comment on anything from the tidiness of the car park and being able to get a trolley, through to the cashier who served them, smiling, um, offering them help, saying hello and saying goodbye. And they mark us on every single area of the store. And then we do, um, accompanied shops, so on a quite regular basis one of the managers in the store will simply ask a customer if they mind if we walk around with them while they do their shopping and then we make a note of the comments they make about their shopping experience.

UNIT 22

② ⑪ Listening, page 104

I = Interviewer, JM = Jane Milton

I: How do you go about finding new customers?

JM: We cold-call, we send a brochure normally and then phone afterwards. But probably at the moment, about 40% of our new work enquiries, people approaching us, come from our website, which was not really why I set the website up. I set the website up so that when people wanted to see examples of our work, I could refer them to it. But I imagined that I'd have already established a relationship with them, but actually some of my biggest jobs have come from people finding us on the Web.

I: What for you is the key to good customer relations?

JM: I think we're always honest and up-front. We quote people for work, and if it takes much longer than we expected it to take, then we stand by that quote and we just have to swallow that cost and be better at estimating another time, but if it takes much less time, we would go back to them and tell them and discount the job, so I think we're very fair with people and we build long-term relationships with them. We've a lot of small clients who initially made very little money for us 'cause they had very li… they only needed help with tiny bits of things, but then they respected that we gave them that help, and as they've got bigger, they've given us more and more work.

I: And how would you deal with a dissatisfied customer?

JM: We're very lucky because I've never had one, and I think a lot of that is initial communication being good and setting up that initial communication, and when we are given a job, either we ask clients to give us a brief, a written brief, and if they can't do that, then I would give them one and get them to confirm it and so we're absolutely clear before we start on anything exactly what's expected of us. I think because of that, we rarely have … have any problems, and if we do, they're small, we know about them because of the relationship we've got with the person and we would clear them up there and then.

UNIT 23

2 12 Listening, page 109

KM = Karl Müller, J = Jolanta

KM: By the way, Jolanta, we really must write to BDD about their late delivery. It caused us a lot of problems.

J: Would you like me to write to them, Karl?

KM: If you could. I've got quite a lot on my plate for the next few days.

J: OK. What would you like me to say?

KM: Well, they sent me a letter the other day saying that we're a valued, long-standing client. Look, here it is. I think we should remind them that that's what they said. See if it's true.

J: OK. But what exactly are we complaining about? The documents arrived late, didn't they?

KM: Mm, five days late, and we specifically asked them to deliver them because in the letter it said that they'd be delivered in 12 hours. I could've done it quicker myself.

J: Of course!

KM: And then you should point out what the results of this late delivery were.

J: Very embarrassing – at least for me.

KM: Sure, since we had the meeting set up to sign the contract, and you had to phone them to postpone it.

J: That's right. Do you think they'll take any notice of our complaint?

KM: They'll have to, otherwise we'll stop doing business with them. You can tell them that, too. I mean, their deliveries must be problem-free from now on.

J: OK, Karl. I'll put all that in a letter. At least that'll make me feel better about what's happened!

KM: Thanks, Jolanta.

UNIT 24

2 13 Speaking, page 112

G = Grazyna

G: I think there are three things which are essential when taking up employment abroad. Firstly, you have to be culturally sensitive. It's no good thinking that you're going to behave in exactly the same way at work as you did in your home country because that way you'll just irritate people and you won't work so effectively. To take a personal example, I come from Poland, where bosses and managers tend to make decisions and staff have to accept them. However, if you're a manager, it's no use being autocratic in the United States, where there's a culture of discussing and consulting before making decisions. Secondly, it's worth learning the language well, both written and spoken. If you don't, you'll have problems doing your job, however skilled you are. You see, people will misunderstand you and they'll get impatient with you. Finally, there's no point in telling people how you do things in your country all the time. You have to fit into their context and understand things from their point of view. If you bear those things in mind, you'll have much less difficulty in achieving success.

2 14 Listening, page 113

I = Interviewer, RL = Rob Liu

I: Can you tell me a bit about your job, what you do and what it involves?

RL: So my job is, um, to market three major service lines we have as a company. We do, um, recruitment, which is targeting Western and Chinese companies based in the UK and, um, in China; and we also do career coaching, that's targeting the Chinese-speaking jobseekers in the UK. Um, so basically, we've got people on a sort of entry level, fresh graduate. We also have people, er, who have worked for, um, quite a while, but who somehow are not happy with their current jobs and would like to make their next move; er, most of the cases they do change their, um, the sectors they work in, in this case, so it's not really headhunting. Um, and also the third, um, major service line is business consulting, and that's again targeting corporate clients, um, in the UK, both Chinese and UK companies. So, my job is to plan and implement an integrated marketing plan, um, to promote these three major services.

I: And what attracted you to this career?

RL: Um, well, it's a, I, my career progression, if you like, um, has been quite interesting. My first degree was in law, and then, um, I did my Master's in journalism, and I did a bit of, er, media production straight after that, and I then moved on to, um, PR – and that was in Beijing. And from there I worked for a media company in Shanghai. So, when this opportunity came up, I very much was looking forward to relocate back to London from Shanghai, as well. So, obviously, the location was something quite appealing to me at that point, and, um, and I do believe that I'm a quite people person, and I do enjoy speaking to people, communicating with people, so marketing would be, um, something, er, perfect for me to utilise those skills and attributes.

I: I'm interested – you coach and recruit Chinese job seekers looking for work in the UK. What do you find are the main differences in working culture between the two countries?

RL: In the West, er, people tend to be very straightforward and direct, and so when it comes to, for example, looking for a job in the job market, they actually see this as a process of rediscovering themselves and also sell themselves in the job market as well. If you go for a job interview in China these days, um, even with a state-owned, big company, they will still ask you things like, um, you know: 'Are you loyal? Are you hard-working? Do you like this company?' Of course, you know, all your questions will be, er, straightforward, 'yes', and that's what they would like to hear from you. But as a jobseeker in the West, you need to show to them that you have the whole set of competencies, for example, and skills, um, that, or transferable skills, if you haven't got any sort of relevant, um, direct experience. And also you have to try to look at your life and your studies to try to find the perfect examples to show to the potential employer that you have all these sets of skills.

I: So, um, alternatively, if you're a European or Westerner going to work in China, what advice would you give?

RL: If you go to big cities like Shanghai, you don't need to actually know anything about China to be able to live there in a very convenient way, er, because of the quite strong sort of foreign expat community. But I would say to be able to work there in the most efficient way, um, you know, to be able to achieve results with Chinese business people, I think one of the most important, um, tactics, if you like, is, um, to try to integrate with the local business culture and mentality.

I: And would that be the same, what about European companies doing business in China – would you suggest the same?

RL: Yeah, I think, I think, yeah, the same would really apply to them. Um, but I think, um, one thing that, um … I would advise them to, to do is to really find someone who really understand the, um, the, the Asian, the Chinese market as a sort of middleman, if you like, to help them. Um, we always say that it is absolutely crucial to have proper Chinese staff, um, even in the core business development team, um, once it comes to cases like that, um, and, um, experience, um, has actually told us that's true. So, to use the core, you know, the core staff, Chinese-speaking staff, as a core team that's, um, very important and, um …

I: And what about when they're actually in the job interviews? I mean, how do you go about coaching, um, some of the applicants that come to you?

R: It's very important to have those sort of soft skills, if you like, um, how to show to them that you're not only one piece of paper, er, with all these academic, you know, qualifications and work experience, but inside you're a real human being, um, and, you know, you have habits and, and you share a sort of, a value and, um, er, emotions, as well. But lots of the candidates we work with are not able to, um, get that message across, um, so they could be brilliant academically, and they could be very hard-working, but that's not enough once it comes

to the employer looking at whether this person would be able to work as a team, er, in that company, um, with other people.

EXAM SKILLS AND EXAM PRACTICE

② ⑮ Listening Test Part 4, Exam skills, Exercise 1b, page 136

I = Interviewer; F = Frances

I: Frances, I'm interested in how you know whether your customers are happy or not.

F: Well, I suppose I've got two types of customer really: the outlets – the hairdressers and beauty salons who buy my products – and the end users – you know, the people who actually buy the products from the outlets. These people tend to tell their hairdresser or beauty therapist more or less how they feel. I mean, I don't get a market researcher going round or anything like that, but at least I do send out a questionnaire twice a year to the outlets for them to fill in, so I do have a sort of semi-formal system. And it works quite well. I mean, people tell me what they think, you know.

I: Do you have any typical difficulties with your customers?

F: Um, well, I suppose there are a few who take their time paying, but they're the minority, really. And I'm pretty understanding. I mean we've all had cashflow problems from time to time, and if you're understanding, you know, people get over them. Most people, though, are pretty decent and pay straight out, cash on the nail. Then there are the types – especially older men – who expect my products to make them look 30 years younger than they are, which is a bit unrealistic. Actually, though, the main problem is that the market is highly seasonal. Something you wouldn't expect, but people only seem to worry about their appearance at the beginning of the summer when they are thinking of going to the beach.

I: And how do you go about winning new customers?

F: People tell each other, basically. I have a website, of course. Everyone has to have one of those nowadays. I've never used things like junk mail or advertising because really they're not cost-effective in my line of work, so basically I rely on selling a good product and letting the news get round on the grapevine.

I: But do you get any customers at all from your website?

② ⑯ Listening Test Part 4, Exam practice, page 137

Section 1: Questions 33–38

You will hear part of a lecture to business students about a transport group called Carter.

For questions **33–38**, circle **one** letter, **A**, **B** or **C**, for the correct answer.

You will hear the lecture twice.

You have 20 seconds to read the questions.

Now you will hear the lecture.

This morning, we're going to look at a major transport group called Carter. The Group, which is based in the UK, operates in over 20 countries around the world. It's organised into several divisions, with the three largest focusing on bus services, passenger train services and rail freight.

The Group's strategy is to expand into new geographical markets by acquiring companies in various countries around the world. Some of its markets will always be weaker than others, of course, but the Group believes this strategy spreads the risks. In addition, Carter aims to carry out its full range of activities in every market, even though that sometimes means that one or more divisions are making a loss in a particular country. Operating in a large number of countries could be a disadvantage – and many companies have failed to manage this successfully. So Carter has developed a system that encourages companies within the group to work together. For example, a train-operating subsidiary in one country might consult a bus operator in another about improving management processes or carrying out customer surveys.

As with many companies, Carter is very aware of environmental issues, and tries hard to keep its impact as low as possible. As an international business, its executives often need to attend international meetings, but whenever possible, they use video-conferencing and other technologies instead. Then, all the Group's bus drivers are trained in eco-driving techniques, to keep fuel consumption to a minimum – in fact, the Group recently won an award for its improvements in this area. Carter also works hard on recycling, so that it generates as little waste as possible.

Carter's Chief Executive, Jenny Thorpe, retired a few months ago. Many analysts expected her deputy, Philip Murray, to step into her shoes, because of his experience and deep understanding of the Group. Instead, Thorpe's replacement was Alexander Harris, who was previously with a furniture manufacturer. Carter's Board wanted the new CEO to have run another business operating around the world.

Now let's have a brief look at finance. Last year, Carter's profits failed to reach the levels that most analysts had predicted at the beginning of the year. This was because some of its major markets experienced economic difficulties for a few months, which seriously affected passenger numbers, and therefore Carter's turnover. The Group reacted quickly by making efficiency savings, with the result that although the final figures failed to meet early expectations, they were slightly higher than in the previous year.

Carter is expected to do well over the next few years. The savings it's made will help it in future, and above all, the Group is in a good position to benefit from the increasing demand for passenger rail travel, particularly on high-speed lines. Its bus services, on the other hand, are likely to grow far more slowly.

Now you will hear the lecture again.

(2) 17 Section 2: Questions 39–44

You will hear a discussion between a man called James and a woman called Trish, who both work in a conference centre's marketing team.

For questions 39–44, circle **one** letter, **A**, **B** or **C**, for the correct answer.

You will hear the discussion twice.

You have 20 seconds to read the questions.

Now you will hear the discussion.

J = James, T = Trish

J: Morning, Trish.

T: Hello, James. Now, as you know, the CEO wants us to revisit our marketing strategy and come up with a better marketing plan. What do you think of our current advertising?

J: Well, we advertise almost entirely in local newspapers and magazines, don't we? And I suppose that's reasonable, as there are conference centres all round the country. At least the ads give an idea of how we're different from other places, but it's buried in all the detail – they include everything that any reader might possibly want to know, like the prices for different types of events, instead of making people visit the website or phone us to find out more.

T: Yes, I agree. The advertising doesn't give a clear image. It risks making people think the centre is untidy and disorganised, like the ads.

J: Or to put it more positively, relaxed and comfortable.

T: Maybe. Whereas really it's a luxury venue. And that's how we should be promoting it. Organisations are willing to pay that bit extra for what we can offer them, but we don't make it clear what they can get.

J: Right.

T: And of course we get a lot of repeat bookings – businesses that have been here once usually come back. But it's getting them here in the first place that's the difficulty. Maybe we should encourage companies to book small-scale events, like meetings or training courses. They'd be more likely to try us for something like that than for a three-day conference for hundreds of people.

J: Yes, and I'd imagine there's greater demand for facilities for that type of event. Do you think we should carry out some market research, to identify exactly what demand there is?

T: Mm. What do you think about an online survey, asking people visiting our website how likely they are to make a booking?

J: That would get filled in by lots of people with no real interest in coming here. Wouldn't it be better to carry out two surveys? One where we send a leaflet to local organisations, showing the facilities, and ask them to fill in a questionnaire on what would make them book. And for the other, I think we should phone past customers, and ask for their suggestions for improvements and whether they're likely to book again.

T: Good idea. We ought to contact that group first, before we write to local organisations.

J: Yes. Do you think we should get a market-research agency to deal with the survey? I'm inclined to do it ourselves – we've both got relevant experience, after all.

T: It won't be just the one survey, though. I doubt if we'll have the time to do it all. Why don't we do a rough version ourselves, then get an agency to do the rest of the work?

J: I see what you mean. OK. By the way, do you know what our budget is for this project?

T: It's going to be decided on Thursday, but I can almost guarantee it won't be enough. Our finance people always seem to hate spending money on marketing.

J: That's true. But as it's the CEO who wants this done, maybe he'll get the budget we're going to need.

T: I hope you're right.

Now you will hear the discussion again.

2 18 Section 3: Questions 45–50

You will hear a radio interview with Sally MacArthur, an executive coach, about conflict at work.

For questions **45–50**, circle **one** letter, **A**, **B** or **C**, for the correct answer.

You will hear the interview twice.

You have 20 seconds to read the questions.

Now you will hear the interview.

I = Interviewer, S = Sally

I: Welcome to our business slot and to my guest, executive coach Sally MacArthur. Hello, Sally.

S: Hello.

I: Now, you're very interested in conflict in the workplace. Is that increasing, do you think?

S: Yes, I think it is. Years ago, in the majority of workplaces the employees had a lot in common. They were mostly men, or mostly women, of a similar age, and with a similar social background. Nowadays, most workforces are far more diverse. And everyone has different needs and expectations, for instance as regards their rights. But company rules generally only change if there are new legal requirements. So they were devised for a workforce which was very different from today's employees.

I: Is there any pattern in the way conflicts at work arise?

S: We generally assume that it's aggressive people who cause most conflict, but in fact they often bring the problem out into the open, so there's a chance of resolving it. It seems to me the problems that go on and on without being resolved are most often caused by people wanting to please everyone. They're afraid of arguments, so they hide their opinions, and say they agree with everyone. So problems remain hidden and unresolved.

I: How should problems be raised?

S: Several things are important. The longer we have an issue on our minds, the more it spirals out of control, and we lose sight of the person we're in conflict with as a human being – they simply become a problem. That's something we need to avoid. We may feel that saying there's a problem somehow makes it worse than saying nothing, but in the long run, saying nothing is potentially far more destructive.

I: I see.

S: Another point is that the way we communicate plays a vital role. Emails aren't subtle. They can seem much ruder than the writer intended. In face-to-face communication, on the other hand, people use facial expressions, body language and tone of voice to express a much more subtle message. This gives a better idea of what each person feels, and you can respond to it, and not just to the words. With emails, all you've got are the words. It takes longer than just writing an email, but it's more likely to be successful, so it'll save time in the long run.

I: So what's your advice about dealing with problems?

S: It's essential to focus on trying to achieve a solution, which will almost always mean you should talk to other people and explain your motives. And if that involves offending them, because you've shown you think they have room for improvement, then handle it. But if all you care about is winning, it'll be difficult to have a healthy, constructive debate, and you'll probably create so much tension with a colleague that you can never restore relations with them.

I: Now, a number of television programmes give the impression that business is an aggressive environment, where bosses shout at their subordinates. What do you think of that?

S: It's a great shame, because it makes it seem that only the strongest people survive, and that puts many young people off the idea of going into business. But it's a very distorted picture. OK, there is some aggression, but the reality is that most of the time, people behave in a far more constructive way.

Now you will hear the interview again.

2 19 Speaking Test Part 2, Exam skills, Exercise 2b, page 159

Well, I'm going to talk about what is important when setting up a new business. Firstly, it depends on the type of business you are starting, but if it has just one or two employees, management experience is not essential. What is more important is knowledge of the product. For example, if you're going to open a clothes shop, you should know a lot about clothes. Another important thing is a knowledge of the market. You have to find out who your competitors are, and your target customers. So you must be sure that people are going to buy your product. I mean, you don't want to invest your life savings in a business which doesn't interest anyone! A further point is that you must have a reasonable working knowledge of finance, so that you can produce a sales forecast, estimate your costs and make a cashflow prediction. This way, you'll be able to persuade a bank to give you a loan or overdraft. But, to conclude, the most important thing is interest in the product and your customers.

Acknowledgements

The author and publishers would like to thank the following teachers and consultants who commented on the material: Austria: Derek Callan; China: Bi Xuqiang; Poland: Andrzej Czaplicki; Russia: Wayne Rimmer; Spain: Inma Sánchez Ballesteros; Switzerland: Trant Luard; UK: Sharon Ashton; David Clark.

The author and publishers would also like to thank the following for agreeing to be interviewed for this book: Harriet Barber; Karl Brundell; Christina Bunt; Adam Evans; Amanda Hamilton; Rob Liu; Duncan Mackintosh; Jane Milton; Charlotte Weston.

Thanks also to Michael Black, Susie-Fairfax Davies (interviewer), Ann Kennedy Smith (lexicographer), and Julie Moore (corpus researcher).

The author would like to give his warmest thanks to everyone who has worked on this book. Particular gratitude to Jane Coates and Catriona Watson-Brown for their enthusiasm, encouragement, patience, expertise and sheer hard work. Also to Dilys Silva, Karen Barns and Una Yeung for their in-house editing, to Sophie Clarke and Elizabeth Knowelden (production controllers), Kevin Brown (photo researcher), Kay George and Michelle Simpson (permissions controllers), James Richardson (audio producer) and Will Harris (sound engineer). Special thanks to the design team at Hart McLeod.

Text acknowledgements

The author and publishers acknowledge the following sources of copyright material and are grateful for the permissions granted. While every effort has been made, it has not always been possible to identify the sources of all the material used, or to trace all copyright holders. If any omissions are brought to our notice, we will be happy to include the appropriate acknowledgements on reprinting.

The publisher has used its best endeavours to ensure that the URLs for external websites referred to in this book are correct and active at the time of going to press. However, the publisher has no responsibility for the websites and can make no guarantee that a site will remain live or that the content is or will remain appropriate.

p. 10: Top Employers China for the adapted article 'Every effort pays off at Deloitte'. Reproduced with permission of Top Employers China, certified by CRF Institute; pp. 16–17: Sony Mobile Communications for the adapted article 'Testimonials' by Suri Maddhula, Angela Zhang, Yoshinori Ito and Laura Hoyle, Sony Mobile Communications. Reproduced with permission; p. 23: About, Inc. for the adapted material 'Phone answering tips to win business', 2004 by Susan Ward. Used with permission of About, Inc. which can be found on the Web at www.about.com. All rights reserved; p. 27: text adapted from 'The mating game' by Patricia O'Dell, *Promo Magazine*, 01/05/04; p. 29: The Economic Times for the adapted article 'Levi's plan to trigger demand with "going viral" marketing' by Sruthi Radhakrishnan, 18/05/11. Source: *The Economic Times*. Copyright © 2012, Bennett, Coleman & Co. Ltd. All rights reserved; p. 29: *The Economic Times* for the adapted article 'Denizen takes Indian trial', 09/09/10. Source: The Economic Times. Copyright © 2012, Bennett, Coleman & Co. Ltd. All Rights Reserved; p. 31: Telegraph Media Group Limited for the adapted article 'If at first you succeed, chai chai again' by Andrew Cave, 22/02/07 *The Telegraph*. Copyright © Telegraph Media Group Limited 2007; p. 39: Dynamic Living for the descriptions of the CorkPops Wine Opener and the Battery-Operated Peeler. Reproduced with permission; p. 40: Business Today for the adapted article 'The Art of Agreeing' by Devashish Chakravarty, 21/12/10. Reproduced from *Business Today* © 2011. LMIL; p. 45: Inc. Magazine for the adapted article 'Should you consider an international franchise?' by Ryan Underwood, 01/02/11 *Inc. Magazine*. Reproduced with permission; p. 53: Technologiepark Heidelberg GmbH for adapted material from www.technologiepark-hd.de. Copyright © Technologiepark Heidelberg GmbH; p. 53: Biopôle for adapted material from www.biopole.ch. Reproduced with permission; p. 64: article adapted from blog post by Jatinder Kaur at Travel Centric Technology. Reproduced with permission; p. 67: Behance, Inc. for the adapted article '5 Tips for Making the Most of a Conference' by Scott Belsky, www.the99percent.com. Reproduced with permission of Behance, Inc; p. 71: Dow Jones & Company for the adapted article 'The New Face of Face-to-Face Meetings' by Joe Mullich, *The Wall Street Journal*. Reproduced with permission of Dow Jones & Company; p. 82: Todd Wilms for the adapted article 'Social Media: 3 Steps from 3 Great Companies' by Todd Wilms, *Forbes Insights* 09/15/11. Reproduced with permission; p. 84: e-skills UK Sector Skills Council Ltd for the adapted article 'Environmentally friendly IT and reducing waste in your business', *Business IT Guide*. Copyright e-skills UK Sector Skills Council Ltd 2000 - 2012. http://www.businessitguide.com/guides/view-guide/88. Reproduced with permission; pp. 92–93: Entrepreneur Media, Inc. for the adapted article 'When to Outsource' by Amy Reinink, *Entrepreneur magazine* 20/04/10. Copyright © 2012 Entrepeneur Media, Inc. 87899:412SH; p. 98: Adams Six Sigma for the adapted article 'Customer satisfaction and customer loyalty are the best predictors of customer retention' by Cary W. Adams, Adams Six Sigma. Reproduced with permission; pp. 98–99: LOMA for the adapted article 'Creating a customer-centric culture' by Stephen Hall. Reprinted from LOMA's Resource Magazine. Visit LOMA at www.loma.org; p. 139: Egremont Group for the adapted article 'Surviving Change' by Natalie Gordon, Egremont Group 2007. Reproduced with permission; p. 140: Telegraph Media Group Limited for the adapted article 'Degrees are not the only route to success' by Louisa Peacock, *The Telegraph* 19/01/12. Copyright © Telegraph Media Group Limited 2012; p. 146: text adapted from *Start and run your own business*, Crimson Publishing.

Photo acknowledgements

p. 8 (T): Thinkstock/Ciaran Griffin; p. 8 (B): Photo used with the kind permission of Flight Centre; p. 10: Top Employers China, Certified by CRF Institute/Deloitte; p. 12 (T): Thinkstock/iStockphoto; p. 12 (B): Ben Edwards/Corbis; p. 13: Catchlight Visual Services/Alamy; p. 14: Courtesy of Tesco plc; p. 16 (T): fuzzbones/Fotolia; p. 16 (CR): Stuart Forster/Alamy; p. 16 (BR): image100/Superstock; p. 17 (TL): BLOOM Image/Getty Images; p. 17 (BL): Fancy Collection/Superstock; p. 17 (TR): Sony Mobile Communications; p. 19: SOMOS/Superstock; p. 20 (T): Image Source Images; p. 20 (B): Shutterstock/PT Images; p. 21: Thinkstock/Huntstock; p. 22: Fancy Collection/Superstock; p. 26 (T): Glow Wellness/Alamy; p. 26 (a): Ian Dagnall/Alamy; p. 26 (b): DBURKE/Alamy; p. 26 (c): LatinContent /Getty Images; p. 26 (d): studiomode/Alamy; p. 26 (e & f): Helene Rogers/Art Directors & TRIP; p. 26 (g TV): Shutterstock/ Ljupco Smokovski; p. 26 (g Car): Thinkstsock/Hemera; p. 26 (logo): Used with the kind permission of Unilever; p. 27: Used with the kind permission of Unilever; p. 28: photo taken by Hart McLeod, with the permission of Tesco plc; p. 29: AP/Eugene Hoshiko/Press Association Images; p. 30 (T): Corbis Images/Image Source; p. 30 (B & inset): Photos used with the kind permission of Drink Me Chai; p. 34 (T): Iain Masterton/Alamy; p. 34 (C): Kevin Foy/Rex Features; p. 34 (B): Sinopix/Rex Features; p. 35: Shutterstock/Blaj Gabriel; p. 37 (T): Martin Barlow/Art Directors & TRIP; p. 37 (B): Helene Rogers/Art Directors & TRIP; p. 38: Thinkstock/Jupiterimages; p. 39 (TL): Courtesy of Cork Pops Inc.; p. 39 (BL): Dynamic-Living.com; p. 39 (BR): Jerzyworks/Masterfile; p. 40 (BL): Courtesy of Cork Pops Inc.; p. 40 (BR): Dynamic-Living.com; p. 44 (T): Blend Images/Image Source; p. 44 (BL): Thinkstock/Jupiterimages; p. 44 (BC & BL): Thinkstock/iStockphoto; p. 45: Courtesy of Dlush; p. 47: Thinkstock/Jupiterimages; p. 48 (T): Thinkstock/iStockphoto; p. 48 (BL): Courtesy of Jane Milton; p. 49: Thinkstock/Jupiterimages; p. 51 (T & B): Karl Brundell; p. 52 (T): Technologiepark Heidelberg GmbH.; p. 52 (R): Thinkstock/iStockphoto; p. 53: Technologiepark Heidelberg GmbH.; p. 55 (T): Piotr Maksys, Gdansk Science & Technology Park; p. 55 (B): Forum/Topfoto; p. 56 (T): Shutterstock/improvize; p. 56 (B): Thinkstock/Jupiterimages; p. 58: Gallo Images – Guy Bubb/Getty Images; p. 59 (T): Thinkstock; p. 59 C): Thinkstock/Jupiterimages; p. 59 (B): Thinkstock/iStockphoto; p. 62 (T): Lou Linwei/Alamy; p. 62 (CR): Thinkstock/Fuse; p. 62 (BL): SOMOS/Superstock; p. 62 (BC): Shutterstock/stefanolunardi; p. 62 (BR): Thinkstock/Photodisc; p. 63 (L): Thinkstock/iStockphoto; p. 63 (R): Bob Masters/Alamy; p. 64: Artiga Photo/Corbis; p. 65: Images Source/Rex Features; p. 66 (T): Shutterstock / improvize; p. 66 (TC): image 100/Superstock; p. 66 (L): Nordic Photos/Superstock; p. 66 (BC): Thinkstock/Hemera; p. 66 (R): Corbis Bridge/Alamy; p. 68: Thinkstock/Hemera; p. 69 (T): Courtesy of Charlotte Weston; p. 69 (B): Shutterstock/Cuiphoto; p. 70 (T): Thinkstock/Jupiterimages; p. 70 (B): Fancy Collection/Superstock; p. 74 (T): Thinkstock/iStockphoto; p. 74 (C): Cultura Creative/Alamy; p. 74 (B): Rocio Muñoz, Brand Manager at Cambridge University Press, Iberian Branch; p. 75: Blend Images/Alamy; p. 77: Thinkstock/Comstock; p. 80 (T): Thinkstock/iStockphoto; p. 80 (CTL & CTR): incamerastock/Alamy; p. 80 (CBL): Andrew Aitchison/Alamy; p. 80 (CBR): Web Pix/Alamy; p. 80 (BL): Thinkstock /iStockphoto; p. 83: Shutterstock/Kzenon; p. 84 (T): Sipa Press/Rex Features; p. 84 (BL): Alan Dawson/age fotostock/Superstock; p. 84 (BR): altrendo images/Getty Images; p. 88 (T): Shutterstock/Dimitry Shironosov; p. 88 (B): Liam Bailey/Photofusion Picture Library; p. 92 (T): David Pearson/Alamy; p. 92 (C): Newscom/UPPA /Photoshot; p. 92 (B): KeystoneUSA-ZUMA/Rex Features; p. 94 (L): Ravi Bhangal; p. 94 (R): Kablonk/Superstock; p. 95 (T): age fotostock/Superstock; p. 95 (B): Danita Delimont/Alamy; p. 98 (T): Image Source/Blend Images; p. 98 (B): Image Source/Getty Images; p. 101 (L): Courtesy of Tesco plc; p. 101 (R): Helene Rogers/Art Directors & TRIP; p. 102 (T): Image Source/Alamy; p. 102 (B): Thinkstock/Digital Vision; p. 104 (L): Thinkstock /Bananastock; p. 104 (R): Ace Stock Ltd/Alamy; p. 105: Thinkstock/iStockphoto; p. 106 (T): Glow Images; p. 106 (BL): Thinkstock/iStockphoto; p. 106 (BR): Image Source/Alamy; p. 108: Thinkstock/iStockphoto; p. 109: Robin Skjoldborg/Getty Images; p. 110 (T): fStop /Alamy; p. 110 (BL): Thinkstock /Jupiterimages; p. 110 (BC): iStockphoto/Pamela Moore; p. 110 (BR): Thinkstock/Stockbyte; p. 111: Exotica/Superstock; p. 112 (T): Shutterstock/SFC; p. 112 (B): Rob Olsen.

Front cover photography by Shutterstock/Serp

We have been unable to trace the copyright holders of the photograph that appears on p. 87 and would appreciate any help to enable us to do so.

Illustrator acknowledgements

Simon Tegg (pages 15, 32, 33, 71, 75, 77, 91)

Audio acknowledgements

Studio: dsound Studios, London
Producer: James Richardson
Sound engineer: Will Harris

Text design and layout: Hart McLeod Ltd

Notes

Notes

Notes